nation dance

nation dance

Religion, Identity, and Cultural Difference in the Caribbean

Edited by Patrick Taylor

Indiana University Press
BLOOMINGTON | INDIANAPOLIS

This book is a publication of

Indiana University Press
601 North Morton Street
Bloomington, IN 47404-3797 USA

http://www.indiana.edu/~iupress

Telephone orders   800-842-6796
Fax orders   812-855-7931
Orders by e-mail   iuporder@indiana.edu

The paper used in this publication meets the minimum requirements
of American National Standard for Information Sciences—Permanence
of Paper for Printed Library Materials, ANSI Z39.48-1984.

Manufactured in the United States of America

Library of Congress Cataloging-in-Publication Data

Nation dance : religion, identity, and cultural difference in the
Caribbean / edited by Patrick Taylor.
        p.   cm.
    Includes bibliographical references and index.
    ISBN 0-253-33835-2 (alk. paper)—ISBN 0-253-21431-9 (pbk. : alk. paper)
    1. Caribbean Area—Religion. 2. Religion and culture—Caribbean Area. 3.
Ethnicity—Caribbean Area.   I. Taylor, Patrick, date

    BL2565 .N38 2001
    200'.9729—dc21

                                                00-040919

1 ` 2   3   4   5   06   05   04   03   02   01

In memory of Eva Fernandez Bravo

Photo by Nancy Mikelsons

Contents

Acknowledgments

This book is the result of the ongoing work of the Caribbean Religions Project at the Centre for Research on Latin America and the Caribbean (CERLAC) at York University. In conjunction with the Canadian Association for Latin America and Caribbean Studies (CALACS) Annual Congress, the Caribbean Religions Project organized a series of keynote addresses, panels and special events related to Caribbean religion, culture, and identity at York University in the fall of 1996. Many of the chapters in the book are revised versions of papers selected from those presentations. Other chapters were added to complement and expand the depth and breadth of the volume. My greatest debt is to the contributors, who usually listened to my suggestions, sometimes humored me, and in all cases worked with me to develop and share their various visions of Caribbean religion and identity. The work benefited from the careful comments and thoughtful suggestions of the reviewers who read the manuscript. Joan Catapano graciously shepherded the project through to publication. I am particularly grateful to the principal team members of the Caribbean Religions Project, Frederick I. Case, Ramabai Espinet, Bernardo Garcia, and Althea Prince, all of whom assisted in many different ways and without whom we would not have been able to pull together the collection. Sean Lokaisingh-Meighoo spent many months providing research assistance and editorial advice, backed up more recently by Makeda Silvera. Adriana Premat and Marshall Beck translated materials with precision and speed. Grace Munroe and Carol Duncan introduced us to Queen Mother Bishop Yvonne B. Drakes and Archbishop Doctor Deloris Seiveright. Nancy Mikelsons, Honor Ford-Smith, and Patricia Swanson ensured that Eva Fernandez Bravo would always remember her trip to North America in a very positive light. Judy Soares widened our research contacts. I am also very grateful to Ricardo Grinspun, my co-chair at the 1996 CALACS Congress and the former Director of CERLAC, who encouraged and supported the book project from the beginning. Jim Handy, President of CALACS, and Kalowatie Deonandan, former President of CALACS, have also been very supportive. Liddy Gomes, former administrative assistant at CERLAC, was always there when needed, backed by cooperative staff, research assistants, and volunteers at both CERLAC and CALACS. The Social Sciences and Humanities Research Council of Canada (SSHRC) remains the principal sponsor of the project out of which this book has grown. Various units at York University also provided financial assistance and other help at different stages, particularly the Office of the Vice-President-Academic, the Office of Research Administration, York International, the Faculty of Graduate Studies, the Faculty of Arts, the Division of Humanities, Founders College, the Latin American and Caribbean Studies Programme, the Department of History, and the Department of French Studies. SSHRC, the Canadian Foundation for the Americas (FOCAL), the Canadian International Development Agency

(CIDA), the International Development Research Centre (IDRC), the Canadian Council for the Americas (CCA), and Latin American and Caribbean embassies and consular representatives in Canada also offered conference support in 1996. To my family, Beverley, Shira, and David, for your love, help, and patience, thanks always.

nation dance

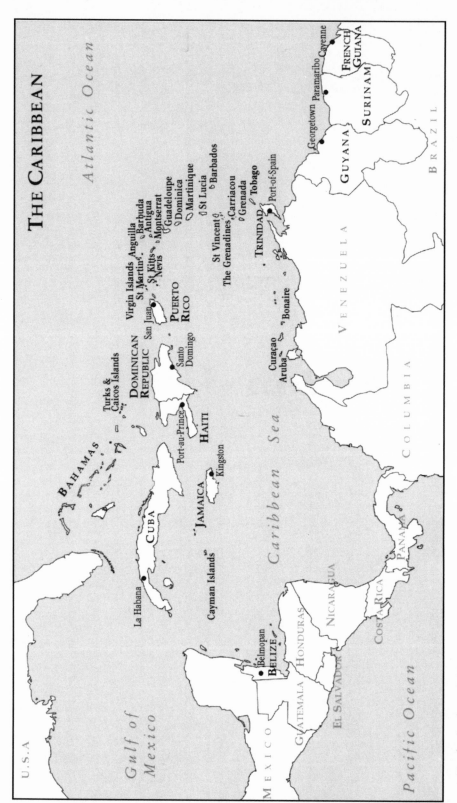

THE CARIBBEAN

Atlantic Ocean

Gulf of
Mexico

U.S.A.

BAHAMAS

Turks &
Caicos Islands

La Habana

CUBA

Cayman Islands

JAMAICA

Kingston

HAITI

Port-au-Prince

DOMINICAN
REPUBLIC

Santo
Domingo

San Juan

PUERTO
RICO

Virgin Islands Anguilla
St Martin Barbuda
St Kitts Antigua
Nevis Montserrat
Guadeloupe
Dominica
Martinique
St Lucia
St Vincent Barbados
The Grenadines Carriacou
Grenada
TRINIDAD Tobago
Port-of-Spain

Caribbean Sea

Curaçao
Aruba Bonaire

BELIZE

Belmopan

GUATEMALA

HONDURAS

EL SALVADOR

NICARAGUA

COSTA RICA

PANAMA

Pacific Ocean

COLUMBIA

VENEZUELA

GUYANA

Georgetown Paramaribo Cayenne

SURINAM

FRENCH
GUIANA

BRAZIL

MEXICO

Map by Stephanie J. Martin

Dancing the Nation

An Introduction

PATRICK TAYLOR

> What's your nation? Arada . . . Cromanti . . . Yarraba . . . Moko . . . ?
> I'm a visitor, a tourist, just someone here for the day.
>
> —Paule Marshall, *Praisesong for the Widow* (Marshall 1984: 167)

> I also, the 'thinker,' dance my dance . . . the thinker is a means of
> prolonging further the terrestrial dance, and in so far is one of the
> masters of ceremony of existence.
>
> —Friedrich Nietzsche, *Joyful Wisdom* (Nietzsche 1960: 89)

In Paule Marshall's *Praisesong for the Widow,* Papa Legba beckons the sterile imaginary of a homogenized middle class to open itself to the world in an ancestral dance into the future. Trickster, guardian of the crossroads, hermeneutical principle *par excellence,* Legba inaugurates the Haitian Vodou ceremonies and opens the gates between the profane and the sacred. Marshall's Legba invites the widowed Avey Johnson to a Big Drum or Nation Dance Ceremony in Carriacou in the Grenadines. She is transported back to her youth in the Shouters Church in Tatem Island, South Carolina: "And for the first time since she was a girl, she felt the threads, that myriad of shiny, silken, brightly colored threads (like the kind used in embroidery) which were thin to the point of invisibility yet as strong as the ropes at Coney Island . . . she used to feel them streaming out of everyone there to enter her, making her part of what seemed a far-reaching, wide-ranging confraternity" (Marshall 1984: 249). Marshall's heroine, Avey Johnson, is a modern American tourist traveling to the Caribbean who finds herself in a dance of black modernity (see Gilroy 1993). Her strange Caribbean cruise provides a way for Marshall the novelist, who is of Barbadian parentage, to assert a diasporic claim to a Caribbean homeland. Modernity devoid of ancestry is the production of the solipsistic ego, rationality without faith, life without meaning. It is living religious traditions and their implications for *Caribbean modernity* that are the subject of the essays in this book.

To dance the nation is to find oneself immersed in a liminal world where tradition informs contemporary experience and ritual takes on new meaning. In the words of Rex Nettleford, Jamaican dancer, choreographer, and cultural theorist, dance is "part of a society's ancestral and existential reality"; it is "one of the most effective means of communication, revealing many profound truths about complex social forces operative in a society groping toward both material and spiritual betterment" (Nettleford 1993: 97–98). Anthropologically speaking, the Nation Dance is an Eastern Caribbean ancestral ceremony in which a community of people pay their respects to their ancestors and retrieve from them the knowledge of the past that will sustain the present and the future: the Nation Dance is an ancestral redemption of the present for the salvation of the future. A legacy of different West African cultures, similar ceremonies can be found throughout the Caribbean region—in the Kumina ceremony of Jamaica, for example, or in the reclamation rite in Haitian Vodou. One very noteworthy aspect of the Nation Dance is its multi-ethnic complexity. If a shared identity is the premise of an individual's incorporation into a group, difference is the play of individuality that forever keeps identity in flux. Whereas identity is a site of unity, difference is the place of tension. The Nation Dance of Carriacou is in fact a ceremony in which the traditions of different dispersed *nations* are celebrated *together* in one sacred space, but in sequence, one after the other, each receiving its due: the Ibo, Cromanti, Congo, Arada, Moko, and others. African steps make way for European as the drums welcome the Old Creole nation. The Nation Dance is *inter*national (see Taylor 1996, McDaniel 1998: 18). Edward Kamau Brathwaite makes an appeal to this meaning of "nation" in its international sense when he refers to the languages of African Caribbean peoples as "nation language" (Brathwaite 1984: 2).

This "dancing of nations" is very typical of the wider Caribbean religious experience. In West African thought, the spiritual world is linked to the physical, and religion is an ever changing symbolic arena in which new spiritual forces reveal themselves as the world changes. If God is a guarantor of meaning, meaning is contextualized and experienced in a multiplicity of evolving divine, ancestral, and spiritual forces. When different peoples come into contact with each other, their differing spiritual forces enter into relationships. The trauma of capture, enslavement, and transshipment intensified contact between Africans of different religious backgrounds and faiths and brought African traditions into contact with new Aboriginal, European, and, later, South and East Asian religious influences. Haitian Vodou consists primarily of four different *nanchon* (nations): Rada (Arada or Dahomey), Petro (of Haitian origin, but with West African and Aboriginal influences), Kongo, and Ibo. As in the case of the Nation Dance, ethnic differentiation in ritual does not signify actual ethnically different communities: most practicing Haitians are followers of both of the two dominant rites, Rada and Petro, and a Rada ceremony may give way to a Petro ceremony. Similarly, under the rubric of Afro-Cuban religion can be found two principal religious orders, or *regla* (rules), each linked to a different African *nación* (nation): Regla de Ocha (Yoruba), Regla de Congo or Palo Monte (Congo). Archbishop Deloris Seiveright refers in her essay in this volume to the flags of the twelve "tribes" or "nations" in Spiritual Baptist ceremony in the Eastern and Southern Caribbean.

This interplay of ethnic difference is not limited to African religious experience. If Petro contains an Aboriginal influence, so too does Winti in Suriname.

Winti goes one step further: given the significant population of Indian descendants of indentured workers in Suriname, it explicitly accommodates Indian spiritual manifestations as well as Aboriginal. Pocomania in Jamaica and Orisha in Trinidad likewise acknowledge Indian spirits of the dance. African Caribbean religions also incorporate aspects of Christianity as taught by Europeans. As has often been observed, African deities share their altars with Christian saints in Haiti, Cuba, Suriname, Jamaica, Trinidad, and elsewhere in the Caribbean. Related processes can be found in some Indian Caribbean religions. Otherwise disparate Indian deities and symbols find themselves in varying relations with each other in the Caribbean as well as with African and European traditions. God, source of all meaning and belief, is the ultimate unity behind all of these symbolic and ritual differentiations, having emanated out of many homelands (the Americas, Africa, Asia, the Middle East) in many guises (Jah, Itzamna, Nzame, Nyame, Olorun, Brahman, Yahweh, Allah).

Scholars have often referred to the overlap and mingling of Caribbean religious systems as "syncretism," a term indicating the extent to which difference has been transposed into unity or synthesis. Syncretism, as opposed to nativism on one hand and assimilation on the other, was the basis for the generation of a new Caribbean culture, the bearer of a new Caribbean nationality. Roberto Fernández Retamar argues that *mestizaje* was for Cuba's José Martí the synthesis of the Aboriginal, the African, and the European and thereby the basis of "our America" (Fernández Retamar 1989: 4). The term "creolization" carried a similar idea: despite differing regional connotations over time, "creole" applied to that which was born in the Caribbean and referred to locally born Europeans and Africans, to their descendants, and to the hybrid language and culture they generated in the region (Allsopp 1996: 176–77). Recent scholarship argues, however, that the term "symbiosis" is more applicable to Caribbean religions than is either "syncretism" or "creolization," in that it accommodates the dance of difference that characterizes them. According to Desmangles, "symbiosis refers to the spatial juxtaposition of diverse religious traditions from two continents, which coexist without fusing with one another" (Desmangles 1992: 8). Following a similar line of thought, Fred Case argues elsewhere in this volume for an "intersemiotic" approach to the study of Caribbean religion that would take into account the dynamic intersection of different cultural codes. The idea of symbiosis helps to pull together two apparently opposing schools of Caribbean social and cultural thought: the creolists and the pluralists. Whereas creolization focuses on the developing unity of the new formative nation, pluralism emphasizes the social and cultural differences that divided and continue to divide a conflictual Caribbean region.

In social and political terms, the Caribbean can be said to manifest a "fragmented nationalism" (Knight 1990). Although inhabited by sovereign, Aboriginal First Nations with their own histories of conflict and cooperation, the region was taken over by various European conquerors, who were often at war with each other and claimed territory in the names of their respective monarchs. The

Africans who were brought to the region against their will and forced to work as chattel slaves looked back to Africa, seeing it as a source of their religion, culture, and identity, home of their *lwa* (divinities of Vodou). Each African nation in the Caribbean preserved, to the extent possible, a sense of that people's link to a particular people or kingdom in Africa. Over time, with creolization, references to specific African regions came to represent Africa in a wider, Pan-African sense. This Pan-African sensibility was reinforced by contact with the Judeo-Christian tradition. Africans in Jamaica and elsewhere identified themselves as a nation in exile and, like the ancient Jews, looked forward to a return to an African Zion. Many identified themselves as Ethiopians, and Ethiopia, a symbol of Africa in general, became the promised land. More recently, the Nation of Islam, drawing from an earlier tradition of African Muslim presence in the Americas, has presented another Pan-African religious ideology. Many Europeans looked back to European nations as their true homes and sources of identity, a process reinforced by Christian ideologies, whether Catholic or Protestant, that legitimated the enterprise of national conquest and colonization. The Indians who were brought as indentured workers originally saw themselves as temporary sojourners in the Caribbean and looked back to India for religious instruction, whether Hindu or Muslim.

Despite this external orientation in Caribbean culture, religion played an important role in the processes leading toward the development of new national cultures and national independence. The ethnic nationalism in which religion expressed itself constantly provided a site of opposition to the European colonial order. The colonial authorities quickly learned the dangers of allowing the slaves to dance, drum, and "have fun," and aspects of slave culture were forbidden. Over time, there was a move toward more creolized, Pan-African ethnic associations that challenged the colonial plantation system, a process that culminated, in the case of Haiti, in a revolutionary transformation (1791–1804). C. L. R. James's famous words express the spirit of this process: "Voodoo was the medium of the conspiracy. In spite of all prohibitions, the slaves travelled miles to sing and dance and practise the rites and talk" (James 1989: 86). According to Haitian oral tradition, the Haitian Revolution began with the dance of the *lwa*, led by a *mambo* (priestess) and the famed Boukman, at a ceremony at Bois Caïman. Christianity, indigenized and reinterpreted in a Caribbean context as a struggle for human dignity, freedom, and equality, reinforced the oppositional process strongly expressed in events such as the 1831 Jamaica Rebellion led by "Native" Baptist preachers such as Sam Sharpe. Likewise, the Indian stick-dancing, drama, and ceremony associated with the Shī'a festival of Tadjah (the martyrdom play reenacting the death of Husayn) was both a symbolic challenge to colonial regimes in Trinidad and Guyana and a vehicle for social change, particularly when Hindus and Africans joined in the Muslim celebrations. This spirit of opposition would ultimately contribute to the movements for national independence in the Anglophone Caribbean. In Cuba, national independence is symbolized by its patron saint, the Virgen de la Caridad del Cobre, a confluence of Taino, Yoruba, and Hispanic mythologies, Atabey, Oshun, and the Virgin Mary in concert, or as Antonio Benítez-Rojo puts it, "a triptych" of "wandering signifiers" (Benítez-Rojo 1992: 13).

To the extent that the "Creole" or "Mestizo" Nation emerges as the dominant concept of nation in the struggle for national independence in the Caribbean, it could be said that a sense of the nation emerges that conforms both to an ancient meaning of nation as expressed in the quest of the Jewish people for a homeland and sovereign state and to a modern notion of the nation state as a culturally homogenous, sovereign political entity. However, the very problematic "forgetting" of the past and in particular of past ethnic diversity and brutality, which Ernest Renan argues is a necessary condition of the modern sense of nation (Renan 1990: 11), is challenged in the Caribbean experience by the ever persistent irruption of ethnic difference and pluralism. National politics as creole politics remained heterogenous. The myth of the singular national identity was expressed at the ideological level: Haitians defined themselves as blacks, Cubans as mestizos, some Anglo-Caribbean nations as creole. However, Caribbean nations never resolved the social and cultural tensions dividing different ethnic, racial, and social groups: not in Revolutionary Haiti or Cuba; not in the liberal Anglophone Caribbean countries; not in heterogeneous Guyana, Trinidad, or Surinam.

Does this mean that the modern Caribbean nation is destined to self-destruct, torn asunder by religion, ethnic chauvinism, and social conflict, on one hand, and the globalization of American religions, communications technology, and free-trade ideology, on the other? Frantz Fanon was one of the most important spokespersons of the twentieth-century independence movements in Africa and elsewhere and also their fiercest critic. His comments are relevant to the Caribbean, his own homeland. Devoid of an independent economic base in a neo-colonial global order, the national bourgeoisie of the new nations transform themselves into authoritarian elites and use religion and other cultural forms to legitimate themselves: ultra-nationalism, chauvinism, and racism are the result, and "nationalism, that magnificent song that made the people rise against their oppressors, stops short, falters and dies away on the day that independence is proclaimed" (Fanon 1968: 203). For Fanon, this degeneration into ultra-nationalism could be prevented only by the practice of an emancipatory culture tied to a democratic politics and a vision of an egalitarian social order. As Ato Sekyi-Otu eloquently puts it, "the modern griot" must "shepherd the writing and the dissemination of the nation's 'vast epic' in a manner radically free from the ancestral complicity of the griot's craft and epic knowledge in 'systems of power and domination'" (Sekyi-Otu 1996: 204). Fanon's ethical imperative is as applicable to the Caribbean as it is to Africa or other postcolonial regions. In the Caribbean it is the dynamic sense of nation that continues to resist and transform both ethnic chauvinism and global homogenization. Laënnec Hurbon's paper in this volume addresses the situation in contemporary Haiti and is a testimony to the role that religion can play in the transformation of the authoritarian postcolonial nation. That Caribbean peoples are fundamentally diasporic; that the nation always oversteps its borders, spatially and temporally; these are the additional guarantees that culture can meet culture, religion meet religion in a dance of mutual recognition and a spirit of common cooperation in the human project.

Dealing with different cultural and religious traditions in the Caribbean, the essays in this volume address some of the major contemporary issues in the study of Caribbean religions as understood by practitioners and scholars who come from the region or who have done extensive fieldwork or research there. The book is divided into three parts and moves in a series of overlapping spirals: from a focus on (1) spirituality and healing, to an examination of (2) theology in social and political context, followed by (3) reflections on religion, identity, and diaspora. The movement from Parts I to II to III is essentially dialectical: from subjective and personal to objective and social, thence to identity as the interplay of the two. This is also a movement outward, from the center out, from home to diaspora, and then on, to the interplay of diaspora and home. Although each essay is a unique contribution, the essays are all related to each other, informing each other and providing wider and deeper understandings of Caribbean religion, culture, and identity.

The Western academic tradition has tended to assume a dualistic conception of the Western "scholar" and *his* "informant." This conception has been put into question by postmodern and postcolonial theorists, among others. This collection explicitly challenges the assumption of the omniscient scholar and the singular, "objective" approach to scholarship. It presumes that scholarship is informed by the location and commitment of the scholar. By virtue of this, scholarship is dialogical and polyphonic. This is particularly true in the case of Caribbean religion and identity, given the plurality of religious discourses, the ideological role of culture, and the ongoing quest for identity in the region. To paraphrase Benítez-Rojo, the Caribbean is characterized by the polyrhythmic play of difference, where traditional and scientific knowledge co-exist and poetry encounters theory (Benítez-Rojo 1992: 17–20).

In this spirit, the collection of essays included here begins with the voices of specific practitioners and then opens into a broad multidisciplinary and interdisciplinary examination of different Caribbean religious traditions and practices from across the region. Essays were selected for inclusion in the volume that offered unique contemporary perspectives and insights relevant to the understanding of Caribbean religion and identity, thus challenging readers to envision new ways of understanding the Caribbean experience. The subjective tone of the first chapters of Part I brings the reader into the lived experience and meaning of Caribbean religiosity: the poetic vitality of practitioners' voices; the importance of listening to these voices and to their spirit; the need to understand different cultures from the inside and the limits to the possibility of such understanding. Subsequent essays do not relinquish this concern with voice even as they deal with wider social, political, and cultural issues. Some are concerned with methodological or theoretical issues, while others are based on fieldwork, archival research, and textual analysis. Issues of race and ethnicity, class and gender, are discussed in various essays and from different perspectives, all uni-fied in their concern to critically address issues of Caribbean religion and identity and advance understanding and scholarship in the field.

An attempt was made to ensure that the major linguistic and geographical areas were represented in the book: from the little-known Dutch Caribbean and Guyana to the more publicized Cuban and Haitian experiences. Most ethnicities and associated religions typical of the Caribbean are also represented: from the less-known Chinese and Indian, both Muslim and Hindu, to more-familiar Afri-can and European traditions. Each subsequent essay is integral to a volume that, as a whole, challenges the reader to address a breadth of Caribbean religious and cultural experiences.

Part I of the book is centered on spirituality, healing, and the divine. The essays in this part range across different Caribbean cultures and regions and focus in large part on the experiences of Caribbean women. The part begins with the words of an *espiritista* (spiritualist) healer, Eva Fernandez Bravo. A daughter of Africa and Europe and a mother 70 years old, Ms. Fernandez left her home in Santiago de Cuba in October 1996 to visit North America for the first time and present this talk. She spoke about her mission and shared her faith and spirit of charity with an international audience. As her ancestors did in Cuba, she used the materials, foods, and spiritual forces that she found when she arrived in Toronto to create a sacred altar, and she led a moving and memorable healing ceremony. Ms. Fernandez began that ceremony by locating and ritually greeting those spiritual leaders who were present. She then invited two Spiritual Baptist leaders, Queen Mother Bishop Yvonne B. Drakes and Archbishop Doctor Deloris Seiveright, to join her in leading the ceremony, despite the fact that she had only met them for the first time that day and they apparently spoke different lan-guages and followed different traditions. In the words of Nancy Mikelsons, a participant-observer who had worked with Eva Fernandez for many years:

> I had never seen Eva work with other women before; it appeared that she had been working with these two wonderful co-celebrants for years. That ceremony was so seamless in its ritual and rhythm that it was a miraculous moment. Until the cere-mony began in earnest, there was a highly sensitive and skilled young woman translating for Eva. Once the spirits entered the room translation of a verbal nature was no longer necessary. While the different elements that came to the ceremony unannounced but destined were entirely different from those in Eva's house, the power of Eva's belief filled the room and embraced every person there, and the atmo-sphere of spiritual truth and safety, in that place for that time, was identical to what Eva created in her home. (Personal communication, Aug. 10, 1998)

Althea Prince, a contributor to this volume, has written an equally moving testimony to the ability of these three spiritual leaders to work with each other across different traditions in the dance of nations that took place at that event:

> Ms. Fernandez invited the two Spiritual Baptist Bishops to participate in the prayers and blessings at an altar that she had earlier constructed. Soon, the "meeting" of

Spirit could be felt and seen in the ease of communication, without translation, between the three Healers.

It was very moving to see Eva Fernandez, while in connection with Spirit, gesture in precise and perfect harmony with the two Spiritual Baptist Bishops. There was flawless, synchronic harmony in the timing of physical movements, as the prayers moved from supplication to benediction. (Newsletter, Caribbean Religions Project, No. 2, Fall 1997)

Eva Fernandez Bravo passed away in 1997 in Santiago de Cuba. This book is dedicated to her, for she is a symbol of the strength of Caribbean spirituality and its ability to reconcile difference without homogenizing the human spirit. Her generous blessing of this academic initiative has encouraged us to make of it a collective offering.

Essays by Queen Mother Bishop Drakes and Archbishop Doctor Seiveright follow Eva Fernandez's presentation. Bishop Drakes talks about Orisha influences in her life in Trinidad, her calling as a Spiritual Baptist, and her practice in Toronto. Archbishop Seiveright traces her own background in the Pentecostal Church in Jamaica, her discovery of her Spiritual Baptist faith, and her role in its practice in Toronto. Drawing from the traditions of their homelands, they both contributed to the building of new communities in the North American diaspora.

Bringing to the scholarly endeavor a deep sensitivity and spirituality, sociologist and fiction writer Althea Prince addresses epistemological issues in the study of Caribbean religion by focusing on the issue of "voice" in the following chapter. The practitioner's voice, expressed in song and prayer, lays claims to the "strange" land in which it finds itself, ritual dance embodies it, and a new Caribbean divine is expressed in the "patchwork" of Caribbean spirituality.

Eva Fernandez, Yvonne Drakes, and Deloris Seiveright are just three of the many Caribbean voices expressed in this volume. Taken as a whole, the collection of essays is premised on the notion that the scholarly endeavor is compatible with religious expression, though neither is reducible to the other. The scholar need not be a practitioner, though some are; the practitioner may not be a scholar, but could be. Though they speak from different intellectual contexts and though the tools of their trades differ, both scholar and practitioner are engaged in a process of disalienation, a quest for meaning, and a work of reconciliation.

Likewise concerned with epistemological issues, Petronella Breinburg raises questions about methodology in the anthropological study of the Surinamese Winti religion in the next essay. She argues that the "insider" should be acknowledged as having a privileged linguistic and cultural knowledge, which the scholar from the "outside" ignores at his or her peril. This is particularly true given that the Winti religion of Surinam, with its complex intermingling of many of the different cultural and national strands that constitute Surinamese culture, has often been perceived through layers of distortion perpetrated by missionaries, anthropologists, and even educated Surinamese. Frederick Case, a literary and cultural critic, addresses a similar problem but does so by making a profound epistemological shift. He argues that one new way to address the complexity of Caribbean religions and their intersemiotic relationships, particularly in the interplay of African and Indian traditions in the region, is to use a number of Arabic epistemological categories. He proceeds to demonstrate how this approach can yield a new understanding of different aspects of Caribbean culture, focusing on several African Guyanese practitioners, all women, who use Hindu Kali Mai practices in the healing process.

To argue that the female practitioner in the Caribbean has a resonant voice that can be heard by those who want to listen should not, however, allow us to romanticize the lot of women in many Caribbean religions. Here the point of view of a Cuban feminist like Margarita Castro Flores is salutary and yields important insights. Drawing on fieldwork in the area of religions of African origin in Cuba, Castro Flores argues in her contribution that these religious expressions, regardless of the African systems or nationalities involved, tend to share a patriarchal understanding of the world with the wider *machista* culture of Cuba. Yet she points out that each system has its own unique gender roles, some of which can be empowering for women, a point that is made in other essays in this collection.

Part II of this volume shifts the discussion of Caribbean religions into a more historical framework, focusing on the transformation of biblical theologies in the Caribbean and their impact on society and politics. Paralleling Prince's commentary on the voice of the psalmist in "a strange land," I begin this part with a Caribbean exegesis of the "Song of Songs." Rastafari "reasoning" lays claim to an ancient African biblical tradition of Judaism, Christianity, and Islam, as expressed in the thirteenth-century *Kebra Nagast,* the narrative of the Ethiopian nation. Quintessentially Caribbean, Rastafari is an expression of a Caribbean national identity that is fundamentally African yet forever marked by Europe and India. The transformation, reinterpretation, and indigenization of European Christianity as Caribbean nationhood is being claimed is one theme in the next chapter. A Church historian with a deep personal knowledge of the Caribbean Church, Arthur Dayfoot shows how the hegemonic and external status of Catholicism in the Caribbean gave way to a plurality of religious expressions as Protestant denominations became influential and were later indigenized. Dayfoot's synoptic view of the Caribbean Church history is complemented by Juanita De Barros's very close historical study of one Christian denomination in Guyana, the Congregationalists. Using a number of primary sources for the first time, De Barros argues that Afro-Guyanese found in Congregationalism ways to resist the colonial hierarchy and position themselves in a conflictual social order. Though Christianity could be read in progressive terms by Afro-Caribbean people, it was most often used to reinforce ideologies of oppression. This was true of most Christian denominations, both Catholic and Protestant. Salvation in heaven was the compensation if not the actual reward for hard physical labor on earth. Women were subordinated to men. The contemporary international surge in Pentecostalism and related "fundamentalist" phenomena has tended to reinforce this conservative practice of Christianity in the Caribbean. Some remarkable ideological transformations are also occurring within Pentecostalism, however, and these are challenging traditional feminist approaches to Christianity. Judith Soares, a political scientist working on gender issues in the Caribbean, traces transformations in gender ideologies in the practice of "fundamentalist" Christianity in Barbados and shows why we must examine "fundamentalist" churches more closely to see how they can empower women.

Part II of the book culminates in a careful analysis of the intersection of religion and politics in Haiti by Laënnec Hurbon, one of Haiti's leading cultural critics. If the upsurge of popular Catholicism, under the influence of liberation theology, was a major player in the political transformation of the Haitian state in the 1980s, Protestantism and Vodou also played important roles. Haitian Vodou, once a progressive force in the formation of a national identity in the struggle against slavery, had been co-opted by a national authoritarian regime. In the *dechoukaj* (uprooting), Vodou, like Christianity, revealed its transformative power. However, both the popular church and progressive Vodou were later restrained. The national imperative, suggests Hurbon, is to recognize the role that different religions can play in deepening the democratic process, to let the nation dance its dance.

Part III of this book explicitly addresses two related themes that are implicit in the earlier essays: identity and diaspora. If religion provides a fundamental source of identity in the Caribbean, diaspora as a religious trope and Caribbean reality has regenerated religious forms and meanings in ways that indicate that identities are ongoing constructions. Historically, people from many nations were dispersed to the Caribbean region; many were once again dispersed, to other Caribbean territories, to Europe, North America, and elsewhere. At each stage they constructed new identities, often drawing from a deeply religious and historical sensibility. Queen Mother Bishop Drakes and Archbishop Doctor Deloris Seiveright, the two Spiritual Baptist leaders who, with Eva Fernandez, opened this book, express the diasporic condition in their very being. Both born in the Caribbean, both are healers to the Caribbean diaspora in North America. Moving beyond religious, linguistic, and national borders, they joined with Eva, a person who had never before left the Caribbean, to weave their curative spiritual "patchwork." All of the essays in this volume are but threads in a tapestry of the global movement of peoples into the Caribbean region from elsewhere in the Americas, Europe, Africa, and Asia and back out again to all the continents of the globe.

Part III opens with the Jamaican sociologist Barry Chevannes in a richly poetic evocation of the Jamaican *yaad* (yard) as a metaphor for home and source of identity. If the Ethiopian in exile looks toward Africa to envision a home, the Jamaican in the Caribbean diaspora in North America remembers and recreates the sacred space of the yard that is home. Without that spiritual return, without name, lineage, nation, there is only rootlessness, and there can be no going forward. That does not mean that the human person must sacrifice his or her subjectivity at the altar of the clan. Diaspora necessitates return, but it is fundamentally about movement. The risk of any claim to identity is that it may be used to deny the ongoing processes of identity formation. The following intervention by Abrahim Khan, a philosopher of religion, challenges those claims to a Caribbean identity that deny cultural difference, lived experience, individuality, and transformation. Examining religion from a cross-cultural perspective that includes two major but neglected traditions in the Caribbean, Hinduism and Islam, he argues that the integrity of the person is at the foundation of religious experience. Religious forms and cultural expressions that deny personhood in the name of identity risk becoming idolatrous.

The Caribbean's First Nations, the waves of Aboriginal peoples who first settled and named the region, were also its first diasporic peoples. Although written out of Caribbean history with the coming of the Europeans, they continue to exert their influence in some islands and in mainland areas such as the Guyanas and Belize and have provided the Caribbean with a vital heritage in ritual, language, and environmental knowledge. Other peoples such as the Chinese were also written out of Caribbean history, as Frank Scherer shows in the next chapter. Drawing from ethnographic fieldwork and bibliographical research in Cuba, he shows how a Chinese Cuban diaspora has responded to changes in Cuban state policy, which have provided new opportunities for religious and ethnic expression. By reinventing aspects of a Confucian heritage and constructing anew their Chinese-Cuban identity, Chinese in Cuba have found themselves participating in a process of self-orientalization.

Part III, and the volume as a whole, concludes with Sean Lokaisingh-Meighoo's theorization of the dialectical relation between diaspora and home, the resulting ambiguities in Caribbean notions of home and styles of identity formation, and the implications of this for understanding Caribbean culture and religion. Picking up on themes posed in the other articles in Part III and, indeed, in the book as a whole, he underscores the dynamism of Caribbean constructs of self and community as they relate to the deep, intercontinental movement of a doubly diasporic Caribbean history: dispersed from Asia and Africa to the Caribbean region, Caribbean people found themselves on the move again, to London, New York, Toronto, and many other places. But to argue that the Caribbean experience is fundamentally diasporic is not to deny cultural difference. Whereas Indian culture and religion have become a celebration of "arrival" in the new Caribbean "home," despite the indignities of indentureship, African culture has focused on the struggle for emancipation.

The modern nation, whether in the Caribbean or outside of it, is the site of difference, plurality, and transformation. In the Nation Dance, the dispersed nations dance their separate dances in the same yard. They borrow from and influence each other, but the dancing of the different nations does not stop. The dance of nations is not ultimately about the dialectic of ethnicity on the stage of History; nor is it simply the immanent expression of a monotheistic God's strange and polymorphous ways. It is about spirit as it manifests itself in the individual in community; and it is about the relations between living communities in a modern globalized world. Religious symbols, rituals, and practices provide inner meaning and define who we are as persons in relation to other persons. But they also commemorate collective history and consolidate group identity. Histories live only in the lives of the individuals and communities. How can this spirit be represented? The scholar and the practitioner each have their own way of experiencing the reality, telling the story, and dancing the dance. Paule Marshall as artist mediates these separate spaces in her praisesong, providing a place for feeling and thought, for the individual voice and collective understanding. The ability to invoke the emergence of a Caribbean person as a voyager in an international world, a person who can dance the terrestrial dance with an identity that is at home with difference—this is one measure of the contribution of Caribbean religions to Caribbean and world culture.

Works Cited

Allsopp, Richard, ed. 1996. *Dictionary of Caribbean English Usage*. Oxford: Oxford University Press.

Benítez-Rojo, Antonio. 1992. *The Repeating Island: The Caribbean and the Postmodern Perspective*. Translated by James Maranis. Durham: Duke University Press.

Brathwaite, Edward Kamau. 1984. *History of the Voice: The Development of Nation Language in Anglophone Caribbean Poetry*. London: New Beacon Books.

Desmangles, Leslie. 1992. *The Faces of the Gods: Vodou and Roman Catholicism in Haiti*. Chapel Hill: University of North Carolina Press.

Fanon, Frantz. 1968. *The Wretched of the Earth*. Translated by Constance Farrington. New York: Grove Press.

Fernández Retamar, Roberto. 1989. *Caliban and Other Essays*. Translated by Edward Baker. Minneapolis: University of Minnesota Press.

Gilroy, Paul. 1993. *The Black Atlantic: Modernity and Double Consciousness*. Cambridge, Mass.: Harvard University Press.

James, C. L. R. 1989. *The Black Jacobins: Toussaint L'Ouverture and the San Domingo Revolution*. 2nd rev. ed. New York: Vintage-Random House.

Knight, Franklin. 1990. *The Caribbean: The Genesis of a Fragmented Nationalism*. New York: Oxford University Press.

Marshall, Paule. 1984. *Praisesong for the Widow*. New York: Dutton-Obelisk.

McDaniel, Lorna. 1998. *The Big Drum Ritual in Carriacou: Praisesongs in Rememory of Flight*. Gainesville: University Press of Florida.

Nettleford, Rex. 1993. *Inward Stretch, Outward Reach: A Voice from the Caribbean*. London: Macmillan Caribbean.

Nietzsche, Friedrich. 1960. *Joyful Wisdom*. Translated by Thomas Common. New York: Ungar.

Renan, Ernest. [1882] 1990. "What Is a Nation?" In *Nation and Narration,* edited by Homi K. Bhabha. New York: Routledge.

Sekyi-Otu, Ato. 1996. *Fanon's Dialectic of Experience.* Cambridge, Mass.: Harvard University Press.

Taylor, Patrick. 1996. "Postcolonial Encounters: Paule Marshall's 'Widow's Praisesong' and George Lamming's 'Daughter's Adventure.'" In *"And the Birds Began to Sing": Religion and Literature in Post-Colonial Cultures,* edited by Jamie Scott. Amsterdam: Rodopi.

I

Spirituality, Healing,
and the Divine

1

Across the Waters
Practitioners Speak

EVA FERNANDEZ BRAVO, YVONNE B. DRAKES,
AND DELORIS SEIVERIGHT

Faith, Hope, and Charity
Eva Fernandez Bravo, Spiritualist
(Transcription and English translation by Adriana Premat)*

I am Eva Fernandez from Cuba. I'm going to speak humbly of things that may be small, but are very interesting. I am a 70-year-old woman, with six children, thirteen grandchildren, and eight great-grandchildren. I am a millionaire. I have been able to attain this wealth, to bring up my family, because of the spirits and because I have obeyed and have done what they have told me and not what I wanted to do.

I came here today because I am driven by the spirits to seek out faith, to unite us, to strengthen the chain because faith, faith is now divided. The spirits have an important mission to the students, the sick; they are important for all needs; but today they are being divided by the monetarization [la metalización] of faith and charity. To save the needy, to give charity to the person who needs it, money [el metal] should not matter. What should matter is the love with which we are going to help human beings because that is what made us missionaries; that is what put us on this mission, making us missionaries who are not bought since we carry it from birth, because the mission cannot be learnt. No. This is a mission given us by the Almighty, wherein lies faith, hope, and charity. What is charity? That I am able to solve a problem for a brother or sister that needs me. But if I go with the money, that is not charity, it is not faith. And it is this faith that we have to seek, in order to continue maintaining it because I know something very great is approaching us in the spiritual field. And this great thing that we are awaiting, we must earn it with faith. And for this I have come here to

*This translation is based on a transcription of an oral presentation in Spanish that was taped at York University, Toronto (1 November 1996). The translator has remained as faithful as possible to the original words of Eva Fernandez, even though this means leaving ambiguities in the English text.

share with you this faith, so that we may unite to make that faith greater and await what the Almighty has for us.

In my faith, when it is time to give charity I invoke the spirits and they make an appearance [*hacen trance*] in my person. I'm not always conscious, but the spirit expresses what it wants to say. Then there are other brothers and sisters around us and they say what the spirit expressed and I do as the spirit orders me.

Well, I saw the spirits when I was 8. My mother did not believe it because she was Catholic. She told me that I was not well. But when I was a young woman I visited the cemetery a lot because a friend of mine, an elderly blind man, had died. So I would pick flowers and I nurtured this spirit. A period of time passed during which I knew nothing more of these things. I got married. I still did not see anything, but I felt things and I loved Santa Barbara, very much. She was my friend. When I had my last son, I had had six children and I was twenty-four and a half. Then, the spirits returned. They made an appearance [*hacen trance*] in my person.

I worked at a factory and my children were single. Two of them got married; there were two women and two men left. And the spirits took me out of the factory to look after my unmarried children and I would say, "Oh, how am I going to support them!" A spirit told me that we would not go without our daily bread. And with my faith, in my house, I worked the spirits. They all got married. And, look, now I'm single because they all got married and I'm grateful to God and to all the spirits. But it was with my faith, because I didn't doubt when they took me away from work.

My "head saint" [*santo de cabeza*] is blessed Santa Barbara and my ritual, after, is of the spirits. My humble mission is to be a missionary and to help my neighbor. But today my neighbors are divided: one has faith and the other doesn't. So the path that we must walk is more difficult, but we are going to carry on and we will prevail. As part of my mission I have a lot of contact with Lázaro, who is a missionary of health and cures many; he's very miraculous. I have Yemayá, the Virgin of Regla, as mother of the deep sea, mother of the spirits. When we gather at the altar we first count on her so that spirits arrive and put us into a trance.

I spoke of Santa Barbara, but my protector spirit is a man, and when I pass through my protector spirit and my guiding spirit, then I can work African, Chinese, French, all spiritual fields. So that woman is not an idol. No. All the spirits, male and female, when we invoke them, a man or a woman may come down. Now I adore Santa Barbara because she is my "head" [*cabeza*], but my protector spirit is a man, and my guide is a nun.

I have no church of my own. My church is Catholic and my home is my center. On Sundays we gather there. That is what we call a spiritual center. Then, we work, trying to find faith because the other side is selfishness, evil, envy. These two parts cannot unite. So we must try with faith to clean this part, to purify it so that we can unite and live better.

So, this is a mission that gives much and this is what I bring you, that we may sustain our faith so that in this world we can reach that which is great and comes from the Almighty.

My Spiritual Journey
Queen Mother Bishop Yvonne B. Drakes

THE SPIRITUAL INHERITANCE AND THE EARLY YEARS

My great-grandmother came directly from Africa; she was enslaved and taken to the island of Grenada. She was a practitioner of Orisha worship and although captured and taken into slavery, her work with the *orisha* (Yoruba divinities), healing and caring for those in need of spiritual guidance, continued on the strange shores of her captivity. Of course I did not know her; however, my grand-mother, the one to whom she eventually passed on her knowledge and work, spoke very highly and favorably about this illuminated soul.

At the passing of my grandmother, the Orisha work fell to my aunt. My aunt was unwilling to carry on the tradition of the family, as she claimed to be a proponent of the "civilized world." After a series of trials and tribulations that plagued her life, a near-death experience and a vision brought about a change of heart and a firm commitment to her destiny. She recounts her vision: "I saw myself dying on my hospital bed, when my mother appeared and used a goblet made of clay to perform certain African death rituals to release me from the jaws of death. But the words were spoken clearly and sternly: 'You must do the work; if not, you die. The choice is yours, choose life or death.'"

For many years prior to her death, my aunt gave this interpretation of the story: "There were certain things in my mother's house which I had to take with me into my new house. These I did not take, hence the reason for my accident." These ancestral artifacts were both sacred and ceremonial, forming the core sym-bols for the Orisha work. My aunt was instructed to make a pilgrimage with the artifacts, taking them from their present resting place into her house. This was a way for her to honor the ancestors. When these artifacts were placed in her new home, my aunt's work in Orisha began, and the ancestors became "alive" through her manifestations. Following this "acceptance" of the Orisha work, she annually offered African prayers in the Orisha way until her death.

It was during one of these annual ceremonies that I first encountered the Orisha powers. At the age of 13, I got the manifestations in the middle of the proceedings, and at that time I was chosen for the Orisha work. Three years after my aunt passed away, the ancestral spirits "searched" for me and "found" me. I started having visions, although I did not realize that the time had come for me to take up the work of the ancestors.

THE TRAINING YEARS

I traveled to Canada and was not actively involved in any of the Orisha prayers or proceedings for a long, long time. When the time came to accept my Orisha heritage, I had to be baptized in the Spiritual Baptist Faith, as I needed knowledge and exposure to this heritage. My "Father" church is St. Anne Spiritual Baptist Faith, Inc., under the auspices of Archbishop Brinsley D. Dickson. The Spiritual Baptist Faith provided me with all of the prerequisites needed for my preparation for the work of the Orisha ancestors. I underwent a period of fasting, praying, and "mourning," in order to be taught the work of the *orisha*. This preceded my initiation into the Orisha work. This retreat of fasting, praying, and "mourning" was a learning experience, and I received visions of my grandmother, instructing and teaching me the fundamentals of the Orisha work. At the end of this training period, I beheld my coronation as Queen of the Seven Orisha Tribes. My baptism in the Spiritual Baptist Faith and my Orisha heritage had finally merged into what I am called today: "an Orisha Baptist." I am therefore under both the banner of the Spiritual Baptist Faith and that of the Orisha Faith.

I experienced an advanced period of training when I journeyed to Trinidad in August 1985, to officially take over the work of the Orisha Queen. This ceremony was performed at my aunt's property in Trinidad, where everything was set up for the transfer of stewardship of the Orisha ancestral work, handed down in my family for three generations. After the "acceptance" ceremony, I returned to Canada to continue my work here.

THE YEARS AFTER "ACCEPTANCE"

Since my initiation and "crowning" as Queen of the Seven Orisha Tribes, I have continued my journey by fasting, praying, and "mourning," receiving along the way first the nine tribes and now the twelve tribes of the *orisha*. I have also grown within the Spiritual Baptist Faith, and two years ago I became eligible to be ordained as a Minister of the gospel. I was ordained as the first woman Bishop in the Spiritual Baptist Faith of Canada.

The Spiritual Baptist Faith was officially accepted in Canada as a denomination on 15 August 1997. Its founding Father, Archbishop Vernon Manswell, and his wife, Judy Manswell, the Mother Abbess, continue to work diligently, along with the founding Committee of Bishops, to promote this Faith and educate Canadians about its precepts and practices. The Faith became more visible in July 1998, through its participation in the host of activities that celebrated Canada Day.

My Orisha "feasts" are held under the banner of Trinity Divine Spiritual Baptist Church. Annually, we host three days of "African Prayers" and feed hundreds of homeless people at shelters in Toronto. This is done during the second week of August and culminates with a water pilgrimage, either to Lake Ontario or to Lake Simcoe.

The work my ancestors have placed on me has served to bring me to full faith in Canada. Through the Spiritual Baptist Faith in Canada, I feel fulfilled that this African inheritance has finally come to fulfill its place within the spiritual boundaries of our Faith. I am proud to look back, honoring those who brought the *orisha* to the world of the Caribbean and the Americas.

The Shouters National Evangelical Spiritual Baptist Faith
Archbishop Doctor Deloris Seiveright

HISTORICAL BACKGROUND

I personally use the word "awesome" to describe this Faith. My Spiritual Father, the late Elton George Griffith, described it as "a diamond." This rich and illustrious Faith can be defined as Christianity with African traditions. The Faith originated in Trinidad through a vision received by a Grenadian, Elton George Griffith. The "call" was that he should lead the people to spiritual freedom with the Shouter Baptist concept of the Divine. However, African people were initially prevented from worshipping in this Faith. The hand clapping, chanting, beating of drums, bell ringing, pouring of sweet oils, shouting and moaning, "speaking in tongues," loud preaching (using the Bible as the main source of inspiration), all were outlawed by the state. Elton George Griffith built the Shouter Baptist Faith out of Shakerism, which originated in St. Vincent. That religion had also been outlawed in St. Vincent by the 1912 Shakerism Prohibition Ordinance. Many Vincentians who practiced Shakerism migrated to Trinidad, where they grew in numbers. Some of the practitioners were put in jail by the authorities, and eventually, in 1917, the religion was prohibited in that island as well.

MY OWN SPIRITUAL JOURNEY

My own spiritual journey and my embrace of the Spiritual Baptist Faith began in Toronto in 1974. I was brought up in the Pentecostal Faith; however, I felt my spirit seeking and searching for something more. As I prayed, I became aware of my limbs and body shaking at the same time that I "spoke in tongues." I also preached and shouted, some thought "like a mad woman," and it was a Guyanese friend who recognized that I was not crazy, but spiritually gifted. We went searching for the "Tie-head" woman or man, as the Spiritualists within the Spiritual Baptist Church are called. Most of the churches we visited were connected to a form of spiritualism that sought to communicate with our dead ancestors. Their practice was very quiet.

Finally, in 1971, I met a Jamaican woman named Mother Brickley, who told me about the churches of African-Caribbean people who worshipped in their basements. I visited these churches and met one Leader from St. Vincent, one from Barbados, and another from Jamaica. Their followers were mostly Trinidadian by birth, with some worshippers from other Caribbean countries. They knew about the Faith, but spoke very little of the Faith. The same gifts and talents were hidden because they could not find a church or other Caribbean people who understood the cultural basis of the religion. As a young student at Ryerson Polytechnical Institute at the time, I was spiritual but curious. I went in search of all of the churches and found two Revivalist churches in the west end of Toronto and two Spiritual Baptist churches in the east end. These two Spiritual Baptist churches that were in the east end of the city are now named St. Anne Spiritual Baptist Faith, Inc. and St. Frederic's Spiritual Baptist Church. In December 1976, I incorporated another Spiritual Baptist church in the east end of Toronto.

The Faith grew as the Caribbean population grew, and in 1975, I was advised by a Trinidadian visitor to go to Trinidad and speak to Elton George Griffith of the Spiritual Baptist Archdiocese. Other Leaders came to Toronto from Trinidad during this period, but were practicing their Faith within the Pentecostal Faith. However, they maintained their Spiritual Baptist customs, and as the Caribbean community grew, the Spiritual Baptist Faith grew. The basement churches changed to store-front churches; Leaders, Mothers, and Brothers established churches in Toronto, securing charters to practice their religion.

I am proud to say that I was one of the Ministers who established the Faith in Toronto, through the late, the Most Eminent, Dr. Archbishop Elton George Griffith and his wife, the late, Her Grace, Archbishop Elaine Griffith. In 1984, a group of Toronto Spiritual Baptist Ministers and business leaders helped me to set up a structured organization and present it to the solicitor general of the Province of Ontario. There are now approximately fifteen to twenty churches in Ontario, with approximately five to ten thousand people living and practicing this Faith. In the summer, we get a permit and preach in the parks and on street corners. Thanks to freedom and rights!

We have overcome a period of struggle in Canada but have been able to unify the Faith by keeping the name and customs of the Faith intact. This has been done with the help of God and of the Trinidad and Tobago Archdiocese, as well as members of the Caribbean community. I honor fighters who stood strong as our Leaders in the struggle for freedom in the Caribbean in 1783, 1912, 1917, 1945, 1950, 1951, 1992, and 1995.

BELIEFS AND PRACTICES

Our beliefs and practices are rich, meaningful, and powerful. We uphold the following beliefs:

• The Bible is the chief authority in all doctrinal and religious matters.

• There is one true God who is the infinite, supreme ruler of heaven and earth and who is omnipresent, omniscient, and omnipotent; the qualities of Father, Son, and Holy Spirit are expressed by Him; God is the Creator and sustains the universe; God is known and unknown and the Holy Spirit is Comforter and Instructor.

• Jesus was incarnated as a son, born of Mary, a Virgin, and fully partook of all human experiences.

• We believe in the resurrection.

• Spiritual retreats are necessary for man and woman to examine his/her conscience and search his/her soul. This period of retreat consists of prayers, partial or complete fasting, meditation, singing of praise and thanksgiving for a period of seven to forty days (it is more commonly seven days).

Washing, Anointing, and Ordinations

The first requirement of this faith is "washing" and "anointing," followed by "baptism." An individual will be placed for a whole night on a sealed chair (sealed with chalk), which is called a "mercy seat" or a "seat of repentance." With singing, teaching, and praying, the candidate will pray and ask for mercy and to receive the Holy Ghost. Lectures will enlighten the new candidate about the Faith, using water, candles, bells, and the Bible. Each candidate is not called by name, but by number.

After the "baptism" is the "mourning" ritual, which is conducted by a "pointer," that is, one who is qualified to do such a ritual. This ritual consists of self-sacrifice, a process that lasts for several days, during which time the candidate is given no food or water and is placed in a secluded, consecrated room. Nurses are in charge of the candidate during this period. This ritual enables the candidate to be cleansed and reach a higher calling in the Faith. This is the unique part of the Spiritual Baptist Faith, which cannot be explained, but must be experienced. Such a journey is called "A Pilgrimage Road," where the candidate meditates and meets teachers and guides from the spiritual realm, including angels and archangels. Again the candidate is not called by name, but by number.

Thanksgiving and Almsgiving

We give thanks for the gifts and all things that occur in our lives. Feasts and festivals are a part of the African culture. We give thanks monthly, semi-annually, and annually. This all depends on the individual. We feed the poor and give thanks for the children. Such a service consists of a table, spread with a white cloth, candles, flowers, offerings of cake, fruits, bread, fish, milk, honey, and different kinds of cooked food. The preparation varies, according to the kind of thanks being offered. There is a spiritual blessing as you give and receive. We believe that to give generously brings prosperity (2 Cor. 9; Isa. 51; Deut. 28).

FAITH AND THE MEANING OF RITUALS

The lighting of candles is a very significant part of worship in this Faith. The wax symbolizes a person, the wick represents the light and glory, and the light is symbolic of continuity and eternity. Practitioners therefore keep a candle burning at all times. It is a part of our worship, with each color representing man and woman to their fullest capacity.

As a Spiritual Baptist develops in the Faith, she/he will develop wisdom, knowledge, and understanding. To attain such wisdom, one needs to follow the rites and practices of the Faith. The church is set up as the four corners, helped by archangels. The center of the church is the pole, which represents the heart of the human and is surrounded by all of the emblems of a garden as well as African symbols and seals. Different-colored flags represent the twelve tribes and nations. The High Altar is a sacred area, and the Bishop, the Ministers, the Mothers and Nurses sit at the side of the altar. This allows them to assist others "in the spirit." The headdress and robes are worn according to each individual's depth in the faith.

During worship, we pray, sing, beat drums, clap hands, and preach. Messengers deliver messages through the spirit, and if they are needed, healings will take place. Olive oil is used in all anointing, and the staff is used to symbolize leadership. Hymns and choruses that have specific meaning are sung during worship, and trumpets are also sounded.

These rituals and practices all have significance in our worship as they do in our daily lives. This Faith can be discussed, debated on, placed in books, preached to all, but having the personal experience of such a rich and cultural faith brings mystery and powerful knowledge. The Faith enables one to strive to attain this knowledge, especially if one is called to minister, using the gifts that one has received.

2

How Shall We Sing the Lord's Song in a Strange Land?

Constructing the Divine in Caribbean Contexts

ALTHEA PRINCE

Prelude

The way they loved, softly and with passion. The way they worked, hard and with understanding that work would bring fruit, when the daylight broke, when the sunlight came. And they would lay the harvest out in the evening shade, as the fire dimmed and the heart stilled and the voices rested with the body, in the moonlight, behind the trees. As feet hurried to places of rest, a lone mongoose scurried across the path, its back unprotected from prying eyes. They saw it and it saw them, and they agreed to be silent, each about the other's presence.

Palm fronds whisper of things to come. Weeping willow mourning the past and future harrowing times. And the woman heard the whispers in the leaves and felt the brown fruit of the sapodilla sweet on her tongue, yet not sweet enough to wipe out the gall and the sting of the bitter-bush of life. Until the rain came.

And the water washed over the whole experience. Rain falling, heralding the hurricane. Winds gusting, clearing the debris, whipping the trees around, changing their direction, forcing them to look out to sea, focus on the horizon, contemplate a distant course, as yet uncharted by a mariner's compass. This path in life so new, not even the sun's light yet brings it into view.

And so they loved, softly and with passion. They worked hard and with understanding that when the daylight broke, when the sunlight came, the fruit would be a witness to their labor.

In the evening shade, as the fire dimmed and the heart stilled itself to listen, they told the Story. The telling went on for many steps in the lineage. In the evening, in the dark, when the Old Ones spoke, the Story unfolded over all of Creation. And the words healed them. And the songs soothed them. And redemption came with the rain.

THE ANTIGUAN PATCHWORK AS METHODOLOGY

My methodology in writing this chapter is to work inward, like an Antiguan patchwork, starting at the outside (which is constructed as a sociological problematic) and moving to the center, to the belly, to the place: the Caribbean. The problematic stated precisely is the following: the sociology of the Caribbean clearly needs to include knowledge of the religious body of the Caribbean. For religion is a part of the whole of the people—a part of what comes out of their belly. In essence, it is a large part of a Caribbean topology of B-E-I-N-G, a part of the universe in which Caribbean people abide.

I begin with a personal experience of "rememory," a term coined by African-American writer Toni Morrison (1987: 215). She uses it to signify sudden, tangible manifestations of something that lies deeper than the memory of events, reclaimed and given voice. First I present my experience of rememory, then the explanation and relevance to a discussion of Caribbean peoples' construct of the Divine.

I receive an Antiguan newspaper every week in the post in Toronto. The other day, I turned the page to a section titled "Hurricane Tips" and registered a rememory of stark terror. Suddenly, I was thrown back to my childhood, when each year, the entire island prepared for the hurricane season. I was catapulted, too, to the four years between 1983 and 1987, when I lived again in Antigua, having left eighteen years earlier. My terror as I read the "Disaster Preparedness" information, put out by the Disaster Preparedness Office, was palpable. I remembered activities that signaled the expectation of the worst possible eventualities of the island being hit by a hurricane. My reclamation, my rememory, made these things as real as if I were experiencing them in the present: the sound of boards being nailed to windows; the sight of people buying bread, dried goods, candles, kerosene oil; cleaning hurricane lamps, which had been ignored since the last hurricane; trimming the wicks, testing the efficacy of the flame; the filling of large clay jars with drinking water. The terror that these activities brought felt so real, I could reach out and touch it.

The relevance of this experience I will use as the thread that will weave the patchwork together. There are two things to consider: (1) location, being inside of a place in your head, in your body, in your belly, or in your womb—being there; and (2) the Experience of "Doing Life," which, in this instance, concerns doing life under threat from the elements, the powerlessness of that part of daily reality. How does one pray as a result of that? The terror of the impending hurricane, the sense of being under siege, the lack of control. How does one make supplication while living under siege? To what God or Gods and in what way? It is a hop, skip, and jump, of course, to connect these questions with the question of the impact on religion of other states of siege: enslavement, indentureship, racism, and colonialism. These states of siege are surely as devastating as a hurricane to the majority of Caribbean people. And they survived them with their soul intact. They survived them, with a firm commitment to and certainty about their connection with the Divine.

THE SOCIAL CONSTRUCTION OF REALITY

How is the social construction of reality—that is, daily life, or "the doing of life"—impacted on and/or designed as a result of the construction of the Divine?

The practice of religious traditions permeating and informing life tells us much of the Caribbean social construction of reality. Their transformation over time tells us more, too, of the genesis of a people's epistemology. The function of these religious traditions does not stop with their impact on the tangible manifestations of life. Their impact on consciousness is critical to our understanding of these questions: Who/what is the Caribbean person? How do Caribbean people express consciousness? Where is consciousness manifest, and what connections can we make between expressions of the Divine and the doing of daily life?

Religion is a part of the whole of the people—a part of what comes out of their belly, out of their womb, out of their heads. I use *belly* and *womb* within specific understandings of those two parts of the anatomy. I speak of "the womb" with the clear definition in mind of the process of procreation. The child stays in embryo in the womb until it is time to give birth to it. When knowledge within the womb reaches, as Rastafari say, "to the fullest overstanding," then the embryonic stage gives way to procreation. So it is that religious form, religious expression, the Divine is birthed. "The belly" I use to refer to the place where emotions are held, the stomach, the center of the body. (When a Caribbean woman really bawls, she does so holding her belly and saying: "Ooi, me belly! Me belly!") I speak of the belly also with the understanding of it as a place where nourishment is processed, the place where food is digested, stored, and then dispersed to the rest of the body.

With these metaphors in mind, I go back to the question: How is the social construction of reality impacted on and/or designed as a result of the construction of the Divine? How is it birthed and how is it nourished? In the scholarly and spiritual quest for an understanding of the Caribbean perception of knowledge, we must explore this. We must explore too the question of how the Caribbean person embraces a religious tradition that is foreign to her/him; how is it transformed, if it is transformed, and why? Does it mean anything, this transformation, if it exists? The process of carrying out what I like to call archaeological digs into the psyche will include odysseys into the religious and spiritual practices that inform Caribbean life. Life comes into being first in the realm of spirit, or within the totality of possibilities. Then life is sustained, that is, moving from spirit to matter, through the embrace of the realm of spirit as a guide in the doing of life. The construct of the Divine is thus the spiritual awareness with which experience is examined in order that people will sustain life.

I watched each year, while I lived in Antigua for those four years from 1983 to 1987, as the hurricane season rolled around, how people responded to what in my mind was a situation of extreme crisis. The CNN weather reports diligently traced the movement of the hurricane, and I listened to North American reporters excitedly predicting which islands would be wiped off the face of the map and which ones might survive. Yet the people were proceeding with life as usual. Some people stoically ignored the suggestions of the Disaster Preparedness Office, saying, "Me nar fret; hurricane will come yes, and even if it come, so what? We going survive. God will provide."

I wondered what kind of spiritual body enabled such an application, such a response in the face of the scientific prognostications? Clearly, there was some other force enabling people to believe that life would continue, despite the obvious, imminent threat to life. Examined within this context, the icons of Divinity matter, not so much in their physicality as in their expanded meaning. What will an archaeological dig uncover? What meanings lie unspoken, but are given purpose in their usage? What lies layers-deep in the collective unconscious that enables some Caribbean persons to embrace or reject Rastafari at the same time that others hold steadfast to Hinduism, Islam, Buddhism, Catholicism, Protestantism, Shakerism, Vodou?

The obvious link between these questions and the patchwork creations of my mother, with her tolerance for a composite manifestation of the Divine, is not lost on me. The patchwork demonstrates an appreciation for many fabrics, in terms of texture, color, and weave. Thread links them, and a unifying border gives them definition and clarity, allowing for continuity. As a small child and throughout my teenage years, I accompanied her to what Antiguans call "Wayside Churches"; they were in small spaces—in one instance, above a rum-shop. I also went with her every Sunday to High Anglican Mass in the eighteenth-century English cathedral. At the same time, I listened spellbound to her stories of the power of Obeah rituals, healings, and curses that she had witnessed. Yet she took pride in the fact that she had never used the services of an *Obeahman* or *Obeahwoman*.

I see my mother's moving between two worlds in her spiritual quest as an interesting example of a Caribbean person trying to make sense of her place in the cosmos, of being there. I connect it to shifts that Caribbean people make in the conceptualization of the Divine between Africa, India, and Europe. I connect it to the following questions: What shifts will be made in the conceptualization of the Divine when the threat of the elements, combined with states of siege, looms large and close in a small piece of volcanic formation? Will it suffice for Mass to be said in a sonorous voice by one person, or will the entire congregation need to harmonize from its belly in order to feel that supplication has been adequately made? What are the implications or connections to be made between liberation and the construction of the Divine? What do Indian people feel when they sing together, listen to the drum, dance to the drum, together? What does the African do in response to the drum? How is that creation different from the Lord's prayer or the Twenty-third Psalm in terms of usage, impact, meaning, feeling? How can we sing the Lord's song in a strange land? And perhaps the answer is: "The land is strange no longer and the people sing their own definition of the Lord's song." For their Gods are creolized, the Divine is their Divine, hence the methods used to conduct inquiry must also move from the strange to the particular. If the subject has arrived at a place of self-knowledge, a further understanding of his/her place in the world, then the researcher must acknowledge that in reporting that experience. It will not do, then, to catalogue and describe the subject's relationship with his/her religion within terms that make it lesser than any external standard.

Within the process itself of conducting intellectual inquiry on Caribbean life, the very method must reflect the Caribbean. Hence my attempt to work my way in from outside, to the center, to the belly, to the womb, walking on the same flat land as the island that spiritually informs the subject.

LOCATION, PLACE, AND SPIRIT

The location must tell me how to examine religion, how to discuss it, how to consider things, how to weave things together. I must pay attention to each piece of fabric, in terms of its weave, its weight (as in body), and its colors. In this regard, I would posit that there is much to be learned in the study of Caribbean patchworks. In addition, the use of human resources will need to be reflective of the Caribbean, racially, philosophically, culturally, regionally, and linguistically. For clearly, location—being able to get inside a place in your head, in your body, in your belly, in your womb—will be hard, if not impossible, to accomplish if the researcher has no sense of the location, place, and spirit of Caribbean people.

ACCEPTANCE OF CARIBBEAN PEOPLE'S COSMOLOGY

The researcher of Caribbean religions needs to be aware of Caribbean people's movement between the universal and their particular. Thus, my acceptance of the certainty with which the people respond to the advent of a hurricane will impact on the conviction with which I respond. My conviction is based on those things that my mind perceives, and the people's certainty of survival is based on their heart-knowledge of their relationship with the cosmos. It is impossible for the mind alone to accept the factors beyond the material constructs. For it is with spirit that those things are perceived and embraced.

It is not necessary that I as a researcher believe people's constructs of the Divine. It is only necessary that I accept that they have a construct of the Divine, their determined relationship with the cosmos. My research requires no evidence of this, no reasons supported by phenomenological manifestations of their belief systems that are acceptable to me. I need only acknowledge and give voice to their cataloguing of the other beliefs that support their constructs of the Divine. It must be their arguments, their reasoning that lends power to concepts of the Divine.

The concept of the Divine is well understood by all Caribbean people to be their way of looking at the world in which they live, the world in which they do life. They are not incapacitated with fear when a hurricane is imminent, because they know that whatever takes place is a part of the larger picture that is their world. Hence they do the things that are necessary, but they do not anticipate that there will be death and total destruction. They have survived other states of siege, and they will survive this one too. They know and do not question the things that occur in the realm of spirit, which others regard askance with a need for proof. It is this knowing that will lead them and guide them. It is this knowing that the researcher needs to notice and give voice to, if he/she is going to be true to the subject's voice.

Allowing the voice of the subject will see to this. The voice of the subject will explain things in a way that comes from the heart and is not restrained by the neat cataloguing that may, in some instances, even deny the efficacy of the religious practice itself.

UNDERSTANDING THE CENTER

Being there, being inside the place, being inside the head, being inside the center of the people's lives, will allow the researcher to do justice to what the practitioner means, feels, and says. The researcher is thus able to recognize what is being said as truth and important when it is said. Cataloguing of religious and spiritual practices will then have authenticity, as it will be the subject's real experience with the Divine. Recognition of false gods will come easily as well to the researcher, for he/she will, in time and with acceptance of the people's voice, be able to tell when someone is not speaking from the heart and is merely giving lip service to a particular teaching or divination.

The simplicity with which people describe their relationship to nature makes it clear that they have a relationship with the Divine that is inclusive of natural occurrences, including hurricanes. There will be some naturalistic explanation of what is occurring. So while CNN will expound the meteorological movements of the hurricane, the people will acknowledge it as nature simply taking its course. They will examine their lives to see how they can be more in rhythm with nature, so that natural disasters do not devastate them. Rightly or wrongly, it is how the people integrate cosmological and practical realities of their life.

Caribbean epistemological libations are things that come from the heart. They come as soothing droplets of healing balm to ease and appease the soul and the troubled heart. The people practice religion in this way, ensuring that what they say to their God is answered in their hearts. Daily life then becomes quite highly integrated with the spiritual realm. There is a certain oneness of mind, body, and spirit that takes place in the non-established churches. This is not to say that it does not occur elsewhere, but that it occurs there very deeply. Thus people are comfortable with shifts and changes in their religious practice that may not occur so quickly and easily in the established churches. Spirituality is close to the belly, the heart, and the life; and the closer to the heart, the more deeply felt is the spiritual connection.

Research carried out within this kind of consciousness makes for the possibility of entering into dialogue easily with the practitioner. This is if one is aware that the practitioner is at peace with the connection he/she has made in spirit. Thus, it behooves the researcher to be aware of the need for allowing the practitioner's voice to have the strongest position in the research. The researcher must step outside of his/her role as the person in authority, the person having authority over what is reported, and allow the practitioner to have the last say. There is thus no need to challenge what the practitioner has to say about how she/he relates to the Divine, for it is their divination. This means that when the people acknowledge the hurricane with a certain mystic, spiritual kind of response, it is because they have an understanding that they will be able to ratify whatever happens with their God.

The final thing that is necessary to say is that in all of our undertakings as researchers, if we can go to the center with the practitioner, that is, open to hear and open to listen, then we will be given a clear vision of their reception of Grace. That is the most that a researcher can do, unless he/she hopes to be captivated and give himself/herself over to the practice itself. That is not a necessary prerequisite to allowing the subject's voice. It is only necessary that we acknowledge the practitioner's voice and allow it to be brought into the light, to be illuminated by an awareness of Caribbean people's construction of the Divine.

The role of the researcher, then, is to enable voice, to enable the practitioner to be heard, and to do that enabling with integrity of purpose and with clarity of vision. If that is all that gets done in the process, it is enough.

Note

The title of this chapter, "How Shall We Sing the Lord's Song in a Strange Land?", is taken from Psalm 137:4, which was popularized in the Caribbean through Rastafari and reggae lyrics.

Work Cited

Morrison, Toni. 1987. *Beloved*. New York: Penguin.

3

Communicating with Our Gods

The Language of Winti

PETRONELLA BREINBURG

Until recent years, the language that Catholics (including a non-Latin-speaking community in the Caribbean) used to communicate with their God was Latin. It was the language used for Mass and chants. There never was any suggestion that the people in the Catholic churches were talking "in tongues," talking "gibberish," talking nonsense. In contrast, there is the common reaction of outsiders to Winti, a religion bearing a striking similarity to the Catholic religion. Outsiders to the Winti community of the Surinamese people refer to Winti variously as nonsense, evil, or "witchcraft," and the image is that of "cute, harmless blacks" dancing, chanting, and talking "in tongues."

To look at the language for communicating with the Winti gods, demi-gods, and ancestral spirits, I have briefly examined the various Creole sub-cultural groups, such as the Banja and the Lakoe players, that are associated with the Winti community. I have looked at Winti as seen by the Creoles (now referred to as Afro-Surinamese) and not as seen by non-Creoles, including anthropologists. I have examined the varieties of Sranan with special reference to lexical items and style as used in relation to religion. Though my emphasis is on the language of Winti, in order to clarify matters I have included a report on a short investigation, with comments on the fusion of deities.

Westerners, whether anthropologists, book writers, or film makers, often depend on sensationalism to promote their work on the religion or the belief systems of non-Western and black people. There are those who, for whatever reason, are intent on degrading or trivializing the system of beliefs of groups such as the followers of the Winti culture. There are sensationalized reports of what are referred to as "cult groups" talking "in tongues." By talking "in tongues," they mean that the people are talking nonsense.

The various black groups (here I am using the term *black* to mean specifically people of African descent but Caribbean origin)[1] also refer to talking "in tongues." However, this group uses the term differently from how it is used by the white "experts" on blacks. The Caribbean people of African descent who respect the cultural factors brought in from Africa by their ancestors refer to talking "in tongues" with pride, even when they may be aware that a watered-down version or fusion of cultural heritage is involved.

One must not indulge in the kind of criticism that can be mistaken for an attack on white researchers, because those researchers only report what they were told and/or have had especially performed for their benefit, or worse, what they have interpreted a ceremony to mean. Interpretation of meaning is a key factor in the study of a culture other than one's own. What we think we are seeing is not necessarily what is in fact taking place. Box-office sensationalism and the need for it is the other factor which is at the root of the deliberate misrepresentation of what are, for the people themselves, strictly religious ceremonies. In films showing "Voodoo" ceremonies we have the stereotypical chicken thrown up in the air, its neck broken by a "Voodoo" priest who chants "in tongues" and dances. All of this makes good box-office material but is not necessarily a true representation of what takes place.

A good example of misinterpretation is seen in a recent event within the Surinamese Creole community in Amsterdam. To outsiders this was simply a twentieth birthday party for a young Creole woman, but to the insider it was also a religious ceremony. The telltale sign was the color scheme of blue and the dress of the birthday girl. She was dressed in Koto Jaky[2] made of the same blue fabric that decorated the community center, including the table on which the "birthday cake" stood. Key African-Caribbean guests were presented with a glass bowl and saucer decorated with blue ribbons. The guests at the party included some white friends. One white guest was very pleased and said that it was nice to see a challenge to the gender stereotype: "blue is for boys and pink for girls but this birthday girl is obviously a feminist and deliberately chose to use blue" (or words to that effect). But to any insider, this was a ceremony in praise of Mama Aisa, who is the mother of earth and fertility and also the muse of the artist; the color used to praise her is blue. Here, we at once note a non-verbal communication with our gods.

Jan Voorhoeven's *Creole Drum* (1975) describes the Lakoe society and its Winti origin. No one would deny that Voorhoeven has done very good work in recording the various folk tales and culture of the Surinamese Creoles; nevertheless, his description of Lakoe, which he spells "Laku," is somewhat different from the Lakoe described by insiders, which was fictionalized in *De Winst van het Lakoe spel* [*The Benefit of the Lakoe Play*] (Breinburg 1982). The language Voorhoeven describes is everyday Sranan, which everyone who knows Sranan can understand, unlike the particular Sranan lexicon used in the case of Winti ceremonies.

As a sharp contrast, Henri Stephen in *Lexicon van de Winti-Kultuur—naar een beter begrip van de Winti Kultuur* [*Lexicon of the Winti Culture—Towards a Better Understanding of the Winti Culture*] (1992) does not confuse Winti ceremony with Lakoe drama—these are two different though related things. In his description of lexical items and semantics, Stephen mentions items specifically related to Winti as well as items specifically related to Lakoe. He points out that the lexical items used in Winti ceremonies are specifically items from Sranan, a language of Surinamese origin although its roots are African, Indian, Spanish, Portuguese, and English. Stephen emphasizes, however, that mainly West African religion, belief systems, and lexical items are used in those ceremonies that are now found in Winti of Surinam.

Stephen cites as a good example of West African retention the names given to Creole children born on a certain day of the week. As Stephen shows, the name based on the day of birth given to a Surinamese Creole baby in a Winti environment is given as the middle name of the child. The first name has to satisfy the Western norm. The child's second name is to satisfy the gods and spirits of the ancestors. A baby outside the Winti community who is a child of a staunch Catholic family will have a name such as Maria, Coba (short for Jacoba), or Jan, which would be more widely accepted, especially in schools and employment situations, than would Akoba (Koba for short) or Yaw.

Stephen lists names of children born within the Winti culture as follows:

Days in Sranan	Girl	Boy
Sonde (Sunday)	Kwasiba	Kwasi
Moendey (Monday)	Adyoeba	Kodyo
Toedewroko (Tuesday)	Abeni	Kwamina
Dridewroko (Wednesday)	Akoeba	Kwakoe
Fodewroko (Thursday)	Yaba	Yaw
Freyda (Friday)	Afi	Kofi
Satra (Saturday)	Amba	Kwami

Source: Stephen 1993, 38–39

For the person in the Winti culture, these names are important and must be used for all ceremonies, including initiations into womanhood or manhood, planting of the umbilical cord, and the birthday of the child. In all these cases, the person is addressed by his/her African name in order to keep the close link with the gods and spirits of the ancestors.

In the following pages, I have some examples of the lexical items generally used in Winti. I commence with names of *ancestors* and *deities*, then *nouns* in general, and finally the *semantic feature* in which the same words have different meanings in everyday use from those they have within the Winti ceremony. Some of the words and phrases used in Winti culture are often referred to as a "secret language." In that case, even those Surinamese who do not have close contact with the Winti culture find it difficult to decode the meaning of the usage, although they know the words. I have used the old spelling "oe," which to me is more authentic than the modern and politically correct spelling of "u" used by Stephen and many others.

I commence with words often confused by researchers who are outsiders to Winti culture. For example, *Gado* means God Almighty of the Christian religion, but *Gadu* is a collective noun for Winti deities. We get *Sonde* (Sunday) and *Sondoe* (or *Sondu*), the latter meaning sin, the former meaning a day of the week. One can see how easy it would be for an outsider to confuse these words.

NAMES ASSOCIATED WITH THE ANCESTRAL SPIRIT

I have put together some words used with the name *Kabra*. Kabra is the head spirit of the ancestors. Each family within the Creole Winti culture has a Kabra. This ancestral holy spirit is often called upon if there is an important decision to be made within that family. A number of prayers and ceremonial dances use the prefix *Kabra-*. The following are explained in Stephen (1986):

Kabrasusa	In Surinam, whether a person belongs to or believes in Winti or not, the prayer to the ancestors is for all Creoles whose ancestors came from Africa. *Susa* is a special ceremonial dance related to ancestral spirits and links directly to the head spirit.
Kabratafra	This is the ceremonial meal prepared as an offering to the ancestors. In this case, we have a feast similar to the Last Supper described in the Christian religion. A problem for the "outsider" is that in everyday Sranan, *tafra* means the wooden structure upon which one places one's meals for consumption, but in Winti culture, *Tafra* refers to a ceremonial meal which need not be eaten from a table. The meal is simple and consists of ground *nanjang* (root vegetables), green vegetables, rice and home-made drinks and tobacco.

THE "KR-" WORDS

Another interesting factor is that a great many names of the deities and spirits (Winti culture makes a distinction between the two) tend to start with a "Kr-." Therefore, for the Winti follower, any chant, ceremonial song, or dance that has as its first two letters "Kr-" is a reference to specific deities. The following is also from Stephen (1986):

Kromantiwinti	This is one of the most respected of the gods in the Winti religion. It is one of the gods of the sky alongside the Sofia Abada (goddess of lightning), the Akantasi (god of thunder), Tata-Yaw, Awese, and many more. These gods of the sky and air are often prayed to and each name is called out in song and chant. When the words in a Kromanti ceremony are chanted rapidly and very emotionally by the leader of the ceremony or a member of the group, to the outside researcher, it may seem like a long mumbling of nonsense words, that is, talking "in tongues."
Krawatra	The water used in special ceremonies is usually plain water, yet another parallel with the Catholic religion. Krawatra is pure water blessed and chanted over by the high priests or some other senior and respected member of the Winti religion. The water is used to bathe a person or

just to wash the face of members before they communicate. Evil can be kept away by the Krawatra just as the use of holy water blessed by a Catholic priest is used to keep away evil. Hence, it is clear that Krawatra of Winti performs the same function for its followers as does the holy water of Catholicism for its people. We use Catholicism as a parallel because of the evidence of a strong missionary influence in Surinam. This present study has not found evidence (as yet) that the use of holy water in religious ceremonies has been brought from West Africa where the Creole Surinamese people originated.

SEMANTICS AND THE OUTSIDER SYNDROME

Communication with the deities of Winti is through a language, the true meaning of which even members of the religion do not understand. The congregation at a Winti ceremony simply recites, chants, sings without any concern about semantics. We can take as a parallel the congregation at a Catholic Mass, which often recites prayers and chants in Latin without knowing any Latin or the meaning of those words.

An interesting example of the above is the *Sokopsalms*. Research on lexical items and their relationship to semantics tends to emphasize literature, narrative, poetry, or drama, rather than song lyrics. However, for this study, data was collected by an insider at a religious meeting where there was praise of the ancestors through what are known as the Afro-Surinamese Sokopsalms. A case-study method was used. The aim was to test the response of both insiders and outsiders to the Sokopsalms. The data was collected from a group of students of Caribbean Studies, who were asked for a general response to the Sokopsalm on tape played to them by a researcher, and from a small number of Winti-culture members living in Amsterdam.

The students responded politely but could not see why the Afro-Surinamese people had a religious ceremony using what sounded like a sort of imitated Latin Mass, as though it were mimicked from a religious Mass of the missionary days. Students who had learned some basic Sranan in an academic setting pointed out that the words did not sound like the ones on a general Sranan tape that they had listened to in class. The words of the Sokopsalms meant nothing to the students, although from the general tape in class they were able to "pick out" words, some being similar to Jamaican Creole.

An individual who had learnt Sranan from childhood, though not a regular speaker, responded by saying that those words strung together seemed to be a copy of some sort of Christian prayer, but the real meaning had no significance for her. Perhaps they meant something to the Winti people but not to her. She was a staunch Catholic and would not tamper with what was clearly Winti.

Individuals of the Winti culture reiterated that they were hearing the Creole people's own religious songs. It was a "culture thing." It was in praise of the African Ancestor, just as the other groups in Surinam, including the whites, had their own religious songs, and so forth, for worship. "Why don't you go and ask the Javanese why they have what they have?" (angrily stated). No, young Creoles do not understand the Sokopsalms, nor would they appreciate them. No, they would not want outsiders to learn the form of language, which is for the Creole people's own private use. No, they did not have to understand the real meaning; all they know is that they are praising their ancestors, not their gods and their spirits. The Hindustanis (Surinamese people of Asian descent) do not all understand the language of their Qur'ān; they just recite it in order to give respect to their gods.

FUSION AND WHOSE GOD?

The question often asked is whether the deities Winti people are communicating with are actually African gods, given the cultural fusion in Surinam. Though the image often presented to the general public and to students of Caribbean Studies is an African-Caribbean one, in reality the Caribbean, certainly Surinam, Guyana, and Trinidad and Tobago, is a multi-racial, multi-religious, and multi-lingual territory. Surinam, in particular, is perhaps one of the most complex areas of the Caribbean. People of Asian descent, for example Indians, Chinese, Indonesians, and Javanese, form about 50 percent of the population. There are also the descendants of Africa who had freed themselves from slavery and went to live in the bush. These people were at one time referred to as *Bosnegers* ("Bush Negroes"). Among these people are the Nduka (formerly spelt Djuka), the Auka (who have developed their own written script), the Saramakaners, the Paramakaners, and the Matawi Maroons.

There is evidence that lexical items from Hindustani, now known as Sarnami, have been taken into the everyday use of Sranan and vice versa. In the case of religious ceremony, the matter is a complex one. Surinamese Winti culture has adopted some non-African deities, and Winti people pray, for example, to "Indian" spirits and then become possessed by what they believe are spirits of the "Indians," both those "Indians" whose forefathers came from Asia and the Aboriginal inhabitants of Surinam. In praising and communicating with the spirits and the deities of the Indians (from Asia), it is not unusual for the words and chants used to be a creolized version of Sarnami. When someone is possessed, what could be taken to be talking "in tongues," nonsense, may well be words or phrases from one of these other ethnic groups. It is in these circumstances that Indian (Sarnami) lexical items may appear.

The term *Basra* is used in everyday Sranan to refer to someone who is of mixed parentage. It follows that some deities are also called Basra Winti, meaning deities of mixed cultural origin, and the talking "in tongues" in this case is known as *Ingitongo* ("Indian" tongue). Again, unless one is part of that particular sub-group, what that person who is communicating with the "Indian spirits" is saying may well sound like a babble of meaningless chanting.

There are numerous other items in Winti that are of "Indian" origin. *Ingiprey* is a religious dance ritual in praise of the "Indian" deities. The general term that covers all deities of "Indian" origin with which Winti members often become possessed is *Ingiwinti*.

Given the above, it is clear that the gods being communicated with are not always of African descent, though a religious form of Sranan is used.

A study of the Winti lexicon is an extremely complex matter because of the cultural fusion that took place in Surinam over the years of colonialism. I have only been able to give a brief indication of the complexity of Winti as a traditional religion of the Surinamese Creoles and of how its language is used to communicate with its deities and its ancestral spirits. This paper points to the confusion and misrepresentation that is possible when an outsider to the Creole people in general, and the Winti culture in particular, investigates the matter. We noted that *Gado* and *Gadu* may sound the same to an outsider when in fact they are two different words, each with their own meaning. Similarly, there is the difference between *Sonde* and *Sondoe* or *Sondu*. Many more items cause confusion; even when the words in use are phonologically the same and appear to be semantically the same, this may not be so. There may well be a difference in usage, hence meaning, depending on whether the word is used in an everyday context or for religious purposes. We also noted the response to the Sokopsalms, which suggested that an attitude study of Winti and its language may have to be undertaken. We noted, too, the multi-cultural and multi-racial nature of Surinam and how this may have resulted in an interesting fusion of belief systems, hence deities, with aspects taken from one culture to another resulting in some non-Sranan lexical items being used.

It is clear, then, that the study of the Winti lexicon of Surinam is an enormous task. It cannot satisfactorily be accomplished without examining the fusion of cultures as a whole. We also cannot ignore the influence of the Catholic religion on Winti, which perhaps can best be studied in parallel with Haitian Vodou or Afro-Brazilian Candomblé. It is hoped that further study of the whole area of the language of Surinamese Creoles will reveal more interesting facts about Winti lexicons.

Notes

1. In the UK the term *black* is often used to include Asians (including Chinese and Vietnamese), Greek, Turkish, and even Spanish people.

2. A large skirt and special blouse unique to Surinam.

Works Cited

Breinburg, P. 1982. *De Winst van het Lakoe Spel*. Bussum, Netherlands: Van Holkema and Warendorf.

Burton, R. 1997. *Afro-Creole: Power, Opposition and Play in the Caribbean*. Ithaca: Cornell University Press.

Dark, P. 1973. *Bush Negro Art*. New York: Alec Tiranti.

De Beet, C. H., and M. Sterman. 1981. "People in Between: The Matawai Maroons of Surinam." Diss., University of Amsterdam/Institute of Cultural Anthropology.

Jan Voorhoeven, J., and Ursy M. Lichtveld, eds. 1975. *Creole Drum: An Anthology of Creole Literature in Surinam*. Translated by Vernie A. February. New Haven: Yale University Press.

Snijders, R. 1995. *Surinaams van de Straat (Sranan tongo fu strati)*. Amsterdam: Prometheus.

Stephen, H. 1986. *De Macht van de Fodoe-Winti*. Amsterdam: Karnak.

Stephen, H. 1992. *Lexicon van de Winti-Kultuur*. Amsterdam: Stephen.

Stephen, H. 1996. *Geneeskruiden van Suriname*. Amsterdam: Drihoek Uitgeverij.

Van Kempen, M., and J. Bongers. 1993. *Sirito: 50 Surinaamse vertelling*. Paramaribo, Suriname: Kennedy Stichting.

4

The Intersemiotics of Obeah and Kali Mai in Guyana

FREDERICK IVOR CASE

The notion of intersemiotics as discussed in this article has two primary written sources. Firstly, it is inspired by Abdelkebir Khatibi's *La Blessure du nom propre* (1974) and it also takes into account Daniel Patte's use of the term "intersemiocity" in his work on semiotics and faith (1982). In the particular case of Obeah and Kali Mai Puja, the analysis of intersemiotics is concerned with the intersection of the codes of two different cultural and spiritual traditions that contribute to the creation of a dynamic of ritual and belief. In this article, we have focused primarily on those elements of Kali Mai Puja that have become an integral part of the ritual and cultural discourse of Obeah. We recognize that the term "culture" and its derivatives are problematic, and we therefore use this term in its Vedic sense of elements that are spiritual, having "roots in the inner life, the life of the spirit" (Siddhantalankar 1969).

In the Caribbean context, it is often necessary to redefine or invent terms to describe social and spiritual phenomena because the European languages that name these elements are inadequate to the task. While such redefinitions can be kept to a minimum, there is a certain basic vocabulary that has to be established from the beginning of this study. The definitions that we propose in this chapter are heuristic hypotheses and are in no way to be considered as the semantics of an established Caribbean epistemology.

A number of Arabic terms will be used throughout: the word *āyat* signifies seme, phrase, sign, and discourse; *dīn* means service to God, spiritual service; *ẓāhir* indicates what is apparent, visible, manifest, or exoteric; and *bāṭin,* that which is hidden, discrete, refers to the esoteric aspects of *āyat* or *dīn*. The polysemy of the Arabic language makes its use appropriate in a context in which we are attempting to establish what occurs when two manners of living and being in the world come into dynamic contact. The social and political appropriateness of Arabic is obvious since it is a sacred language with which African and Hindu systems of *dīn* have come into close contact in Africa, India, and Guyana. Arabic is therefore used to provide us with semantic and conceptual tools and is in no way a philosophical or theological determinant. On the contrary, the polysemic dimensions of the terms adopted will lead us to a greater sensitivity and a deeper understanding of the processes of intersemiocity described below. For what we witness in Guyana is an unstructured polysemy in which *āyat* are hardly attached to the *ẓāhir* but are deeply rooted in notions of the esoteric.

In this reflection on Obeah and Kali Mai Puja, we are concerned with the cultural aspects of belief originally expressed, separately, by two different ethnic groups united in their poverty and political impotence. Obeah in Guyana remains the spiritual resource of the dispossessed seeking inner and physical healing as well as the experience of nearness to God. The literature on Kali Mai Puja confirms the same social class bases of those who practice this form of *dīn* (Bassier 1994; Karran 1996). Whatever the ancestral origins of these two systems, in Guyana they have been similarly stigmatized and ostracized. They have both fulfilled similar social and psychological roles and have sustained the inner life of those who, in their quest for God, adhered to their beliefs. The two axiological systems are compatible as the class motivations are ethically and ideologically shared and as both peoples have been obliged to forge a new imaginative process based on changed circumstances of place and time. In this intellectual recreation of the sacred, they have enshrined the concept of myth in a positive manner as a "symbolic expression of original and universal realities" (Arkoun 1982: 10).

In Trinidad, the phenomenon of Kali Mai at the Catholic shrine of La Divina Pastora in Siparia is evidence of Kali's versatility (Sirju 1996). The creative imagination of Kali devotees who have recognized in Mary, Mother of Jesus, their own Mother Kali is a transcendence of La Divina Pastora. The Hindu devotion in Siparia is not merely an acknowledgment of the universal principle of motherhood; it is the recognition of Mary as a principle of mediation and a deepening of her experience as benevolent shepherdess of a vastly diverse flock. There are no theological treatises to confirm or to name this original coming together of two traditions in a dynamic myth of reciprocal appropriation. Mary claims Kali and Kali claims Mary. In the creative imagination of the Kali worshippers, there is constructive dialogue of Mary and Kali to the point that they enunciate one discourse.

In Siparia, Mary/La Divina Pastora is highly respected and embedded in a textual code interpreted by a priestly caste. Kali is the spiritual resource of those who are in desperate need of help and whose rites and beliefs are, in this specific case, not textually coded. The written text and its preservation by priests limit the creative spiritual imagination and leave little room for the dynamic development of myth as a process of understanding. The discursive path of Kali worshippers is not the same as that of Catholic worshippers. However, for the Kali worshippers, the two paths converge since the Kali myth is inclusive and the other is exclusive in its adherence to Catholic orthodoxy. Orality generally permits, encourages, and even provokes inclusion as an essential aspect of dialogue, renewal, and conservation.

Obeah is essentially oral, and this attribute has always permitted this *dīn* to be receptive to others. During the centuries of slavery and even after, the intersections of ritual and belief with the Aboriginal populations have been many. The use of hallucinogens to induce states of trance and a number of other specific practices like "blowing" have been learned, acknowledged, and perpetuated through oral means that ensure their constant renewal as the dialogue of spirituality continues.

In Guyana, at least, both Obeah and Kali Mai as systems of *dīn* have been primarily orally transmitted traditions. The oral discourse confers great power in the spiritualization of the real and creates the marvelous and mythical in *dīn*. The marvelous is sustained by myth and evoked as an exoteric manifestation of a syntactical relationship of diverse aspects of *āyat*. The marvelous is the dramatic and most often visible evidence of magic. Magic, as defined by Bisnauth (1989: 91–92), is a frequent characteristic of Obeah and of Kali Mai in which change is engendered through successful communication with the spirits and/ or divinities. Such communication is often aided by ritual, sacred, or simple words. Aichele writes, "Words are attached not to reality (as in realism) but to our thoughts about reality" (1997: 10). In the context of Obeah and Kali Mai, the use of metaphor is eloquent in its ability to capture the esoteric meaning through the imaginative process of the individual.

The power in and of the spoken word is precisely the ability to produce dimensions of the *bāṭin* that the written text is incapable of evoking. African spirituality is transmitted primarily in this form (Mbiti 1970). Though the ritual of Kali Mai Puja is contained in the written texts of Hinduism, it appears that the Guyanese *pujārī* ("practitioners") have conserved their knowledge through orality, and just as remnants of African languages survive in Obeah, so do remnants of Tamil and Hindi survive in Kali Mai Puja. Kali Mai, as we know it, is the coming together of two distinctive *dīn*: worship of Kali from North (East) India and South India, and Tamil village worship of Mariamma (Bassier 1994; Sulty and Nagapin 1989). Obeah is said to have its origins in the country that is now called Ghana, and the origins of the word have been traced to Efik/Akan/Edo/ Twi (Dalgish 1982; Morrish 1982; Williams 1979; Cassidy and Le Page 1967). Obeah in Guyana has long been associated with negative practices and rituals evoking notions of sorcery. Williams's work enumerates many of the prejudices surrounding and undermining this system of belief, and the connotations of his insensitive and ethnocentric analyses deny the elements of *dīn* that are clearly apparent in Guyanese practice. In fact, there is a tendency, based on ignorance, to associate all systems of belief or rituals that are African with Obeah and to reject such manifestations of *dīn* as worship of the Devil. These condemnations of superstition and evil often reveal the extent to which detractors have fallen victim of their own vision of the world.

Obeah has evolved in its new Caribbean context (Bisnauth 1989; Morrish 1982; Williams 1979), and Morrish's work clearly shows the processes of interaction with Myalism and Christianity in Jamaica. Kali Mai has also undergone major transformations in its *ẓāhir* manifestations (Bassier 1994; Karran 1996; Sulty and Nagapin 1989). In the social and cultural readjustments of slavery and indenture respectively, both systems have adopted and adapted elements from other *dīn* of their respective regions of origin, and in Guyana, both have come into conflict with Christianity and its diverse orthodoxies. Obeah and Kali Mai are liberating spiritual and social forces that impose few daily constraints on adherents. Persons of all ethnicities and religious affiliations present themselves for consultations in either *dīn* and participate in their rituals. These adherents communicate and are communicated with on the bases of what Khatibi calls "*les signes migrateurs*" ("migratory signs" [Khatibi 1974: 13]). This set of mobile semiotic codes is particularly appropriate to the volatile cultural and demo-graphic context of the Caribbean.

In Guyana, the particular area of our fieldwork has been in Berbice, where Obeah reveals the unambiguous spiritual presence of "Dutch" spirits. Histori-cally, all of Guyana was at one point a Dutch colony, and the spirits that manifest themselves may be Aboriginal,[1] African, Indian, European, Jewish, Christian, or Muslim. However, Berbice shares a common border with Surinam, and there is frequent movement of individuals from one country to the other. Historically, in order to survive on the plantations, African systems of spirituality had to be versatile and to put in practice their ability to be inclusive (Bisnauth 1989: 98–99). Details of diachronic and synchronic, cultural and spiritual proximity be-come important in the tendency of Obeah in Berbice to be adaptable and to integrate elements from outside its own system.

According to Karran (1996), Kali Mai has displayed similar tendencies of eth-nic, social, and spiritual inclusion. It is therefore significant that there are prac-titioners who have produced a synthesis of these two systems that is a dynamic process of viewing and living reality. Karran also emphasizes the universal moth-erhood of Kali and stresses her concern for all of her children. In this respect, intersemiocity can be understood as the active acknowledgment of otherness and the tendency to interact and produce innovative semantic and mythical systems.

The term *fromu* is used to describe "the process of amalgamation of parallel institutions into new systems or at least the integration of culture elements from various cultural systems belonging to the same culture area" (Wooding 1979). In this way, *fromu* could be applied to Obeah and Winti, which are both African systems having their origins in the same general region of Ghana, but the "amal-gamation" of Obeah and Kali Mai presents us with different questions of concep-tualization. We are attempting to explore what Arkoun calls the "re-membering of sense in a given cultural tradition" (1982: 81). In this particular case, it is the re-membering of one sense emanating from two or more traditions. Such a re-membering is based on the implicit or explicit acknowledgment of otherness. Daniel Patte writes that "this recognition of an otherness is the acknowledgment of the phenomenon of intersemiocity. Besides the semiotic system which I hold, there are other semiotic systems to which I must relate" (1982: 107). We will study the question of intersemiocity in relation to four aspects as practiced in Berbice by three African Guyanese practitioners: iconography, purification, sacrifice, and the sacralized object.

ICONOGRAPHY

In an article on Hindu art in Guadeloupe and Martinique, Max Sulty writes that it is a "transfiguration of reality or of the sense of a community and its relationship to its environment." The iconography of Kali in Guyana corresponds entirely to this context of transfiguration "implying the manifest necessity of another order on the spiritual plane" (Sulty 1994: 289). Kali is generally depicted as a dark-skinned female, sometimes blue, black, or purple. Her skin color association with Tamils or Madrasis makes her also acceptable to Africans in much the same manner that Our Lady of Perpetual Help, with her dark skin and scarifications, has been adapted by and in Vodou and Santería. Théophile Obenga's detailed analysis of color symbolism shows black as a "colour of suffering; of mystery; of strength and of magic" (1985: 186–93).

But if Kali is the terrible aspect of Durga and one of the wives of Shiva, she is also the embodiment of power and thus an invaluable companion/protector of the powerless. One Obeah spiritual person, M. A., calls her "my mother" (interview) and explains that with Kali on her altar, she is fully represented and protected as woman, mother, and African. She sees Kali as the African mother of all humankind, and even if her picture is surrounded by those of Ganesh, Hanuman, and Lord Shiva, M. A. experiences no cultural tension and is comfortable receiving her clients of all Guyanese ethnic origins. The images on her altar are garlanded with flowers and incense, and candles burn in front of them. Red, green, and yellow cloths flow horizontally and vertically behind the objects on the altar. Unlike several other practitioners of the Kali *dīn*, M.A. has no *jhaṇḍi* (flags) erected in her yard. In those cases where *jhaṇḍi* are raised, they tend to be red in honor of Kali's bloody encounter with the *asura,* but in at least one case black *jhaṇḍi* abound and submerge the red.

Guyanese Obeah relies heavily on the Christian scriptural tradition. It is generally acknowledged by a number of African Guyanese Obeah practitioners and believers that Europeans deliberately misled entire populations in the interpretations of the Old and New Testaments. Mother M., in her annual ceremony of the Planting of the Ensigns, commemorates God's giving the *jhaṇḍi* to the African Moses during the exodus from Egypt. The Africanization of the Christian scriptures is accompanied by the discursive inclusion of Hinduism in the narrative of Obeah. The *jhaṇḍi* were given to each of the twelve tribes so that God could identify each tribe from above (Num. 2: 2; Isa. 10: 11, 30: 17). Hence the integration of *jhaṇḍi* within the iconographic code of Obeah. Kali's *jhaṇḍi* occupy a logical place in the mythic structures of Obeah. They underline the legitimacy of Kali as a divinity deriving her spiritual strength from God of the Old Testament.

Kali's numerous hands, each holding a significant object, emphasize her power and her ability to make several things happen at the same time. The radical initiation of dynamic change is the single most urgent aspiration of the dispossessed, and the depiction of Kali is the *āyat* that embodies the concept of change as she bears a saber in one hand and a bloody head in another. Her necklace of skulls and her belt of severed heads attest to her terrible will and powers of execution. She is the mighty slayer of evil and will act accordingly on behalf of her followers. There is no contradiction between this terrifying depiction and the notion of universal motherhood. After all, God of the Old Testament is at times terrifying in His punishments and His threats.

The tension within the *āyat* resides between the depiction and the significance attached to it. It is in this moment of tension that myth exists as a structured epistemology that fills the conceptual gap between *z̤āhir* and *bāṭin*. In this sense, myth does not connote that which is not real but denotes the reality of spiritual relationships that are not attainable through logic but through subjective reason in the heart. It is the "transfiguration" that Sulty mentions in his article. Myth is therefore a conceptual means of understanding, the epistemology of a highly sophisticated cultural process that permits Kali to be a universal Hindu maternal principle, a Tamil village divinity curing cholera and smallpox, and at the same time the mother of all Africans torn from their ancestral home. Myth therefore becomes a dynamic creative system of reconceptualization and renewal.

The Kali Mai myth in Guyana represents a new understanding of the universal mother. It could be said that in crossing the *Kāla Pāni* (the Black Water), Kali assumed new dimensions of being and thereby assumed new responsibilities and the power to inspire new visions. In Obeah, references to the black water, the black triangular *jhaṇḍi,* and the use of black candles are frequent codes that give coherence to a sacred discourse that the uninitiated see but do not fully understand. The *āyat* creates a pattern of coherent meaning based on what are apparently disparate theories of knowledge. The *z̤āhir* of this discourse can even be misleading, but to initiates the *bāṭin* is readily apparent, and the process of intersemiocity leads to a deeper and innovative consciousness of spirituality. In this context, the psychological benefits of social and cultural *rapprochement* should not be minimized. Even if Kali Mai and Obeah are sometimes associated with "lower" means of spiritual communication, they have succeeded in creating spiritual solidarity between two rival ethnic groups.

PURIFICATION

In Obeah as in Kali Mai Puja, before any major spiritual work is undertaken the practitioner and at times the person on whose behalf the work is to be done will live through a period of purification. The purification consists of prayers, special baths, fasting, and abstinence from sexual activities. Purification should be understood from two major perspectives that are intricately linked: cleansing and preparation. It is obvious that the physical cleansing is a ẓāhir process with profound bāṭin implications. It would be dangerous for the practitioner or adherent to approach the spiritual work in a state of impurity. Retribution by the divinity could be swift and devastating. Furthermore, it is a sign of disrespect to defile the sacred ceremonies and places by the presence of an unworthy body and spirit.

Such restrictions and high ethical principles are common to African and to Hindu practices. There is no compromise possible, and though the means of arriving at a state of purity might be different, the outcome is the same. Purification of the human body renders it sacred in the sense that it is then restricted to particular spiritual uses. The body is then capable of approaching the divinities without fear and with openness. Purification of the mind and the spirit accompanies purification of the body.

It would be superfluous to enter into the many detailed rituals of purification in Obeah and in Kali Mai Puja, but it is necessary to indicate the major principles underlying this code. In both cases it is true to say that what appears from the outside to be obscurity is from the inside spiritual light. The abstinence from certain foods, from alcohol, and from sexual activity appears from the outside to be so much "foolishness" that shrouds the practitioner or adherent in mystery. Within the confines of the ritual, there is no mystery, in the sense of obscurity of meaning or deliberate mystification, but what can be called the marvelous in the sense of the ẓāhir phenomena that elucidate and give form to the bāṭin. Arkoun writes that "the marvellous changes nature and function depending on whether it is experienced by the believer or the unbeliever" (1982: 90). There is a dialectic of reality between ritual and consciousness of the marvelous. For example, the marvelous resides in the contact engendered by the process of purification and the catalytic effect of profane phenomena—water, candles, incense, herbs, particular vestments of particular color, chants, prayers, bells, and so on—that are dynamic agents of psychic and sometimes physical metamorphosis.

Bathing and chanting are the most apparent external aspects of the purification, while fasting and sexual abstinence are the most discreet. It is the abstinence from the profane, the cleansing of the things of this earth, and the striving after a closer relationship with the divine that confer the experience of the power of intermediary. In this enlightened state, the officiant can rise to the heights of esoteric experience in a process of involution that is not at all introspective. In her work on Kumina, Maureen Warner Lewis likens the spiritual experience of the retreat to "a return to the womb which is at the same time a journey into the tomb" (1977: 64). For the person undergoing purification is not doing so for her/his own sake, for her/his own salvation, but so as to be worthy of closeness to the divinity in order to obtain certain favors. Purity, as much else in Obeah and Kali Mai Puja, is functional.

The purification of the liturgical space is yet another aspect of bodily purification. It sets aside what is sacred and what is reserved for divine usage. The

yard is purified by the erection of the *jhaṇḍi,* whose color and form place ritualized space and ceremony under the protection of a particular divinity. In the
absence of the *jhaṇḍi,* it may be the "boundary master" who protects and perhaps
even cleans the yard. The "boundary master" is usually Dutch, powerful, and
persistent. Characteristically, he is meticulously clean.

SACRIFICE

Animal Sacrifice

There are two major forms of sacrifice to be considered: animal/blood sacrifice and vegetable sacrifice. Animal sacrifice is less and less favored by certain
Obeah as well as Kali Mai communities, and this is a major point of divergence
cutting across the two *dīn.* Warner Lewis writes of the "life-sustaining quality of
blood" that makes sacrifice "the most eloquent symbol of . . . Self-denial" (1977:
57). The life-giving force that is shed in an offering to the divinity or to God is a
formal handing back of life to its source and creator. The earth that absorbs
the blood of the fowl or goat is integrating into itself a nourishing element of
transcendence. Sacrifice is also an element of purification as it renders the earth
and/or altar sacred.

The external view of the Obeah sacrifice is negative and usually associated
with evil. As in Kali Mai Puja, the severed head of the animal is seen as a reflection of the heads worn around Kali's waist. However, the animal chosen, its size,
color, gender, and species are all carefully determined by the particular divinity
or spirit to be honored and the nature of the request to be made. The principle
of returning vital energy to its source in an effort to reinforce protection and help
is central to the idea of African sacrifice. It is a coded mediation that of itself
brings about transformation. It is at one and the same time enunciator and enun-
ciated in a discourse that sometimes elevates the person offering sacrifice to a
state of epiphany. This latter term has been used by Guérin Montilus (1989: xv,
48) to identify what is commonly called "possession," a term coined through
ignorance and the desire to discredit heightened spiritual experience.

Nagapin (1994: 246–47) recounts that in Kali Mai Puja the sacrificed animal
is considered as part of the being of the person offering sacrifice. Her/his antici-
pation of liberation from the troubles that inspired the sacrifice puts her/him
into a state of agitation. The experience of trance is common to Obeah and to
Kali Mai Puja, and the various stages are not dissimilar: initial period of contact
with the world of spirits and travel beyond the social realities of the site; "speaking in tongues" of Africa and/or India; transmission of messages/healing; the
process of leaving the state of epiphany.

Sister G., an African *pujārī,* apologized for the sacrifice of the fowl as it
hopped around her yard without its head, but she considered it necessary for
the spiritual work that she had in hand. She had already passed the live fowl
over the body of the person offering the sacrifice in a ritual of purification and
cleansing. This process is sometimes used as part of a healing ceremony in which

the spirit of illness passes into the fowl. Once the fowl has been decapitated, there is a liberation of vital energies. In Sister G.'s ceremony, the blood of the black fowl was spattered all over the yard and against objects and individuals in a showering of blessings of life. Expediency and the demands of the divinities, as much as individual squeamishness of practitioners and adherents, seem to determine the choice of sacrifice. There are few officiants who appear to be motivated by ethical principles in this context.

Vegetable Sacrifice

Mother M., an African "spiritual person," performs this type of sacrifice in her annual ceremony of the Planting of the Ensigns. The plate of vegetables to be sacrificed by the black water is carefully arranged and carried in procession. Camphor is spread among the uncooked vegetables as hymns are sung and prayers recited; then the officiant begins to speak in a man's voice in African tongues. Unmistakable in this dialogue with God and the divinities are the Arabic words *"Allāhu Akbar"* ("God is great"). Considerable care is taken in setting out the plate of sweet rice, bananas, and coconut, for this is the ceremony of reenactment of God bestowing identity on His people. The miniature *jhaṇḍi* prepared by Mother M. herself are planted in the bank beside the black water. These miniatures of every appropriate ritual/liturgical color become the dynamic mediation between the adherents and the *jhaṇḍi* on the masts before Mother M.'s establishment. It is these miniatures of self-identification that give significance to the full-sized *jhaṇḍi*.

The discourse of African identity is enshrined in bloodless sacrifice as the earth, air, fire, and water combine to consume the sacrificial elements. As the smoke rises, so does the epiphany of Mother M., whose trance is very controlled and very deep. The relationship between the ensigns of the Old Testament and the *jhaṇḍi* of Hinduism is one of complementarity. The ensigns inscribe Mother M.'s group in an ancient written tradition that is as respectable as that of the Hindus whose identity is proclaimed by their *jhaṇḍi*. Since other followers of the Bible ignore the significance of this fundamental detail of identification, Mother M.'s group are the guardians of interpretation as eisegesis, abandoning blood sacrifice while holding steadfastly to other aspects of fundamental Old Testament teachings. Is the adherence to vegetable sacrifice an attempt to create an ethical distance from bloody aspects of some Kali Mai ceremonies? (However, it is well known that certain *pujārī* perform only vegetable sacrifices to Kali Mai [Karran 1996] and that these are burned, the smoke rising to propitiate the divinity.)

It is at this juncture that the principle of intersemiocity—the positive acknowledgment of otherness and its adaptation—becomes functional. Most of Mother M.'s followers appear to be poor urban Africans whose knowledge of the Bible is impressive. The ensigns are a proclamation of social identity in the community and the ultimate evidence of God's acknowledgment. The Kali Mai *jhaṇḍi* serve similar purposes of proclaiming allegiance to the divinity. The triangular forms of the *jhaṇḍi,* always pointing in whichever direction the wind turns them, are forever sacred, and, as with the ensigns of Mother M., they seem to grow out of the earth. The black *jhaṇḍi* testify to Kali's synthesis of all energy and the red, to her terrible retribution. In the same way that the ensigns are sacralized, the *jhaṇḍi* too before being erected are carefully wound around the mast, perfumed, aspersed, and prayed over. They are also "planted" in a specific position and in a particular spot and confer an identity on the yard or property on which they stand.

THE SACRALIZED OBJECT: THE COCONUT

We have isolated this single ritual element in order to give an example of how and why "profane" objects become sacred. The coconut is widely used in Obeah and also in Kali Mai Puja. Every part of the coconut tree, from the roots to the nuts, can be used for medicinal purposes (Ouensanga 1983, 1: 65–66) and it also has other well-known uses that have been exploited for centuries by Africans and Indians. Its place in the pharmacopoeia has necessarily given it profound significance in the context of *dīn.* Apart from its medicinal and culinary uses, coconut oil has often been used by African and Indians to groom hair and particularly to care for the skin. Its usage is therefore personal and aesthetic. In certain Afro-Caribbean forms of divination, the coconut is smashed on a floor and the spiritual reading is given according to the disposition of the various pieces, their number and location. In this way the divinity or spirit is seen to create a coherent code that is read and interpreted by the officiant. This form of mathematical literacy is often accompanied by seeing or hearing spirits.

In Obeah, there are many uses of the coconut. The everyday object becomes sacralized, and its usage is experienced as a series of symbolic acts with ritual ramifications. There is nothing spectacular in splitting a coconut open, nor is there necessarily anything sacred about such an act, but in the context of the Obeah ceremony, the object and its manipulation are eloquent elements of communication, creating the dynamic of myth that nourishes and sustains faith.

The coconut is an *āyat* of Kali insofar as they both give the outward appearance of obscurity but contain much light in their very nature. The coconut is dark brown on the outside and resplendent on the inside, where the clear water is to be found. Not only is the oil of the coconut used for giving light, but the shells are often used as lamps. Light born of obscurity is one of the fundamental esoteric principles. It is the light of transcendent Truth because it is the light of Knowledge that resides in the heart.

In Kali Mai Puja, the coconut is used as a food offering, as lamp, and as decoration. It can be cut in two with a machete as a symbolic replacement for the decapitation of an animal. The water that flows to the earth symbolizes the blood, and the two or more pieces that litter the ground are the body of the animal. Significantly, the water from the coconut can be used to replace serum in cases of emergency (Ouensanga 1983, 1: 65–66). The emphasis is therefore on the life-giving qualities of the coconut. In a Kali Mai yard where vegetable sacrifice is offered, there can be a mound of dry coconut shells attesting to numerous ceremonies. In Sister G.'s case, the sacrifice of a fowl was accompanied by the "decapitation" of a coconut. Both sacrificed elements were cooked, and because the officiant and the man making the sacrifice were pure, they could eat the sacrifice.

The coconut, high above the heads of humans, is truly an element of air and of earth; the tree itself is a symbol of the mediation between earth and air, water and fire. Its sacred use further elevates it, this time to a transcendent sphere as it is invested with spiritual characteristics. The profane becomes sacred, and the object speaks eloquently as it fulfils a role in the mythical sphere that corresponds to the importance of its curative medicinal properties. These medicinal properties as well as the culinary uses of the coconut have tended to anchor it in the "really real" of Caribbean life. However, its sacred use has set it aside as restricted and special in a transcendence that acknowledges a close relationship between *ẓāhir* and *bāṭin*. Indeed, these two notions are by no means exclusive and should be considered only in their function of interdependence. The coconut and its uses are the best illustration of the meaning of the relationship of these two terms. The full polysemic connotations of the *āyat* can be best appreciated in this manner.

From the examples that have been given, it is readily apparent that neither Obeah nor Kali Mai Puja can be understood only from their exoteric manifestations. Often the exoteric is misleading in that it reveals a semantic code that appears banal, profane, and incoherent, while the esoteric discourse is a coherent communication between humans, spirits, and/or divinities. This communication takes place at the level of myth with its own syntactical structure and understanding of reality.

The relationship of intersemiocity should not be confused with syncretism. This notion implies a power relationship characterized by linguistic or cultural diglossia in which there is tension between two discourses. Syncretism implies a hierarchy within a heterogeneous juxtaposition of principles and practices corresponding to the acrolect/mesalect/basilect paradigm of ethnocentric linguistic analysis. Obeah and Kali Mai Puja intersect in their epistemology and their phenomenology. Grounded as they both are in an ethos of the dispossessed, they have come to create a common axiology and often differ only in their lexical choices. Since their mythical codes function in approximately the same manner, the transmission of knowledge from one system of *dīn* to another is not complicated by ideological considerations of superiority/inferiority. The differences that are sometimes cited concerning practices and beliefs of the two *dīn* tend to be superficial and evidently racist.

We have discussed the integration of elements of Kali Mai Puja into Obeah because these are most evident and verifiable. It can be generally said that Obeah has integrated *ẓāhir* elements and has fully explored and exploited their esoteric depths. The question of elements of Obeah in Kali Mai Puja would necessitate another study undertaken from a different perspective. The integration of Obeah elements into Kali Mai Puja appears to have taken place at the level of the *bāṭin* in the same way that Aboriginal spirituality has permeated aspects of African and Hindu worship.

It is perhaps in the domain of healing that the two *dīn* are closest in their *bāṭin* aspects. However, a specific discussion of healing in these two *dīn* would have to take into account the major contribution of Aboriginal healing. Much of the activity in and around Obeah and Kali Mai Puja is concerned with healing physical, mental, and spiritual illnesses. Individuals travel from near or far to be treated by the practitioner in whom they have greatest faith. The *pujārī* Samaroo has set up his Kali Mai infirmary close to the Timehri International Airport and receives patients from elsewhere in the Caribbean and also from North America. Such is the light emitted by Kali Mai and the healing power of her *dīn*. Sacrifice, animal or vegetable, is central to healing in Obeah and in Kali Mai. The medium of trance is one of the major means of identifying and naming the sources of the illness. Trance and its highest point, epiphany, are shared experiences of the spiritual in which it is relatively easy to move from Obeah to Kali Mai and vice versa. The experience of epiphany not only depends on the subject but is indicative of the close collaboration of the spirits and/or divinities. The effects of epiphany are physical, mental, and psychological as well as spiritual, and that is why precautions are taken to prevent the uninitiated from falling deeply into this stage. To avoid possible harm to the individual, there has to be a solid protection from the dramatic infusion of energy when the individual is *monté* or *chevauché*.[2] This is one of the most important reasons why the practitioners and some adherents undergo a period of thorough purification before undertaking spiritual work.

Obeah and Kali Mai present similar phenomenological characteristics and visions of the world that coincide on many important points. These convergences are cemented by the contributions of Aboriginal spirituality that are varied and very deep. It is clear from this study that the application of semiotic theory to Caribbean *dīn* can lead to innovative perspectives on the formulation of a Caribbean epistemology. Such an undertaking requires historical consciousness and knowledge, sincerity, the social and cultural aptitude to be comfortable in different milieus, and sympathy and openness toward a variety of discourses. There are few remaining complete solitudes in the Caribbean, a region that has the pretensions and the characteristics of being a crucible of the Universe.

Notes

1. The word "Amerindian" is commonly used in Guyana but has connotations that are increasingly rejected by those named in this manner. There are also objections to the use of the term "indigenous." "Aboriginal" appears, at the present time, to be the most acceptable term in English.

2. These two words in Haitian both mean "mounted" and describe how the contact of the spirit or divinity is perceived in relation to the individual experiencing epiphany.

Works Cited

Aichele, George. 1997. *Sign, Text, Scripture: Semiotics and the Bible*. Sheffield: Sheffield Academic Press.

Arkoun, Mohammed. 1982. *Lectures du Coran*. Paris: Maisonneuve et Larose.

Bassier, Dennis W. M. Z. 1994. "Indian Lower Caste Cult Worship in Guyana: Their Fate in 1988." In *Présences de l'Inde dans le monde*, éd. Gerry L'Étang. Paris: L'Harmattan/GÉREC/PUC.

Bisnauth, Dale. 1989. *History of Religions in the Caribbean*. Kingston: Kingston Publishers.

Cassidy, F. G., and R. B. Lepage. 1967. *Dictionary of Jamaican English*. Cambridge: Cambridge University Press.

Dalgish, Gerard M. 1982. *A Dictionary of Africanisms: Contributions of Sub-Saharan Africa to the English Language*. London: Greenwood.

Karran, Kampta. 1996. "The Guyana Kali Mai Puja: A Worship's Metamorphosis." Paper read at Caribbean Religions Project Workshop on African, Indian and Indigenous Religions of the Caribbean. St. Augustine, Trinidad, and Tobago: Institute of Caribbean Studies/University of the West Indies, 16–18 August 1996.

Khatibi, Abdelkebir. 1974. *La Blessure du nom propre*. Paris: Denoël.

M. A. Personal interview. August 1996.

Mbiti, John. 1970. *African Religions and Philosophy*. London: Heinemann.

Montilus, Guérin. 1989. *Dompin: The Spirituality of African Peoples*. Nashville: Winston Derek Publishers.

Morrish, Ivor. 1982. *Obeah, Christ and Rastaman: Jamaica and its Religion*. Cambridge: James Clarke.

Mother M. Personal interview. December 1996.

Nagapin, Jocelyn. 1994. "Les rites antillo-hindous." In *Présences de l'Inde dans le monde*, éd. Gerry L'Étang. Paris: L'Harmattan/GÉREC/PUC.

Obenga, Théophile. 1985. *Les Bantu: langues-peuples-civilisations*. Paris: Présences Africaine.

Ouensanga, Christian. 1983. *Plantes médicinales et remèdes créoles*. 2 vols. Paris: Désormeaux.

Patte, Daniel. 1982. "The Interface of Semiotics and Faith: Greimas' Semiotics Revisited in the Light of the Phenomenon of Religion." *Recherches Sémiotiques/Semiotic Inquiry* 2 (2): 105–29.

Siddhantalankar, Satyavrata. 1969. *Heritage of Vedic Culture. A Pragmatic Presentation*. Bombay: D. B. Taraporevala Sons.

Sirju, Martin. 1996. "La Divin-Suparee (Kali) Mai Devotion and the Empowerment of Hindu Women." Paper read at Caribbean Religions Project Workshop on African, Indian and Indigenous Religions of the Caribbean. St. Augustine, Trinidad and Tobago: Institute of Caribbean Studies/University of the West Indies, 16–18 August 1996.

Sister G. Personal interview. August 1997.

Sulty, Max. 1994. "L'Art religieux hindou de la Guadeloupe et de la Martinique." In *Présences de l'Inde dans le Monde*, éd. Gerry L'Étang. Paris: L'Harmattan/GÉREC/PUC.

Sulty, Max-André, and Jocelyn Nagapin. 1989. *La Migration de l'Hindouisme vers les Antilles au XIXe siècle après l'abolition de l'esclavage*. N.p.

Warner Lewis, Maureen. 1977. *The Nkuyu: Spirit Messengers of the Kumina*. Mona, Jamaica: Savacou.

Williams, Joseph J. [1934] 1979. *Psychic Phenomena of Jamaica*. Westport, Conn.: Greenwood.

Wooding, Charles J. 1979. "Traditional Healing and Medicine in Winti: A Sociological Interpretation." *ISSUE* 9 (3): 35–40.

5

Religions of African Origin in Cuba
A Gender Perspective

MARÍA MARGARITA CASTRO FLORES

(ENGLISH TRANSLATION BY ADRIANA PREMAT AND MARSHALL BECK)

To tackle the issue of gender in the study of religion constitutes a challenge in Cuba today, given that the subject has not received much previous attention. Moreover, the topic is of interest because, in spite of the widespread legitimation of women's rights in contemporary Cuba, such recognition has not necessarily translated into a widening of the scope of action for women, particularly in the religious sphere, where they are subject to socio-historical factors in the form of norms and prohibitions.

The presence of factors tending to marginalize women at the core of religious beliefs in today's Cuba reflects the influence of the different religious systems that were brought together as the result of colonization. The European colonial presence was accompanied by two main religious currents that nurtured the Cuban religious expressions of today. One was the *sui generis* Catholicism professed by the European colonizers, plagued with discrimination against women and influenced, in turn, by several centuries of domination by Islam, a religion that in its practice excluded women from consideration as independent social entities.

The other current, consisting of the beliefs that arrived with African slaves of various ethnicities, is the main object of the present analysis. These beliefs were carried by men and women who were selected randomly, based on the utilitarian criterion of their economic potential, and gave rise to some of the main religious systems in Cuba today, such as Regla de Ocha or Santería, Regla Conga or Palo Monte, and the male Abakuá secret societies, among others. In time, the religions brought by the slaves underwent modifications, but they also retained certain principles and precepts. Even today, among the values that were maintained, the subordinate role of women in the exercise of many religious practices stands out. This is a reflection of the secondary role attributed to women in society. The roots of this subordination must be sought in the socio-historical framework within which contributing ethnic groups developed until the moment of their brusque uprooting, as well as in the social context into which they were subsequently inserted.

The discriminatory treatment of that which is feminine in aspects of African culture was reinforced in the Caribbean by the conquerors' attitude to women—particularly African women, given the conquerors' Eurocentric racism and contempt for other peoples. A characteristic element of this process was "evangeliza-tion,"[1] a project that resulted in and justified the mistreatment of blacks. A different culture and religion were imposed, with the final goal of destroying the African's original vision of the cosmos. According to the civil and ecclesiastical laws that established norms for the Catholic education of slaves,[2] conversion had to encompass baptism, communion, confirmation, marriage, and training into the Christian doctrine. In practice, these regulations were retained mainly in form, though they generated a transculturation process in some cases, and in other cases resulted in forced acculturation.[3]

As a consequence, some African values disappeared and others survived, hidden and incorporated, transformed—without being dissolved—into the substratum of a new nationality that was slowly forming. These surviving values contributed to an explicit, qualitative differentiation within the religious sphere, evident in the features of the deities, among other things. In the words of Fernando Ortiz: "the black gods are generally very happy; they do not feel the philosophizing agony and ethical interventionism of the white gods, and they like to come down [to earth] to have fun with their faithful, like over-familiar pals" (1991: 92).

In summary, the African woman was the object of *machista* reaffirmation, the result of the imposition of a series of patriarchal regimes. The feminine was subordinated not only to the colonizer, but also to the colonized male. This abused woman became the carrier of racial, cultural, and religious *mestizaje* (mixing).

STEREOTYPES AND ETHNIC GROUPS IN AFRO-CUBAN RELIGIONS

In any society, stereotypes of human groups are formed and become social preconceptions. In Cuba, these stereotypes affect the religious sphere in a number of ways, manifesting themselves in a multiplicity of extant expressions about religion, and more specifically, about those of African origin. This stereotyped vision is present in some sociological approaches to the topic.

On the one hand, there exist material and spiritual factors that make the practice of religions of African origin in Cuba accessible and attractive. From a certain perspective, they are positively judged by sectors that consider the initiated practitioner as an individual with power and wisdom because, from the perspective of the believer, he or she possesses explanations and, in many cases, even precise solutions to problems of various kinds, be they related to health, work, or marriage. Here, the practitioner enjoys high social esteem, so that on occasion he or she is subject to compliments and gifts from his or her godchildren. This is not necessarily a commercial practice, although such distortions may also be observed, because the regular practitioner in Cuba generally does not differ in his or her standard of living from the rest of the population.

On the other hand, a different aspect of the subject becomes highlighted when we focus on religion in Cuba as one of the realms where racial prejudice is most manifest. This inherited pattern is expressed in the manner in which some members of the population[4] evaluate skin color, characterizing the black person as "scandalous, crude, delinquent and indolent" and the white person as "discrete, educated, and one that strives to live better and knows how to behave."[5] As can be seen, values are correlated here with apparent racial affiliation rather than behavior, so that the white person constitutes the ethical, aesthetic, and cultural model. Such prejudices have historically burdened the appreciation of black culture and religion in Cuba, in many cases reducing it to the realm of folklore and limiting any acknowledgment of its social role. Thus, for example, religious beliefs and practices of African origin have been typified pejoratively as "religions of blacks" and have been identified as such in accordance with the prevalent pattern of racism.

Although these religious systems continued to be practiced primarily by blacks and *mestizos* (mixed persons), nowadays their social status has undergone a degree of change, and we can observe their extension into the white sector[6] as this social recognition has deepened. The explanation for this phenomenon merits more attention. One of the influencing factors is the situation Cuba is currently undergoing, in which material needs have increased, generating conflicts requiring immediate solutions; the faithful expect solutions to result from their beliefs. Another possible factor is that active practice of these religions provides access to certain economic benefits, as mentioned earlier. To these influences must be added those who become incorporated naturally through family tradition, or in order to meet their spiritual needs. These reasons are not exclusive, and indeed in some cases overlap.

It is important to note the role played by the Fourth Congress of the Cuban Communist Party in 1991, when believers were accepted into the heart of the organization. If one considers the politicization of Cuban society and the support for this leading force in the populace, it is clear that many people who were believers in religions of African origin concealed or did not show their beliefs so as to avoid a certain ideo-political rejection in the social arena. Even if the opening made by the Congress did not represent a stimulus to the growth of these religions, it indisputably contributed to the public exhibition of religious affiliation by believers who previously concealed their faith. This may constitute the reason for the rapid "increase" in the number of new practitioners, something that, in many cases, is actually the exteriorization of an old practice.

An element to take into account when considering these religious expressions is the fact that in everyday life they are accessible to people of any social background. A basic prerequisite to exercise the status of *oriaté*[7] is memory and popular wisdom. These represent bastions of the African inheritance, as is clear when we consider that the transmission of the cultural and religious norms of Africans, forcefully introduced into the "New World," was achieved exclusively through oral means. Not only were their languages non-literary, but in the majority of cases the slaveholder mixed individuals from different ethnic groups as a precaution against revolts, making communication between slaves more difficult but at the same time facilitating the necessary search for a common language.

If we take a broad look at the current religious panorama in Cuba, we can see that, as is the case in other social spheres, women occupy an important place, as much in their role as believers-practitioners as in their position as mothers transmitting their own beliefs as part of their function as educators in the home. Nevertheless, if we take a more in-depth look at religions of African origin present in contemporary Cuban society, we find that such an active social role does not correspond to that which is permitted to women at the religious level. Evidence for this can be found in the hierarchical structures and the divining systems of the most common African religious expressions in Cuba. These have undergone a process of religious transculturation encompassing the various intermingled religious expressions from Africa, as well as Spanish Catholicism and some vestiges of Aboriginal beliefs.[8]

Below, we will broach, in summary fashion, the phenomenon of the presence of women in these religions, paying particular attention to the Regla de Ocha, also known as Santería. As will be seen, evidence demonstrates that in the various hierarchical levels around which these religious expressions are structured, women play a role that is at once limited yet transcendental.

Palo Monte, or Regla Conga

This practice has its origins in the beliefs of African slaves of Bantu ethnic origin (see Lachatañeré 1992: 168; López Valdés 1985: 201). The maximum hierarchical position is that of the *tata nganga,* who possesses the authority to make the *nganga,* a receptacle that contains various elements of nature (including mineral, animal, or vegetable, and even human bones) and that represents the base or foundation of Palo Monte. The *tata nganga* also has the authority to initiate new believers through *el rayamiento* (incisions are made in various parts of the body in the process of religious initiation). The *tata* decides on the validity of any act of communication with the deities. Etymologically speaking, the term *tata nganga* means "father of the *nganga,*" a status that is generally valid only for men, because a woman may accede to this status only when she has stopped menstruating, a factor that is also present in other religious expressions in which, as here, menstruation is associated with impurity.

It is interesting to note that a practitioner considered that the *kiyumba* [cranium] of a woman was more suitable "because she doesn't know about reasoning; people that know a lot, are not willing or open, are not good for *nganga*" (Cabrera 1993: 126). It is not very common in Palo Monte to find women in the highest role, although there are important "houses" that are "ruled" by them. As a general trend, other functions are reserved for women: to bless, to confirm initiation, to participate in the ceremonies, and to cook the foods consumed therein.

Male Abakuá Secret Societies

In the case of the male Abakuá secret societies, originating from the Nigerian Calabar region, women cannot even be initiated as members. This restriction has its basis in the origin myth-legend, according to which a woman (princess Sikán) committed an act of indiscretion, considered treasonous, that stigmatized her forever and for which she was condemned to death: she revealed a secret that indirectly resulted in the destruction of the fish Tanze, the only being capable of reproducing the sound of the god Abasí. This sentiment of rejection is expressed, among other ways, in the act of initiation where aspiring members (known as *indísemes*) swear before the sacred drum, Ekué: "The *indíseme* swears not to be effeminate. That is another very serious sin. Ekué hates females. The secret is exclusive to men . . . fags [*los maricas*] cannot get close to Ekué, just as women cannot" (Cabrera 1958: 245). Even "the wood of the Ekué cannot be from a female tree, because nothing in Abakuá can belong to the feminine gender" (116). For the Abakuá practitioner, one's sense of honor resides in one's manliness, a concept that relegates women to the status of mother-mate, a *machista* criterion that prevails in the rest of the society and that reaffirms this feature. Nevertheless, for the initiate of this religious system, one of the basic principles is respect for the mother and the wife. This notwithstanding, within the Abakuá ethical code, this respect does not presuppose, but rather excludes, the status of women as equal.

Regla de Ocha, or Santería

The rationale behind discriminatory practices in the Regla de Ocha system has a more complex character, given that this is a more structured religious system. Here, women, even when present at various levels, do not have access to certain functions. This religion has important cults, such as that dedicated to Ifá, whose maximum figure is the Ifá priest or *babalawo*, who is endowed with the knowledge of the deepest secrets of his religion. Etymologically, the term *babalawo* means "father of the secrets." His role is essential, indispensable; however, as with the religious expressions discussed earlier, women's access to this highest level is limited. Women cannot, for example, have access to the divining systems used by the *babalawo*. Other cults present in the Regla de Ocha are that dedicated to the *orisha* (deities), whose initiates are named *babalocha* or *iyalocha*, according to whether they are men or women respectively, and the Cult of Añá, the deity that allows the playing of the *batá* drums, the ritual act that closes the religious initiation process and that is open only to men. There exist other auxiliary functions that, in the majority of cases, are prohibited to women. Among these is that of *pinaddo*, known by the expression "to take the knife," which permits the initiate to sacrifice animals of various types, including the four-legged variety, for initiation ceremonies. Equally, women are prohibited from the function of *osainista,* he who knows of the plants offered to each deity in the process of initiation and who provides individual attention to initiates.

On the other hand, we can mention another interesting function that is fulfilled by women: that of *apetebbí,* which, in one of its variants, entails service as personal helper to the *babalawo.* One task among others of the *apetebbí* is to present the food that is offered and served to Orula, *orisha* of divination. In order to achieve such status, the designated woman goes through a ceremony known as *cofá,* where she receives necklaces and other attributes that entitle her to assume these responsibilities. Without the presence of these females, the ritual cannot be carried out. Herein lies, in grand measure, the essential significance of women in the Regla de Ocha.

Feminine Image and Practice in Religions of African Origin: The Present Context

What has been said thus far excludes those women who have contributed in outstanding ways to the development of these religious expressions, and who have even been considered the founders of some of their branches. Women constitute an important element in the reproduction of values in the religious sphere. This role can be better understood if we take into account the fact that among the great majority of believers (primarily black and *mestizo*), the maternal dyad predominates, with single, female heads-of-household in extended family nuclei (including various generations and collateral relations). Here, it is in fact the woman who assumes the responsibility of caring for the children and the home, and for this reason, it is also she who is in charge of transmitting the main traditional values.[9] This widespread phenomenon carries with it for women the implicit contradiction of, on the one hand, being the economic pillar and transmitter of essential values within the family, roles of utmost importance, while, on the other hand, being barred from the possibility of performing the highest roles within the religion they profess.

Such restrictions on women as those mentioned above are not limited to the framework of religious life. Given their pervasive character, they exercise a strong influence upon important sectors of the female population. A process of mutual influence reaffirms tendencies already present at both the social and religious levels, tendencies that are as active within the religious framework as they are outside that ambit. As much on the individual as on the social level, it so happens that, in a conscious or unconscious manner, women themselves can be the carriers of self-limiting values that contribute to slowing down the process of their own emancipation.

It is interesting to assess how women's participation in these religious expressions has increased over the last years, a trend that promises to continue, in a national context that, nonetheless, shows a high degree of female independence. In this sense, a question that has not been sufficiently investigated is that of the perspective of the female believer toward her subordination within these religious practices. It is known that fears of mystical origin have long accumulated in the gender imaginary and have circumscribed female actions within certain limits that are impossible to surpass. What factors contribute to the increased involvement of women in these religious practices?

To address this question, we can turn to preliminary results of fieldwork. Findings revealed the following tendencies: an overwhelming participation of women who are housewives and have no occupational links; an increase in the number of young women (between 15 and 35 years of age); an increase in the educational level of participants (of middle-level preparation); and an increase in the racial mix of religious participants, which expresses itself in the incorporation of white women into the religions under study. It is evident from the research data that among the women surveyed, attraction to these religious expressions has as a primary cause the search for solutions to health problems and other matters of a personal character; participation appears to be conditioned by utilitarian reasons more than by mystico-spiritual convictions. Similarly, there exists a correspondence with other religious expressions, for example, *Espiritismo* (Spiritism). In general, it is very common to find people who simultaneously practice more than one of the religious expressions discussed here.

As for the perceptions held by female participants themselves, a majority accepts the limits imposed on their status within religious practice as something that should not be questioned. Some, accepting concessions by men that benefit them, go so far as to overvalue the place assigned to them. Another group accepts the place given to them, with the difference that they admit to the discrimination entailed—though without proposing a change that would transform this situation. It is evident that to confront such subordinating practices would require, in the first place, women's self-awareness of their situation; this is the prerequisite *sine qua non* for the real overcoming of any such limitation. Such an overcoming is not impossible, if one takes into account the changes in both form and content that have taken place within these religious expressions in the past, as well as the existence of other comparative cases where the situation of women practitioners manifests itself in conditions different from those of Cuba. Such is the case in Brazil, where the female *mae de santo* is the center of the religion and constitutes its maximum persona, as well as in Nigeria, where, as an exception, when the *babalawo* has no masculine descendants, his eldest daughter succeeds him.

Regardless of one's perspective, it is important to emphasize that even in a situation of subordination, women have an essential role in the realm of religions of African origin in Cuba and represent the bastion on which rests the survival and reproduction of these religions in present conditions. There is evidence of a notable expansion of female participation in these religions.[10] Nevertheless, these women have been converted into the natural reproducers of a model of self-limitation. In general terms, the analysis of the current topic from a sociological perspective tends to be different from that of the intra-religious vantage point, something that opens doors to other approaches and generates points of disagreement. On the other hand, the topic has many other dimensions yet to be explored, particularly regarding the valuable contribution made by women.

This must be the object of other investigations that will carry us more deeply into the problematic of women in religion in Cuba.

Notes

1. Evangelization really developed in a purely formal character, since in practice it was reduced to the mass baptism of African slaves and the imposition of a name derived from the Catholic calendar of saints' days.

2. See *Reglas para los hacendados que aspiran a proporcionar a sus esclavos la instrucción religiosa,* cited in Fraginals 1991.

3. The term *transculturation* was coined by the Cuban anthropologist Fernando Ortiz (1995: 97–103) to refer to the process by which different cultures can interrelate and contribute to the formation of a new one with features that differentiate it from those that gave rise to it, such as in the case of Cuban culture. Such a perspective is equally applicable to Caribbean culture in general, which has nourished itself upon diverse sources.

4. It should be noted that the criterion of racial affiliation, in the analysis of this phenomenon in Cuba, does not have a referent informed by anthropometric measurements, for which reason we adhere to the conventional category of white-*mestizo*-black, according to skin color.

5. These criteria have been confirmed by the results of fieldwork carried out by Rodrigo Espina and Magdalena Pérez, researchers from the Centre of Anthropology at the Ministry of Science, Technology and the Environment, and were presented at Antropología 94, an international event held at the Centre (La Habana, Dec. 1994).

6. White people participated in these expressions in previous periods, without ever constituting a majority. To give one example, in the mid-nineteenth century, the Abakuá secret society created an order, or "land," of whites.

7. The *oriaté,* in religious language, is the initiate who has the authority to exercise some divining systems and to sponsor or guide new believers.

8. The presence of Aboriginal vestiges are evident in some of the liturgical elements of the religious beliefs of African origin, such as the petal-like axe associated with the *orisha* Shangó, the offering of maize to certain deities, the use of tobacco, and other practices, all of which Fernando Ortiz (1951) called "a sort of selective survival."

9. This data was derived from the results of an investigation by Marcos Marín and Odalys Buscarón, from the Centre of Anthropology at the Ministry of Science, Technology and the Environment, presented at the international event, Antropología 94 (La Habana, Dec. 1994).

10. See the research presented by the Department of Socio-Religious Studies, Centro de Investigaciones Psicológicas y Sociológicas (CIPS), at the I Encuentro Internacional de Estudios Socioreligiosos, La Habana, 1995.

Works Cited

Cabrera, Lydia. [1954] 1993. *El monte.* La Habana: Editorial Letras Cubanas.

Cabrera, Lydia. 1958. *La sociedad secreta abakuá.* La Habana: Edic. CR.

Espina, Rodrigo, and Magdalena Pérez. 1994. Paper presented at Antropología 94, Cuban Ministry of Science, Technology and the Environment, La Habana.

Fraginals, Moreno. 1991. *El ingenio.* La Habana: Editorial de Ciencias Sociales.

Lachatañeré, Rómulo. 1992. *El sistema religioso de los Afrocubanos.* La Habana: Editorial de Ciencias Sociales.

López Valdés, Rafael L. 1985. *Componentes africanos en el etnos cubano.* La Habana: Editorial Ciencias Sociales.

Marín, Marcos, and Odalys Buscarón. 1994. Paper presented at Antropología 94, Cuban Ministry of Science, Technology and the Environment, La Habana.

Ortiz, Fernando. [1947] 1995. *Cuban Counterpoint: Tobacco and Sugar.* Durham: Duke University Press.

Ortiz, Fernando. 1951. *Los bailes y el teatro de los negros en el folklore de Cuba.* La Habana: Ediciones Cardenas.

Ortiz, Fernando. 1991. "La música sagrada de los negros yorubas en Cuba." In *Estudios etnosociológicos.* La Habana: Editorial de Ciencias Sociales.

II

Theology, Society, and Politics

6

Sheba's Song

The Bible, the Kebra Nagast, *and the Rastafari*

PATRICK TAYLOR

We must return to the point from which we started. Diversion is not
a useful ploy unless it is nourished by reversion: not a return to the
longing for origins, to some immutable state of Being, but a return to
the point of entanglement, from which we were forcefully turned
away; that is where we must ultimately put to work the forces of
creolization, or perish.

—Glissant, *Caribbean Discourse* (1989: 26)

I start this Caribbean story with a detour or diversion, as Edouard Glissant
would call it, or rather a series of diversions, in the expectation of arriving at a
point of entanglement in modernity referred to as creolization. My first detour
is centered around the passionate poetry of two young lovers. The woman ex-
claims:

Kiss me, make me drunk with your kisses!
Your sweet loving
is better than wine

My lover, my king, has brought me into his chambers.
We will laugh, you and I, and count
each kiss,
better than wine

I am dark, daughters of Jerusalem,
and I am beautiful!
Dark as the tents of Kedar, lavish
as Solomon's tapestries. (Song of Songs 1:2–5)[1]

Now, King Solomon was a lover of women and women loved him. (The Bible
tells us so.) He had many wives, seven hundred, and many concubines, three
hundred. Many were foreigners, like the Pharaoh's daughter (1 Kings 11:1–8).
Solomon is mentioned in the Song of Songs, and the great love poem, a very
intimate dialogue between two lovers, has traditionally been attributed to him,
despite internal evidence that this is improbable (Bloch and Bloch 1995: 10–11,
21–23). Let us assume, however, that Solomon did love some of his queens and
they him with the intensity of our two lovers. Now, Solomon was famous: for
his wisdom and righteousness, for the prosperity of his kingdom and strength

of his God. So we are told that the Queen of Sheba determined that she would visit him. She showered him with wealth and he "gave to her all that she desired, whatever she asked . . . and she turned and went back to her own land, with her servants" (1 Kings 10:13; see also 2 Chron. 9:12).

Solomon's father David had willed that "Ethiopia hasten to stretch out her hands to God" (Ps. 68:31; see also Ps. 72). Could the Queen of Sheba be Queen Makeda of Ethiopia who, according to Ethiopian tradition, fulfilled David's wish by becoming Solomon's lover, thereby conceiving the child that would bring Judaism to Ethiopia? Was this the origin of the dispersed Jews of Cush (Isa. 11:6, 11, 12), including the author of the Book of Zephaniah (Zeph. 1:1, 3:10)? The Bible suggests that Ethiopia became Jewish, then Christian. According to the Christian Bible, Christianity was first introduced in Ethiopia by an Ethiopian eunuch, a minister of Queen Candace, who was a converted Jew; he had come from Ethiopia to Jerusalem to worship and was reading Isaiah when the disciple Philip met him and converted him to Christianity (Acts 8:27–38).

I start with this diversion because of its entanglement in cross-cultural, indeed cross-racial, encounters: Can the Song of Songs, and the biblical text as a whole, be read as a passion of hybridity?

> Do not see me only as dark,
> the sun has stared at me.
>
> My brothers were angry with me,
> they made me guard the vineyards.
> I have not guarded my own.
>
> Tell me, my only love,
> where do you pasture your sheep,
> where will you let them rest in the heat of noon? (Song of Songs 1:6–7)

The Bible's silence around the relationship between King Solomon and the Queen of Sheba begs for further readings. One such reading is provided in the Qur'ān with the references to Bilqis, the Queen of *Sabā'* (the Arabic word for Sheba). With the poetic richness of the Qur'ān, a messenger informs Solomon of a great queen who worships the sun: "I come from Saba with positive news. / I found a woman reigning over them, / and she has been favoured with everything; / and she has a throne that is magnificent" (27:22–23). Solomon sends an envoy to the queen, requesting that she not rise up against him, but instead surrender to God. Bilqis consults her advisors and decides to send a gift to Solomon; he rejects it, and has his assistants transport her throne to him. The queen visits Solomon, recognizes his greatness, and surrenders to God: "I submit to the Lord of all the worlds with Solomon" (27:44). Commentary on the Qur'ān presents Bilqis as being a beautiful and powerful woman, whose great wisdom lies in her submission to God (her *Islam*). In some Muslim legends, she marries Solomon after converting and they have a son (Stowasser 1994: 64–65).

Neither in the Bible nor in the Qur'ān is the story of the Queen of Sheba fleshed out. Post-biblical Jewish commentaries, however, share many additional legends about the queen with Muslim commentaries in what amounts to a remarkable intertextual play between these two traditions, despite their differences. It is notable that in both the queen is a wise woman who tests Solomon with riddles and tricks but ultimately loses to his superior wisdom (Lassner 1993: 38–41). Although, as Lassner argues, a patriarchal order can thereby be asserted by the male interpreters of Jewish and Muslim tradition (35), it is worth bearing in mind that the Queen of Sheba retains her status as a great, independent queen in the Bible, while in the Qur'ān her submission is to God, not Solomon, and she may thereby be read as having become Solomon's equal before God (Stowasser 1994: 66).

Although modern scholarship identifies Sheba in geographical terms as having been in Southern Arabia (Yemen), it is in Ethiopian tradition that the legend of the Queen of Sheba receives its fullest treatment: the queen is the centerpiece of the Ethiopian *Kebra Nagast* (Glory of Kings), "the foremost creation of Ethiopic literature" (Prouty and Rosenfeld 1981: 113). The origins of the *Kebra Nagast* remain obscure, but the book seems to be based on a number of early works of Jewish, Christian, and Muslim expression that were compiled and modified after the restoration of the Solomonic dynasty in Ethiopia in 1270 C.E. (Brooks 1996: xxv). The text relates the origins of the Jewish tradition in Ethiopia, extols the "truth" of Christianity, and reworks the Muslim traditions about Queen Bilqis. According to the *Kebra Nagast*, the Queen of Sheba was the Ethiopian Axumite queen, Dabra Makeda. Her empire extended from Egypt to Yemen, and her merchants traded with nations as far away as India (119).[2] As a narrative of divine kingship and sacred history, the *Kebra Nagast* established the lineage of the Solomonic dynasty and legitimated that dynasty's rule of Ethiopia from the thirteenth century to the Revolution of 1974.

At the center of the text are the related stories of Makeda's visit to Jerusalem and the subsequent journey of the Ark of the Covenant to Ethiopia. Solomon seduced Makeda and she bore him a son. Menyelek I ("Son of the King" [Giday 1992: 11]) would later return to visit his father, where he would be anointed in the temple in Jerusalem by Zadok, the Jewish high priest, and crowned King David of Ethiopia. Together with a host of first-born sons of Israel, he would come back to Ethiopia, Ark of the Covenant in hand.

The seduction of Makeda by Solomon and the subsequent removal of the Ark of the Covenant from Jerusalem to Axum, two resonating silences in the biblical account, set the stage for much of the plot of the *Kebra Nagast*. The seduction scene, though apparently based on a consensual act, is not without its ambiguities: thirsty, the virgin queen releases Solomon from his oath of chastity if he will provide her with water. Solomon dreams that a brilliant sun appears over Israel and then flies west to Ethiopia, where it will shine "with exceedingly great brightness forever" (31–32). The seduction scene in the *Kebra Nagast* necessitates a reworking of Ham's biblical legacy. According to Genesis, Ham and his descendants, including Canaan, Egypt, Put, and Cush (and thereby Seba and Sheba), were cursed and would suffer enslavement by the descendants of Ham's brothers Shem and Japheth (Gen. 9:20–10:7). Yet Solomon marries Canaanite and Egyptian women (among others) and seduces the Queen of Sheba. Indeed, in the *Kebra Nagast,* Solomon tells one of his wives, the pharaoh's daughter, that both she and the Queen of Ethiopia are "black" and as such "the children of Ham."[3] He has chosen them as mothers of his children but he will not worship their idols (87). His seed and the seed of his sons will spread Israel's glory. (Solomon has four hundred queens and six hundred concubines, according to the *Kebra Nagast!* [28].) Though race and color are not issues for Solomon, religion clearly is. In a strong patriarchal motif, the seed of Shem, the male line, will cleanse the stain on the female seed of Ham.

The *Kebra Nagast* could have left the story here: Judaism goes to Ethiopia and the imperial lineage is extended. However, the text is insistent in its counter-narrative. The queen comes to Jerusalem on her own accord, the sun shifts from Jerusalem to Ethiopia, and Menyelek visits his father in Jerusalem and is recognized and welcomed as a son and king by him. Ethiopia is not a colony of Israel. Most importantly, God has chosen to have a special relationship with the Ethiopian people, for the Ark of the Covenant, Lady Zion, will henceforth be found in Axum, not Jerusalem. The narrative accomplishes this feat quite cleverly. Solomon delegates first-born sons of Jerusalem, including the son of the high priest, to accompany Menyelek, Solomon's first-born, and settle in Ethiopia to extend the glory of Israel. He blesses Menyelek, wills that the Tabernacle of the Law of God, Lady Zion, be his "guide" "at all times," and gives him one of the "coverings" of the Tabernacle (63). What Solomon does not know is that Menyelek takes this charge literally: he will take the actual Ark with him. This will be done in the name of the first-born sons of Israel who will not have to suffer the sorrow of the loss of their Lady Zion. Azariah, son of the high priest, devises the plan and it is authorized by the Angel of the Lord: "For Israel has provoked God to wrath, and for this reason He will make the Tabernacle of the Law of God to depart from them" (61). This Ethiopian counter-narrative does nothing, however, to challenge the inherited patriarchal motif: the story of Makeda, Queen of Axum, gives way to that of Menyelek, Son of Solomon. Although the Ark of the Covenant is feminized, kingship is in the hands of the descendants of the male line, who are in effect the protectors of "Lady Zion."[4]

The irony of the biblical text, as read by Christians, is that the descendant of Solomon, Christ the Savior, is rejected by his own people, the Jews. Thus, it is the Roman Emperor Constantine who spreads the true message. But Christianity does not escape its own bitter irony: those who accept the teachings of the Jews are those who condemn the Jews in the most virulent terms. Born out of Judaism and propagated by Rome, Christianity is necessarily a cross-cultural construct. The *Kebra Nagast* deepens this hybridity. The text establishes Menyelek as the founder of a hybrid, Axumite-Jewish national population. However, the Ethiopian descendants of Solomon's first son, Menyelek, "believed in one trustworthy disciple" and converted to Christianity (129). The Romans, the descendants of Solomon's third son Adranis (husband of the daughter of the king of Rome), likewise accepted Christianity and, under Emperor Constantine, spread the faith. The Ethiopians broke with the Romans because the latter became "corrupted" by Satan and "introduced heresies" (125–26). In contrast to both the Romans and the Ethiopians, the Jewish descendants of Solomon's second son Rehoboam rejected the possibility of their own salvation. The Romans therefore dispersed the Jews and took their land. The *Kebra Nagast* concludes with a vision of a unified future: the Ethiopian king and the Roman king meet in Jerusalem to divide the world between them, the Romans ruling the North and the West and the Ethiopians the South and the East as far as India. The Jews, the killers of Christ, would be "condemned to the fire which is everlasting" (128) and "pass into everlasting punishment" (171). Yet there is a contradiction in the text between this dualistic vision of salvation and damnation, and a conflicting vision of an age of Jewish redemption: "He will not leave in Sheol His people Israel by whom the pearl hath been carried" (96).

There is a history, or rather, there are a series of histories around which these literary detours can be narrated. These histories remain largely undocumented and are variously contested, but they continue to be told in "Falasha" legends, Ethiopian nationalist ideologies, Western travel narratives, and "orientalist" scholarship. Ethiopia has always existed as a relation between cultures: Semitic, Hamitic, Cushitic in the first instance; Middle Eastern, African, Asian, even European in the second. The term *Ethiopia* itself is marked by this hybridity: it comes from the Greek words for *burn* and *face*, echoing the very words of the Song of Songs. The Greek term referred to the same geographical entity as the Egyptian term *Cush,* that is, the ancient civilization of Meroë in Northern Sudan. In the eighth century B.C.E., Meroë conquered Egypt and established the "Ethiopian dynasty" of pharaohs. When Meroë was conquered by Axum in the fourth century C.E., Meroë merged with Abyssinia, and the terms *Cush* and *Ethiopia* came to refer to Abyssinia, today's Ethiopia (Kessler 1996: 20–21).

Because of its location, the region shared much of that migratory experience that characterized the ancient civilizations of the Middle East. But again because of its location, it was able to maintain its distance and uniqueness. Scholars still debate the origins of Judaism in Ethiopia. While the dominant scholarly opinion is that Judaism spread from a Jewish kingdom in Southern Arabia (Yemen) between the seventh and fourth centuries B.C.E., there is a strong case to be made that it moved through the Nile Valley (from Egypt, through Nubia and Meroë, to Axum). Although *Sabā'* (Sheba) could refer to Sabā' in Southern Arabia, Jewish and Christian sources, following the biblical text, have traditionally linked the Queen to Ethiopia, and it is possible that the Sabean name was a later imposition on the biblical text (Kessler 1996: 18–21, 26–27). In any case, the Agaw, the ancient Cushitic population that lived in the region, came under the influence of Semitic culture, and a new "Ethiopic civilization" that was predominantly Semitic was born. While the dominant Amharic and Tigrayan cultures grew out of this new culture as it became Christianized, the Agaw were never entirely assimilated, and there remained pockets of "pagan," "Hebraic-pagan," and "Hebraic" Agaw who spoke Cushitic rather than Semitic languages (Gamst 1969: 12–13).

The story of the Queen of Sheba is, first of all, the story of the Jews of Ethiopia, who are thereby privileged as the originators of a unique Ethiopian civilization. Most remarkable in this story is the leadership of the Agaw Jewish queen, Jodith, who, true to her biblical namesake, responded to Christian repression of Jews in the ninth century by assembling a large army, capturing Axum, and setting herself up as monarch. For a period of time, Christianity was repressed and Axumite books and monuments destroyed (Giday 1992: 132–37). The fact that Ethiopian Jews were largely unknown to the West, that once known they seemed to be of the wrong color, and that they were largely unaffected by the transitions in Judaism that had taken place elsewhere in the world, including the teachings of the Midrash and the Talmud, made it at first difficult for world Jewry to recognize them as Jews. However, Ethiopian Jews were recognized by the Chief Sephardi Rabbi and his Ashkenazi counterpart in 1973 and 1975 respectively. With war and famine in Ethiopia, Israel and the United States organized Operations Moses and Sheba (1984–85) and Operation Solomon (1991), transporting most of Ethiopia's Jews to Israel. Ethiopian Jews have adopted the name *Beta Esrael* (House of Israel) as a replacement for the name *Falasha*, meaning "foreigner," "immigrant," or "exile" in Amharic and thereby suggesting that Ethiopian Jews did not belong to Ethiopia, although, paradoxically, it is as "exiles" that they have returned to the "promised land" (Barnavi 1992: 266–67; Kessler 1996: 4).

Although Christianity first came to Ethiopia through the work of individual disciples, as recorded in the Christian Bible and other sources, it is Frumentius, a Greek Christian who lived in Ethiopia, who is credited with its spread. Named Ethiopia's first bishop by the Egyptian Coptic Patriarch in Alexandria in 320 C.E., Frumentius converted King Ezana, who then ordered that all Ethiopians be baptized. (An Ethiopian Orthodox Church publication gives the date for the official adoption of Christianity by the Axumite state as 332 C.E. [Wondmagegnehu and Motovu 1970: 4].) Christianity developed on the basis of the strong Jewish traditions already present in the country and continues to have a strong Hebraic mold. Despite the Egyptian Coptic influence and patronage, Ethiopian Christianity assumed a distinctly national form within the wider Oriental Orthodox non-Chalcedonian tradition (which includes the Coptic, Armenian, Syrian, and Indian Churches). However, it was not until 1959 that the Ethiopian Church became fully independent from Alexandria and appointed its own Abuna, or Patriarch (Giday 1992: 95–96, 103–5; Wondmagegnehu and Motovu 1970: 96–100).

Islam first made its mark on Ethiopia in the seventh century, when Muslim refugees sought and received the protection of Ethiopia's Christian rulers. They were followed by merchants who entered the country to trade peacefully and settle. Some Ethiopians converted to Islam, but Christian-Muslim conflict arose over trade routes through the Red Sea. In the sixteenth century, the Amir of Harar, Imam Ahmed Ibn Ibrahim Al Ghazi (Gran), invaded large portions of the kingdom of Ethiopia with the assistance of the Turks and Ethiopian Jews, converting many Christians to Islam. Ironically, it was only with military help from Catholic Portugal that Gran was defeated in 1543; the Ethiopian Jewish Kingdom that had assisted him was liquidated (Giday 1992: 141–44; Pankhurst 1990: 277–80; Barnavi 1992: 267).

Although the *Kebra Nagast* legitimates a Christian Kingdom at the expense of Ethiopian Jews and Muslims, its ideological role has much to do with ethnic and political conflict within the Christian feudal hierarchy itself. From 922 to 1268 C.E., Ethiopia was ruled by the Zagwe dynasty, which was of Agaw rather than Axumite descent. After a civil war, the Axumite line was restored. The *Kebra Nagast* was written in the fourteenth century: legitimating the Axumite line, it established a Judeo-Christian foundation for an African feudal kingdom and a divinely ordained lineage for its "Solomonic" dynasty (Giday 1992: 140). This imperial line would endure to the twentieth century.

A third detour takes me back to Glissant's Caribbean: "Our Redeemer is calling us home. / We see there is no truth in Rome. / Our Heaven is in Ethiopia / With King Rasta and Queen Omega" (Simpson 1980: 215). This early Rasta chant is but one "verse" of a living Rasta "song," the text of which consists of African diasporic interpretations of biblical and Ethiopian traditions. Expressed in the upsurge of the oral into the written, Rastafari is an "irruption into modernity," to use Glissant's terms (1989: 146–47). Rastafari developed out of a long tradition of Ethiopianism in Jamaica. Both in Africa and in the Americas, African Christians had been identified by European missionaries as Ethiopians in accordance with references to Ethiopia in the Bible; sometimes, African Christians assumed this identity themselves, albeit in a redefined way. In 1852, Martin Delany, an African American who took up exile in Canada, appealed to the words of the psalmist, "Princes shall come forth out of Egypt; Ethiopia shall soon stretch forth her hands unto God" (Ps. 68:31), and wrote, "we shall boldly advance, singing sweet songs of redemption, in the regeneration of our race and restoration of our father-land" (quoted in Gilroy 1993: 20). Edward Blyden, a West Indian who committed himself to the development of modern Liberia, was influenced by Jewish thought in the Danish West Indies, where he was born in 1832. A "son of Ham," he identified the struggle of his people with that of the ancient Hebrews: "Africa had fostered the development of civilization among Jews," and both Africans and Jews had a contemporary mission to regenerate humanity (Gilroy 1993: 210–11). In South Africa in the 1880s, "Ethiopian" and "Israelite" churches broke away from their missionary progenitors (Davidson 1969: 278). "Black Baptists" in Jamaica, led by an African-American missionary,

George Leile, and his Jamaican deacon, Thomas Swiggle, had already identified their followers as a "Church of Ethiopia" by the end of the eighteenth century (Turner 1982: 11; Chevannes 1994: 33–37). A number of Jamaicans would later claim to be of royal Ethiopian descent (Hill 1983: 26).

It was Marcus Garvey, founder of the Universal Negro Improvement Association (UNIA), who would become the most influential spokesperson for Ethiopianism in Jamaica, the United States, and other areas of the African diaspora. In 1896, the Abyssinians had defeated the Italians under Menyelek II at the Battle of Adwa, thereby preserving Ethiopia from direct European colonialism. The "UNIA Anthem" (1920) would both reflect this fact and elaborate a Pan-African vision of a strong, unified, and free African people. With the rallying cry "Let Africa be free," the anthem invokes a new order: "Ethiopia, the tyrants falling, / Who smote thee upon thy knees, / And thy children are lustily calling / From over the distant seas" (Garvey 1986, 2: 140). Garvey, like Delany, quotes Psalm 68 and continues: "At this moment methinks I see Ethiopia stretching forth her hands unto God, and methinks I see the Angel of God taking up the standard of the Red, the Black and the Green [UNIA's colors], and saying 'Men of the Negro Race, Men of Ethiopia, follow me'" (Garvey 1986, 1: 96; see also 1: 81).

Garvey was reported to have told his followers: "Look to Africa, when a black king shall be crowned, for the day of deliverance is near" (quoted in Smith et al. 1978: 5). Word became prophecy when in 1930 the Ethiopian nobleman Ras Tafari was crowned emperor, assumed the name Haile Selassie ("Might of the Trinity"), and, tracing his descent to the line of Solomon, took the title "King of Kings, Lion of the Tribe of Judah." Many Jamaicans looked in awe at the photographs in the Kingston papers showing European leaders respectfully bowing down to this new African leader. Prophets began to preach the divinity of Ras Tafari. Leonard Howell was one of several people to proclaim that Christ had returned and now the white race would bow down to the black race. Europeans who called themselves Jews and Christians had distorted the biblical teachings and appropriated the place of God's chosen people, guardians of the Ark of the Covenant, the black race. The Messiah would come to redeem his people from the land of colonialism and slavery and lead them out of Babylon into the promised land, Ethiopia (Barrett 1988: 80–84).

Caribbean creative writers such as Roger Mais and Derek Walcott have been able to invoke some of the beauty and spirituality of the Rastafari. Mais, a Jamaican novelist attentive to the Jamaican idiom, recovers the spirit of the story in the words of his main character in *Brother Man*: "But de spirit of de Lawd passed over into Ethiopia, after the Queen of Sheba came to Solomon and learned all his wisdom, an' passed over back to her own land. So it was black men out of Africa who became God's chosen people, for they had learnt de Way" (1974: 74). In a similar vein, there issues forth from the mouth of the character named Sufferer in *O Babylon!* the inspired words of that great Caribbean poet, Derek Walcott:

In him [Emperor Selassie] is beauty. In him is wisdom.
For when Sheba travel to Ethiopia,
her jangling procession on the horizon
a moving oasis of palms and banners,
lions in the desert rise up to look.
She couple with Solomon, and from their seed sprang
Ras Makonnen, the vine and the fig tree
of fragrant Zion, Selassie himself. (1978: 167–68)

Despite the polysemic potency of the lion symbol (Lion of Judah, African Lion), the messianic message—wait for the coming of the savior—may seem to be a passive compromise with reality. This is the sense of one version of Garvey's UNIA anthem reworked by the Rastafari as the "Ethiopian National Anthem." Whereas Garvey's anthem privileges active support for the Ethiopian ideal with the words "Our armies come rushing to thee" with swords "thrust outward to gleam," in the Rastafari version there is a passive appeal to the Fatherland: the emperor will "shield us from wrong" as "Thy Children are gathered to thee." The threatening dreadlocks of the Rastafari—at once Nazarite vow and lion's mane— give way in this redemptive moment to vows of truth, peace, and love (Garvey 1986, 2: 140; Simpson 1980: 214). Though a fundamental messianic under-standing would remain central to Rastafari in its various expressions, it would be reasoned out in different ways: some would wait, others would act; a few would emigrate to Ethiopia, others would build their own "Ethiopia" in Jamaica; some would reason only with persons of African descent, others would share the teachings regardless of race (Taylor 1990). Ironically, some Jamaican Rasta-fari would reach the new Zion and settle on the emperor's land grant to persons of African descent in Shashamane, only to find the imperial state transformed by revolution, the emperor assassinated, and the country in ruins. Doubly ironic is the case of those members of the Ethiopian Beta Esrael population, discrimi-nated against by Christian Ethiopians for centuries, rescued by the Israeli state and transported to Israel, only to find themselves pushed by racism to emigrate to the Caribbean.

The Rastafari counter-narrative is not without further twists, ambiguities, and diversions as the lived experience of the Caribbean finds other points of inser-tion. Rastafari was primarily a men's movement: the sons of the father, Solomon, maintained his traditions. However, just as the Bible could produce a female voice in Song of Songs and in Sheba, or Ethiopian tradition a Makeda or a Jodith, so too the Rastas recognized the dignity of women: the "daughters" were also "Queens." More and more Rasta women began to claim their space in the religion beginning in the 1970s (Rowe 1980; Chevannes 1994: 255–62).

Rastafari was Pan-African in its orientation. However, Jamaica was not only African or even African and European: Indian indentured workers were also brought to the island, albeit in relatively small numbers. In an inclusive leap, a typical mark of the Caribbean creolization process, Howell is reported to have assumed as his own ritual name, Gangunguru ("Teacher of Famed Wisdom") Maragh ("King"), a title given to him by his Hindu adviser, Laloo. The Rastafari took up the practice of smoking ganja (sometimes called "Kali" after the Hindu Goddess) for ritual purposes and developed their own version of the doctrine of reincarnation (Hill 1983: 32–37; Bishton 1986: 115–17). Rastafari is hybridity at its grandest, narrated as dispersion and return, Africa and Europe mutually implicated, pushing the meaning of the other to its limits, ingesting, transforming, humanizing.

The Bible, the *Kebra Nagast,* the Rastafari story, through the diversion of these texts I have been arguing the case for Caribbean creolization. The Bible is a Caribbean text; in general, people in the Anglophone Caribbean know their Bible better than North Americans! The *Kebra Nagast* is a Caribbean text. The Rastafari have known about this book for many years. I purchased a copy of the Red Sea Press edition in Addis Ababa. Published in 1996, it was edited by Miguel Brooks, a Panamanian-Jamaican Seventh Day Adventist, and dedicated to the memory of Marcus Garvey. In 1997, edited selections of the *Kebra Nagast* were published under the title *The Kebra Nagast: The Lost Bible of Rastafarian Wisdom and Faith from Ethiopia and Jamaica.* It contains a preface by reggae artist Ziggy Marley, son of the legendary Bob Marley, as well as selections of contemporary Rastafari reasoning. In an interpretative process in defiance of both biblical hermeneutics and liberation theology, the Rastafari have brought the oral into the written text to become the bearers of a Caribbean textuality at its fullest.

According to Edward Kamau Brathwaite, the term *creole* (from the Latin *creare,* to create or suckle, through Spanish and Portuguese, to create or found) was used with different nuances throughout the Americas to refer to locally born persons, regardless of racial or cultural origin. Creolization was the foundation for a dynamic new national society in the Caribbean. The problem was that this national potential was never fully realized by the colonial and later neo-colonial elites in the society. Creolization gave way to assimilation (into European modernity) and denial (of an African-based popular culture) (Brathwaite 1971: 306–11). Indeed, the pluralism also characteristic of colonial society marks the very limit of creolization. According to M. G. Smith, plural societies are characterized by distinct cultural and social groups in a single political system that can be maintained only by the monopolistic exercise of power by one of these distinct groups (Smith 1960: 767, 773). The white plantocracy in the Caribbean maintained the social order by force while subordinate groups, such as African slaves and Indian indentured workers, resisted it.

In 1970, the Black Power Movement in the Caribbean challenged the creole elite to acknowledge its history and confront its African heritage. The Rastafari had always spoken from within the context of a conflictual, plural society. Challenging the legacy of the plantation colony, they put into question the legitimating ideologies of white racial and cultural supremacy. This critique extended into the period of national independence when black, colored, and white elites worked for international capitalism and allied themselves with American consumer and evangelical culture. The Black Power youth were catching up with the Rastafari, and the Rastafari were there, as Rodney put it, to "ground" with them (Rodney 1983: 60–68). As a decidedly anti-assimilationist, historically and culturally grounded, Pan-African movement, the Rastafari had always challenged the elite concept of creolization. (The Indian population, a major player in the plural society of some Caribbean countries, would issue their own challenge beginning in the 1980s.)

At the same time, Rastafari is quintessentially creole in Brathwaite's and Glissant's sense. As C. L. R. James has pointed out, Africa is a Caribbean desire (James 1989: 399). Rooted in a radical Afro-Christian, Jamaican tradition, Rastas have forged a new religion and culture out of African, European, and even Indian roots. The Bible of King James was reread through the *Kebra Nagast* of Ethiopia and both texts reflectively applied to a Caribbean historical reality in an upsurge of orality that Rastas refer to as "reasoning." Rasta ingenuity helped to awaken first in Jamaicans and then in other peoples of African descent a new sense of themselves as Africans in a struggle for social and political change. At the same time, its universal appeal, popularized in reggae, thrust it into the global arena, attracting people of different races and creeds, including both Jews and Christians.

Contrasting Mediterranean civilizations (Hebrew, Greek, Roman, and Arabic) with the Caribbean, Glissant argues that in that inner sea surrounded by land, thought is concentrated into "the One." The Caribbean is instead a "sea that explodes the scattered lands into an arc"; it is a site of "Relation" (1997: 33–34). At their most philosophical, the Rastafari are the bearers of relational thinking in its fullest: the subject knows itself only through its relationship with its other. The Rasta term for the plural subject *we* is *I-n-I*, the relation of separate selves through Rastafar-*I,* Selassie-*I,* the unifying one. The "I-and-I" logic of Rastafari discourse is thereby itself reflected in other discourses, in the "I-Thou" relation of Martin Buber, for example, or Søren Kierkegaard's "God-relationship" (see Owens 1979: 65). As a Derridean "supplement" to a European Judeo-Christian tradition told in accordance with the doctrine of "the One," Ethiopian Judaism and Ethiopian Christianity likewise explode the myth of "the One." It would be fair to say, therefore, that the mountains of Ethiopia, rising beside the Red Sea, cross-cut for eons by the lakes, rivers, and waterfalls that flow north to the great Nile Valley civilizations and south to the Indian ocean, are explosions of hybridity not unlike the volcanic cones of the Caribbean Sea. Exposing the radical "difference" of the biblical text, the Rastafari reversion to Ethiopianism reveals, in Glissant's terms, the "point of entanglement" that unleashes the creolization process to its plural histories.

I close with words from one of the Caribbean's most famous songs:

Emancipate yourselves from mental slavery
None but ourselves can free our minds

Won't you help to sing, these songs of freedom
cause all I ever had, redemption songs
all I ever had, redemption songs
these songs of freedom, songs of freedom. (Marley and the Wailers 1980)

Notes

Early versions of this paper were presented at the Annual Meeting of the Modern Languages Association (Toronto, December 1997) and the Eastern Regionals of the American Academy of Religion (Toronto, April 1998).

1. Song of Songs references are to the Bloch and Bloch translation (1995). All other biblical references are to the Revised Standard Version (1973).

2. Unless otherwise indicated, references are to the Brooks translation, which is now readily available in both Ethiopia and North America. Brooks states that he retranslated the text from the1528 Spanish translation and separated out the "authentic" from the "legendary" portions (xiv, xxx). Much of Brooks's English text is the same as Wallis Bridge's translation ([1922] 1932).

3. The Bridge translation suggests that the term "race" is implied (hence it is in square brackets) whereas Brooks uses the term outright, even in cases where Bridge uses "kin." It should be noted that Brooks's explicit intention is to "establish the truth of the origins of the Solomonic Dynasty of Kings and the current abode of the Ark of the Covenant" (xv). Moreover, Brooks dedicates the book to Marcus Garvey and hopes that the reader will find "some useful insight into the majestic role that divine providence has set aside for the black race" (xxvii).

4. The Ark of the Covenant is said to be housed in the Church of St. Mary of Zion in Axum, as are many other Church treasures. While the Ark is kept out of sight, the other treasures were open for viewing by men. Women, largely non-Ethiopian, were invited to see these for the first time in November 1997, and were given a formal apology by the Abuna.

Works Cited

Al-Qur'ān. 1988. Translated by Ahmed Ali. Rev. ed. Princeton, N.J.: Princeton University Press.

The New Oxford Annotated Bible. 1973. Rev. Standard Version. New York: Oxford University Press.

The Queen of Sheba and Her Only Son Menyelek (I) Being the "Book of the Glory of Kings" (Kebra Nagast). [1922] 1932. Translated by Wallis Bridge. 2nd ed. Oxford: Oxford University Press.

Song of Songs: A New Translation. 1995. Translated by Ariel Bloch and Chana Bloch. New York: Random House.

Barnavi, Eli. 1992. *A Historical Atlas of the Jewish People.* New York: Schocken.

Barrett, Leonard. 1988. *The Rastafarians: Sounds of Cultural Dissonance.* Rev. ed. Boston: Beacon.

Bishton, Derek. 1986. *Black Heart Man.* London: Chatto and Windus.

Brathwaite, Edward. 1971. *The Development of Creole Society in Jamaica: 1770–1820.* Oxford: Oxford University Press.

Brooks, Miguel F., ed. 1996. *Kebra Nagast (Glory of Kings)*. Lawrenceville, N.J.: Red Sea Press.

Chevannes, Barry. 1994. *Rastafari: Roots and Ideology*. Syracuse: Syracuse University Press.

Davidson, Basil. 1969. *The African Genius: An Introduction to African Cultural and Social History*. Boston: Little, Brown and Company.

Gamst, Frederick. 1969. *The Qemant: A Pagan-Hebraic Peasantry in Ethiopia*. New York: Holt, Rinehart and Winston.

Garvey, Marcus. 1986. *The Philosophy and Opinions of Marcus Garvey*. Edited by Amy Jacques-Garvey. 2 vols. New York: Atheneum.

Giday, Belai. 1992. *Ethiopian Civilization*. Addis Ababa: n.p.

Gilroy, Paul. 1993. *The Black Atlantic: Modernity and Double Consciousness*. Cambridge, Mass.: Harvard University Press.

Glissant, Edouard. 1989. *Caribbean Discourse: Selected Essays*. Translated by J. Michael Dash. Charlottesville: University Press of Virginia.

Glissant, Edouard. 1997. *Poetics of Relation*. Translated by Betsy Wing. Ann Arbor: University of Michigan Press.

Hill, Robert. 1983. "Leonard P. Howell and Millenarian Visions in Early Rastafari." *Jamaica Journal* 16 (1): 24–39.

James, C. L. R. 1989. *The Black Jacobins: Toussaint L'Overture and the San Domingo Revolution*. 2nd ed. rev. New York: Vintage-Random House.

Kessler, David. [1982] 1996. *The Falashas: A Short History of the Ethiopian Jews*. 3rd rev. ed. London: Frank Cass.

Lassner, Jacob. 1993. *The Demonizing of the Queen of Sheba: Boundaries of Gender and Culture in Postbiblical Judaism and Medieval Islam*. Chicago: University of Chicago Press.

Mais, Roger. 1974. *Brother Man*. London: Heinemann.

Marley, Bob, and the Wailers. 1980. "Redemption Song." *Uprising*. LP. Island.

Owens, Joseph. 1979. *Dread: The Rastafarians of Jamaica*. Kingston, Jamaica: Sangster's Book Stores, 1976. Reprint, London: Heinemann.

Pankhurst, Richard. 1990. *A Social History of Ethiopia: The Northern and Central Highlands from Early Medieval Times to the Rise of Emperor Tewodros II*. Addis Ababa: Institute of Ethiopian Studies.

Prouty, Chris, and Eugene Rosenfeld. 1981. *Historical Dictionary of Ethiopia*. Metuchen, N.J.: Scarecrow Press.

Rodney, Walter. 1983. *The Groundings with My Brothers*. London: Bogle L'Ouverture Publications.

Rowe, Maureen. 1980. "The Women in Rastafari." *Caribbean Quarterly* 26 (4): 13–21.

Simpson, George Eaton. 1980. *Religious Cults of the Caribbean: Trinidad, Jamaica and Haiti*. 3rd ed. Rio Piedras, Puerto Rico: Institute of Caribbean Studies.

Smith, M. G. 1960. "Social and Cultural Pluralism." In *Social and Cultural Pluralism in the Caribbean*, ed. Vera Rubin. Annals of the New York Academy of Sciences 83.5. New York: Academy of Sciences.

Smith, M. G., Roy Augier, and Rex Nettleford. [1960] 1978. *The Rastafari Movement in Kingston, Jamaica*. Mona, Jamaica: Extra-Mural Studies, University of the West Indies.

Stowasser, Barbara F. 1994. *Women in the Qur'ān, Traditions, and Interpretation*. New York: Oxford University Press.

Taylor, Patrick. 1990. "Perspectives on History in Rastafari Thought." *Studies in Religion* 19 (2): 191–205.

Turner, Mary. 1982. *Slaves and Missionaries: The Disintegration of Jamaican Slave Society, 1787–1834*. Urbana: University of Illinois Press.

Walcott, Derek. 1978. *The Joker of Seville and O Babylon!: Two Plays*. New York: Farrar, Straus and Giroux.

Wondmagegnehu, Aymro, and Joachim Motovu, eds. 1970. *The Ethiopian Orthodox Church*. Addis Ababa: Ethiopian Orthodox Mission.

7

Themes from West Indian Church History in Colonial and Post-colonial Times

ARTHUR C. DAYFOOT

It is commonly believed that the history of the churches of the West Indies—and indeed of the western hemisphere in general—is basically an extension of European Christianity. This may be true in terms of the structure of ecclesiastical institutions, and when considered from narrow denominational standards. However, it is also true that the pattern of corporate Christian life in the "New World," and in the West Indies in particular, has gained a character of its own, both in practice and in theory, distinct from that of Europe.

There is much in common west of the Atlantic in the historical demographic circumstances of the mingling of populations through European colonization, through contact and conflict with the Aboriginal occupants, and subsequently through the bringing in of millions of African and Asian, as well as later-arriving European, groups. These factors have created a variety of new societies in two continents and the neighboring islands. A great number of churches and missions have conveyed old and new Christian beliefs and practices to the people in these societies. These traditions have provoked indigenous responses of various kinds, and these responses in turn have spread beyond their home base to other parts of the New World (and sometimes back to the "Old World" as well). Non-Christian religions of Aboriginal, African, and Asian origin have led both to controversy and to syncretistic adaptation in the new environment. Such factors have created a "New World ethos" in the life of the churches as well as in society as a whole. The resultant pluralism is a religious pluralism quite different from that of Europe (Zavala 1962; Conference on the History of Religion in the New World during Colonial Times 1958).

Within this New World ethos, each area has developed a character of its own. Language and culture are only part of the reason for this variation. In plantation America, the exploitation of estate labor incited a struggle against slavery, and even over European and Asian indenture, which underlay the life of the Church in the West Indies, in this respect resembling the American South. The biblical theology of the Exodus and the divine demand for justice, as well as the natural desire for freedom among the exploited people, played a part in the story of both earlier and post-emancipation aspirations, which has a kinship with the American movement of the black churches.

In other particulars, Christian life in the West Indies is distinct from that of the two other English-speaking areas of this hemisphere—the United States and Canada. American church historians were first to begin rewriting the religious history of their country. Among other factors, they pointed to the influence of revolutionary democratic ideas and of the western frontier on the pluralistic style of religion in their country (Sweet 1939, 1950; Littell 1962). In Canada, democracy and even the frontier had a different history, and with its two language areas there have been more conservative loyalties to the traditions of Catholic and Reformed Christianity (Walsh 1956; Grant 1966: 72).

In the English-speaking Caribbean, colonial conditions continued much longer than in North America. Class-and-color stratification of society made advance to democracy more difficult. Frontiers in the West Indies had been at first only "coastland frontiers," like the earliest settlements of North America. Later, small communities were formed by ex-slaves and ex–indentured workers, especially in remote parts of the larger territories. Rather than novel orthodox and unorthodox Christian movements like those of western continental United States, these West Indian communities produced other kinds of religious novelty. These included forms of Afro-Caribbean practice and belief, and the mingling of Asian and African religious traditions with those of Christianity. Throughout the entire society, the spiritual aspirations of the people run very deep.

To a much greater extent than on the northern continent, widespread poverty resulting from centuries of exploitation by the metropolitan powers, and also from limited natural resources, has hindered the establishment of strong economic foundations for indigenous development. In many ways, attitudes of colonial dependence and imitation still persist even since the achievement of political independence.

In the face of these limitations, the story of Christianity in the English-speaking Caribbean is marked by a number of motifs that were deeply colored by the colonial experience and that are still working themselves out in the life of the new West Indian nations. This chapter attempts to identify some of these themes, to trace briefly their origins and development, and to consider their survival and modification in the post-independence era.

FROM STATE-CHURCH TO PLURALISM

Caribbean church history records a slow transition from the monopoly position held by the early-sixteenth-century Spanish Catholic Church (in the Spanish Empire, including Jamaica and Trinidad) to the great diversity of Christian and non-Christian religious bodies flourishing in the English-speaking Caribbean of the twentieth century. The religion brought to the New World by the Spaniards was the faith of late medieval Christendom as it prevailed in the Iberian peninsula at the end of its seven-century struggle, called the Reconquest, for independence from Muslim rule. The Church, which was the focus of identity in this struggle, remained as a bulwark of Spanish national as well as religious life. Ironically, Christians, who in the years of the New Testament and the early Church had suffered persecution from the Roman empire, were now centuries later using state power and the Inquisition to persecute Muslims, Jews, and, later, the new heretics called Protestants. These other religious groups were to be excluded from the new Spanish empire as well as from Spain itself. Moreover, in that empire the Aboriginal people were subjected to forced Christianization by the *encomienda* system and "pacification."

By the mid-sixteenth century, however, France and later the Netherlands and England began to challenge Spanish political and religious monopoly. Protestant sailors played an active part in this opposition, which was expressed through trade and hostile attack. Then in the seventeenth century, non-Spanish colonies were planted in the Lesser Antilles and in Guiana. Jamaica was captured, and Spain finally had to concede that other nations and other churches would be existing in the New World it had claimed to own.

For decades of this period of early non-Spanish colonization, a variety of European settlers lived in close proximity and mutual toleration in their island and coastland territories: Anglicans, Puritans, and Quakers, Irish and French Catholics, Huguenots, Jews, and others. Mainly for pragmatic reasons, the pluralistic style of this pioneer period displayed a level of religious freedom unusual for that time (Dayfoot 1999: ch. 6).

By the beginning of the eighteenth century, in the heyday of slavery in the English colonies, the new plantation order brought this pluralism to an end. As other groups dwindled or moved away, the Church of England was left virtually alone. The "planters' church," controlled by vestries and assemblies, was not interested in opening its doors to the slaves around it—in spite of efforts from afar by Royal Instructions (to the governors), by the Bishop of London, and by the Society for the Propagation of the Gospel to promote their Christianization (Labaree 1935, 2: 482–512; Bennett 1958; Dayfoot 1999: ch. 7).

With the coming of the eighteenth-century evangelical movement, Moravians from Saxony and later also from England, English Methodists, and African-American free Baptist preachers began to befriend and preach to the slaves. Later, new missionary societies with Anglican, Congregational (London Missionary Society), and English Baptist connections also formed congregations. In addition, African-American ex-soldiers, who had been granted land in south Trinidad, established their own Baptist churches in their "company villages." Meanwhile, as the Windward Islands and Trinidad were taken from France and Spain and a scattering of Catholic refugees settled in Jamaica, many thousands of Roman Catholics (including slaves) were added to the British West Indies. Religious pluralism was now firmly reestablished.

A new surge of diversification came before and after Emancipation. In connection with the British government's policy of "Amelioration" (1823), two bishops were appointed for the Church of England in the West Indies, centered in Barbados and Jamaica. They were mandated to promote conversion and education of the slaves under established Church auspices. Scottish Missionary Society workers, and some from the Secession Church began to form congregations in Jamaica and in Trinidad. Anglican missions ("Slave Conversion Society," Church Missionary Society, and the long-established Society for the Propagation of the

Gospel), the several nonconformist missions, a profusion of missionary schools, and those of the Mico Charity greatly advanced literacy among eager slaves and ex-slaves as well as people of color. Many of these were now ready to count themselves as Christians. After Emancipation, new missions and schools from the London Missionary Society and, from the United States, Oberlin College, the American Missionary Association, and the Church of Christ (Disciples) came to Jamaica.

Some groups among the slaves, such as the "Native Baptists" of Jamaica, found in the Bible a theology of liberation—while also retaining African beliefs and practices. Their urge for freedom helped to inspire rebellions such as those in Demerara in 1823 and Jamaica in 1831 and 1865 (Heuman 1994). Then, as an indirect consequence of the Morant Bay crisis, crown colony governments officially recognized religious pluralism as a fact. In and around 1870, the Church of England was disestablished, except in Barbados.

Following Emancipation, indentured workers from India brought with them their religions of Hinduism and Islam, mainly to the Southern Caribbean. Also, the long-existing presence and influence of African traditional religion was slowly beginning to be recognized, notably as a by-product of the Jamaican "revival" of 1861–62 (Curtin 1975: 168–72).

Later in the century, the Society of Friends from the American Midwest, the African Methodist Episcopal Churches from North America, and the Salvation Army from England began work in the Caribbean. American colporteurs introduced Seventh-Day Adventism. In the twentieth century, other missionaries founded Christian denominations of the new "Holiness" and "Pentecostal" traditions. Various indigenous groups and congregations under this influence have added to the complexity of the religious scene down to the present day. This pluralism, although in some ways resembling that of North America, created a pattern of its own.

RELIGIOUS FREEDOM AND SEPARATION OF CHURCH AND STATE

The growth in religious tolerance and the idea of separation of church and state were by-products of the slow and halting transition from state-church to pluralism. Other factors also played a part in this process, such as the need for security from external enemies and the requirements of trade in the seventeenth-century pioneer settlements. Huguenots, for example, at most times were tolerated in French colonies because otherwise they could easily escape to neighboring British or Dutch territories (Reyss 1907). In the emerging sugar-producing society, white slave-owners felt the need of "deficiency men," whatever their religion, to guard against slave rebellion.

On the other hand, in those episodes where tolerance was denied, there were non-religious as well as religious motives. For example, Quakers were persecuted because they refused to serve in the militia or to remove their hats before their "superiors"—and because sometimes they invited slaves to their religious meetings (Besse 1753). During the English Civil War, royalists and Puritan sympathizers in Barbados had political reasons to demand or to reject use of the Book of Common Prayer, while giving lip-service to "liberty of conscience in matters of religion." Roman Catholics were distrusted because of the external threat of Spain or France. Nonconformist missionaries and their converts were persecuted because their teachings to the slaves—that duties to God came first, such as church worship, Sunday-observance, scripture-reading, and sexual morality—clashed with the exclusive claim of masters over the lives of their chattels, and also because their teachings ran counter to the prevailing social mores of the whites themselves. Even in the twentieth century, the worship of Shouter Baptists in St. Vincent and Trinidad was prohibited for decades largely because upper-class people regarded it as a noisy "nuisance" (Thomas 1987).

Separation of church and state has not been as complete as in many other parts of the world. Education was pioneered by churches, and in many places it retains these links, partly for practical reasons. Christian, and in some places other denominational, schools are often state-supported. Continuing cooperation with government in education is due also to the religious ethos of the people, among whom "Western" secularism is not widely adopted.

ECUMENICAL COOPERATION

Over time, the scattered state of Christian groups and pluralistic tendencies began to be questioned and modified by a cooperative and ultimately an "ecumenical" movement. Evangelical missions in the eighteenth and nineteenth centuries had a common cause—to reach slaves and others with the message of the gospel—and usually carried on in friendly relationships. Early in the nineteenth century, the British and Foreign Bible Society distributed New Testaments to slaves and ex-slaves of all denominations who were learning to read, and several West Indian Auxiliaries of this interdenominational organization were formed. Their agent in Jamaica, "Bible Thomson," inspired the formation in the western part of the island of the first Ministerial Association. Such unofficial "fraternal" gatherings of clergy from time to time have played an active part in the life of the churches and the larger community, sometimes conducting interdenominational evangelistic "crusades" and at other times speaking out on moral and social issues. In some territories, church councils with official (rather than simply individual) standing, such as the Jamaica Christian Council, the Federal Council of Evangelical Churches in Trinidad, and the Christian Social Council in Guyana, also began to address community problems.

Another area of common concern was ministerial training. After many decades when this was conducted by individual missionaries or in denominational institutions such as Codrington and Calabar Colleges, interdenominational cooperation in theological education emerged in the twentieth century. For a generation, Baptist, Methodist, Moravian, Presbyterian, Congregational, and Disciples of Christ denominations shared classes at Calabar and Caenwood in Jamaica. In

1959, Presbyterian Theological College in Trinidad began to welcome students of other denominations and accordingly renamed itself "St. Andrew's." In 1966, eleven Caribbean churches established the United Theological College of the West Indies (UTCWI) at the university center at Mona. The provision for a licentiate, a B.A., and ultimately higher degrees in theology through the University of the West Indies (UWI) accompanied these developments. Roman Catholic seminaries, St. Jean Vianney in Trinidad and St. Michael's in Jamaica, as well as historic Codrington College in Barbados became similarly associated with UWI. At about the same time, the Jamaica Theological Seminary, under the designation "evangelical," was formed in Kingston, serving another group of Christian churches, mainly with American associations. Education and training for church clergy and other personnel was now increasingly interdenominational in method and conscious of Caribbean identity. Theological teachers were soon predominantly West Indian rather than expatriate.

In the 1950s just before independence, churches had begun to see the need for other forms of organized cooperation (Caribbean Consultation 1957). The Caribbean Council for Joint Christian Action (CCJCA) was formed and an interdenominational Sunday School curriculum produced. In accord with the worldwide Ecumenical Movement, the Caribbean Conference of Churches (CCC) was established in 1973. It was the first such church council in the world to include the Roman Catholic Church as a charter member. A variety of joint social and economic activities and consultations on theological and related topics have been carried on by the CCC (Cuthbert 1986).

In such ways, the extreme diversity of Christian denominations has been somewhat counterbalanced and given a new Caribbean identity in the post-independence era. The idea of cooperation and even the word "ecumenism" have been used sometimes in a still wider sense. There has been increasing recognition of, and especially in the 1990s dialogue with, non-Christian religions (Bisnauth 1996). This is notably so in the Southern Caribbean including Suriname (Sankeralli 1995). Some Hindu and Muslim schools and non-Christian religious holidays have been officially recognized by governments. In Trinidad at least, an Inter-Religious Organization has become established for consultation and common action.

REDUCTION OF DEPENDENCE UPON OVERSEAS PERSONNEL AND FINANCIAL SUPPORT

Colonial circumstances perpetuated dependence by the European- or North American-centered churches upon leadership from abroad. As early as 1511, bishops from Spain were placed in authority in the New World. Although Bishop Zumárraga in Mexico had opened a school for local priests, the European-style training was unsuited to Aboriginal youths. Prejudice against Aboriginal people, mestizos, and Africans kept them from the priesthood, and distrust of *criollos* denied these American-born whites promotion within the Spanish Church.

The "planters' church" in English colonies in the slavery era was theoretically under the care of the Bishop of London, but active episcopal oversight and consequently local ordinations and confirmations were lacking. Clergy came from Great Britain or, in rare cases, traveled to England to be ordained. The appointment of Bishops Coleridge and Lipscomb to the West Indies was an epochal step forward. After disestablishment, West Indian synods (at first of bishops only and in London) began to meet. Provincial synods, established in 1883, finally in 1959 came to embrace three houses of bishops, clergy, and laity (CPWI 1983). West Indian–born bishops were rare until after independence, and clergy of non-white ancestry were recognized only very slowly (Stewart 1992: 94–109).

In the evangelical churches, originally expatriate missionaries were the only clergy, but training of local preachers and ministers began early, at first by individual missionaries in their stations. Secondary schools, such as Calabar College, Montego Bay Academy, York Castle, Buxton Grove, and the Naparima Colleges, were founded in connection with the need for teachers and preachers to supply schools and churches. In Jamaica, Baptist self-support was declared as early as 1842, and the Jamaica Baptist Union enabled local ministers to move into leadership from about the 1880s, although theological teachers were still sent from England (Russell 1993). In other churches, advance toward independence was slower and in some instances suffered temporary reversal, as when the Lutheran Church in British Guiana became a "mission" of the Lutheran Church in the United States (Beatty 1970). Yet missionary societies abroad often favored "devolution" and promotion of local leadership. Some simply forced it by withdrawing missionaries and financial support. In other cases, grants of money left considerable influence over their use, even when missionaries were no longer the local leaders.

Progress toward self-government and self-support was hampered by poverty, absentee ownership of property, the cost and loss of time due to geographical distance between colonies, and lack of educated leaders and of any university—until the founding of the University College of the West Indies (later UWI) in 1948. The Methodists, for example, set up two Caribbean Conferences (Western and Eastern) in 1883 but had to return to mission status in 1903 (Findlay and Holdsworth 1921, 2: 453–62). Finally in 1960, better financial arrangements, improvement in education including theological training, and air travel made it possible to establish the regional Methodist Church of the Caribbean and the Americas (Sherlock 1966). A little later, the Presbyterian Church in Trinidad and Grenada negotiated its independence from the support of the United Church of Canada, and missionaries were withdrawn in 1975.

In the later twentieth century, some began to question the irrelevant denominational divisions resulting from the variety of missions from overseas. Discussions on Church union took place, notably in 1955 in Jamaica among the Congregational, Disciples, Methodist, Moravian, and Presbyterian Churches (Jamaica Church Union Commission 1957). One such union was achieved in 1965 when the (Scottish-affiliated) Presbyterian and (English-originated) Congregational Churches joined to become the United Church of Jamaica and Grand Cayman. Later in 1992, the Disciples of Christ in Jamaica (founded from the United States) entered the union, forming the United Church of Jamaica and the Cayman Islands. Overcoming as it does a number of ecclesiastical differences as well as overseas connections, this is one of the notable church unions of the twentieth century.

THE STRUGGLE FOR LIBERATION: FROM FEUDALISM, SLAVERY, INDENTURE, POVERTY, AND DISCRIMINATION

In spite of the power of vested interests in colonial society, signs of a Christian conscience asserted themselves from time to time. In Spanish times, many "Indianist" protagonists such as Antonio Montesinos challenged the *encomienda* system as well as slavery among the Aboriginal people (Hanke 1965; Zavala 1964). They achieved some modification of this exploitation, and Bartolomé de Las Casas in his *De Unico Modo Vocationis* set forth the principle that Christianization must be by persuasion, never by force (Las Casas 1992). There were even some individuals who began to question African slavery, for example Las Casas in his later years, Tomás Mercado, Bartolomé de Albernoz, and Alonzo de Sandoval (Williams 1963, docs. 125, 152–157; Maxwell 1975).

In the English colonies, a small but growing number criticized the slave system: for example, Quakers George Fox and William Edmundson; Anglicans Morgan Godwyn and James Ramsay; and missionaries John Wray, John Smith, William Shrewsbury, and William Knibb (Godwyn 1680; Ramsay 1784; Shyllon 1977; Shrewsbury 1825: 211–33, 251–75). From the later eighteenth century, there were contacts with Christians in Britain and North America who were active in the anti-slavery movement. On their part, as already noted, from time to time slaves who had had connections with the missions challenged the system on biblical grounds: for example, slaves at Le Resouvenir in Demerara in 1823 and Sam Sharpe in Jamaica in 1831(Williams 1952, doc. 294; Turner 1982: 152, 163, 199).

After emancipation had been won, the struggle for justice was not as clear. Participation in education through primary and secondary schools was the usual method used by church leaders in all major denominations to improve the lot of the people. A few schools offered training for trades, domestic science, and agriculture. In some places, community services for economic betterment were sponsored by the Jesuit order or by Christian Action for Development in the Eastern Caribbean (CADEC). The CCC in recent decades has carried out a program of advocacy and social development under its mandate: "the promotion of ecumenism and social change in obedience to Jesus Christ and in solidarity with the poor."

In the later twentieth century, some church leaders and scholars have advocated a form of "liberation theology." Latin American liberation theology, North American black theology, and other third-world Christian thinking have had some influence upon this, but basically it has been a response to the surrounding poverty and the realization of the long history of metropolitan domination and colonial exploitation of the West Indies. Other issues are also discussed in relation to the search for "a Caribbean theology," or as some prefer to call it, "Caribbean perspectives in theology" (Hamid 1971; Davis 1990; Gregory 1995). As the churches of the Caribbean prepare to enter the twenty-first century, it is still a question for discussion—and perhaps controversy—as to how they will continue and improve upon their somewhat ambivalent history of social concern during the last five centuries.

Works Cited

Beatty, Paul B. Jr. 1970. *A History of the Lutheran Church in Guyana*. South Pasadena, Calif.: William Carey Press.

Bennett, J. Harry. 1958. *Bondsmen and Bishops: Slavery and Apprenticeship on the Codrington Plantations in Barbados, 1710–1838*. University of California Publications in History 62. Berkeley: University of California Press.

Besse, Joseph. 1753. *A Collection of the Sufferings of the People called Quakers*. 2 vols. London: Luke Hinde.

Bisnauth, Dale A. 1996. *A History of Religions in the Caribbean*. Kingston: Kingston Publishers, 1989. Reprint, Trenton: Africa World Press.

Caribbean Consultation. 1957. *The Listening Isles*. New York: International Missionary Council and World Council of Christian Education.

Conference on the History of Religion in the New World during Colonial Times. 1958. *The Americas* 14. Reprinted in *Studies Presented at the Conference on the History of Religion in the New World during Colonial Times*. Washington, D.C.: Secretary of the Conference.

The Church in the Province of the West Indies (CPWI). 1983. *This Is the CPWI: A Commemorative Brochure 1883–1983*. Barbados: CPWI.

Curtin, Philip D. 1975. *Two Jamaicas: The Role of Ideas in a Tropical Colony, 1830–1865*. Cambridge, Mass.: Harvard University Press, 1955. Reprint, New York: Atheneum.

Cuthbert, Robert W. M. 1986. *Ecumenism and Development: A Socio-Historical Analysis of the Caribbean Conference of Churches*. Bridgetown, Barbados: CCC.

Davis, Kortright. 1990. *Emancipation Still Comin': Explorations in Caribbean Emancipatory Theology*. Maryknoll, N.Y.: Orbis.

Dayfoot, Arthur C. 1999. *The Shaping of the West Indian Church 1492–1962*. Mona, Jamaica, and Gainesville: Press University of the West Indies and University Press of Florida.

Findlay, George G., and W. W. Holdsworth. 1921. *The History of the Wesleyan Methodist Missionary Society*. Vol. 2. London: Epworth.

Godwyn, Morgan. 1680. *The Negro's and Indian's Advocate: Suing for their Admission into the Church*. London.

Grant, John W., ed. 1966. *A History of the Christian Church in Canada*. 3 vols. Toronto: McGraw-Hill Ryerson.

Gregory, Howard, ed. 1995. *Caribbean Theology: Preparing for the Challenges Ahead*. Mona, Jamaica: Canoe Press.

Hanke, Lewis U. 1965. *The Spanish Struggle for Justice in the Conquest of America*. 1949. Reprint, Boston: Little, Brown and Company.

Hamid, Idris. 1971. *In Search of New Perspectives*. Bridgetown: Caribbean Ecumenical Consultation for Development.

Heumann, Gad. 1994. *The Killing Time: The Morant Bay Rebellion in Jamaica*. London: Macmillan Caribbean.

Jamaica Church Union Commission. 1957. *The Proposed Basis of Union*. Kingston: JCUC.

Labaree, Leonard Woods. 1935. *Royal Instructions to the British Colonial Governors, 1670–1776*. 2 vols. New York: Appleton-Century.

Las Casas, Bartolomé de. 1992. *The Only Way*. Translated by F. P. Sullivan. New York: Paulist Press.

Littell, Franklin H. 1962. *From State Church to Pluralism: A Protestant Interpretation of Religion in American History*. Garden City, N.Y.: Doubleday.

Maxwell, John Francis. 1975. *Slavery and the Catholic Church*. Chichester: Barry Rose Publishers and Anti-Slavery Society.

Ramsay, James. 1784. *An Essay on the Treatment and Conversion of African Slaves in the British Sugar Colonies*. London: James Phillips.

Reyss, Paul. 1907. *Étude sur quelques points de l'histoire de la tolérance au Canada et aux Antilles, XVIe et XVIIe siècles*. Genève: W. Kündig et Fils.

Russell, Horace O. 1993. *Foundations and Anticipations: The Jamaica Baptist Story, 1783–1892*. Columbus, Ga.: Brentwood Christian Press.

Sankeralli, Burton, ed. 1995. *At the Crossroads: African Caribbean Religion and Christianity*. Port of Spain, Trinidad: CCC.

Sherlock, Hugh. 1966. *Methodism in the Caribbean with Particular Reference to Autonomy* (William Fish Lecture). Kingston: Methodist Church.

Shrewsbury, William J. 1825. *Sermons Preached on Several Occasions in the Island of Barbadoes*. London: Butterworth and Son.

Shyllon, Folarin O. 1977. *James Ramsay: the Unknown Abolitionist*. Edinburgh: Canongate.

Stewart, Robert J. 1992. *Religion and Society in Post-Emancipation Jamaica*. Knoxville: University of Tennessee Press.

Sweet, William W. 1939. "The Frontier in American Christianity." In *Environmental Factors in Christian History*, edited by John T. McNeill, M. Spinka, and H. R. Willoughby. Chicago: University Press.

Sweet, William W. [1930] 1950. *The Story of Religion(s) in America*. New York: Harper.

Thomas, Eudora. 1987. *A History of the Shouter Baptists in Trinidad and Tobago*. Ithaca, N.Y. and Tacarigua, Trinidad: Calaloux Publications.

Turner, Mary. 1982. *Slaves and Missionaries: The Disintegration of Jamaican Slave Society*. Urbana: University of Illinois Press.

Walsh, Henry H. 1956. *The Christian Church in Canada*. Toronto: Ryerson Press.

Williams, Eric, ed. 1952. *Documents on British West Indian History, 1807–1833*. Trinidad: Trinidad Publishers.

Williams, Eric, ed. 1963. *Documents of West Indian History, Vol. I, 1492–1655*. Trinidad: PNM Publishing Company.

Zavala, Silvio Arturo. 1962. *The Colonial Period in the History of the New World*. Translated by Max Savelle. Mexico: Instituto Panamericana de Geografía y Historia.

Zavala, Silvio Arturo. 1964. *The Defence of Human Rights in Latin America*. Paris: UNESCO.

8

Congregationalism and Afro-Guianese Autonomy

JUANITA DE BARROS

When Henry Kirke—sometime attorney general of British Guiana—described the colony's Congregational ministers as obliged to "consult every sentiment and weakness of their flocks to attain their ends; jealousy, emulation, love of dress and display, [were] all appealed to, and not in vain," he was not far wrong.[1] In the late nineteenth and early twentieth centuries, Afro-Guianese congregations exploited the tenets of the British Guiana Congregational Union (BGCU)—its independence from government support and its willingness to allow congregations to "call" their ministers—to achieve temporal and spiritual ends. Thus, Kirke's comments describe a power imbalance, a dependence of pastors upon church members, which congregations manipulated to realize a limited degree of autonomy. As Congregationalists endeavored to negotiate some freedom within colonial Guianese society, they demonstrated the oppositional value of Congregationalism as providing an alternative vision of social order, one where Afro-Guianese called the shots. Yet ironically, this vision had a conservative cast and suggested an adherence to a Congregationalism where the traditional verities reigned.

The mission churches had a long history in the Anglophone Caribbean. Protestant missionaries began arriving in the region in the late eighteenth century, providing first slaves and then the newly emancipated not only with spiritual guidance, but also with education and leadership roles. During the period of slavery, these churches saw the emergence of a culture of resistance: membership widened individuals' horizons, and church gatherings could shroud explicitly political meetings. Jamaica's 1831 slave uprising is but one example.[2]

In British Guiana, the London Missionary Society (LMS) was the first religious organization to minister to the colony's enslaved population, posting its missionaries not far from the capital of Georgetown (or Stabroek as it was then known) in 1808 and 1809. By 1817, the LMS had four missionaries in British Guiana; following the 1823 slave rebellion in Demerara and the involvement of LMS adherents (and the suspected complicity of its ministers), the church declined in the colony. By 1824, two of its ministers had died (John Smith succumbing in prison, where he had been held following the uprising) and a third had left, leaving just one working in Berbice. The arrival of Joseph Ketley in 1828 saw something of a slow resurgence for the LMS as he attracted enslaved Afro-Guianese to the Sunday school, prayer meetings, and religious classes.[3] The LMS subsequently withdrew from British Guiana, leaving the work in the "hands of the native Christians," but in the 1880s worked with local ministers to create a congregational union there.[4]

Historian Monica Schuler—in her examination of the BGCU's predecessor, the LMS, in early post-emancipation British Guiana—demonstrates church members' agency during the early post-emancipation period. She argues that congregations' willingness to exploit their "rights" under the LMS system—most notably their ability to call a minister—enabled them to compel planters, who were desirous of securing a stable plantation laborer force, to provide schools and chapels. Indeed, even during the period of slavery, Afro-Guianese exercised a measure of control in LMS churches, acting as deacons and teachers.[5]

To an extent, the attainment of this local power can be attributed to the peculiarities of Congregationalism. The origins of Congregationalism, or Independency, lay in sixteenth-century England, when a group of Puritans left the Church of England and its hierarchical form of church governance to found independent congregations that emphasized their right to choose their ministers and deacons. Congregationalism constituted the core of the London Missionary Society. The LMS was established in the late eighteenth century and, though intending to be interdenominational, was primarily Congregational.[6]

From such a position, Afro-Guianese Congregationalists exercised a limited degree of autonomy and articulated an alternative social vision. Throughout their intertwined history, the LMS and Congregationalism contained oppositional possibilities, both culturally and politically. In part, this opposition was subtle, lurking in the dissonance implicit in the simultaneous acceptance of African and Christian belief systems. Historian Brian Moore argues that although by the 1830s most Afro-Guianese were enthusiastic Christians, recipients of "Euro-Christian values," their retention and adaptation of aspects of African religious practices permitted a measure of opposition.[7] Schuler also posits a complex and dynamic relationship between Christianity and African religious beliefs in British Guiana. She maintains that African LMS converts in British Guiana outnumbered creole members and that these individuals—who helped found LMS congregations in the colony—probably saw Congregationalism as "a vehicle of social regeneration," aided as they were by the "temporal orientation of African and African diaspora religions and their tendency to adopt new ideas and symbols during periods of change." Thus, missionary demands that new converts relinquish traditional beliefs may have been accepted by African converts willing to abandon, for example, "the pursuit of private interest [Obeah] . . . in favour of a renewal of the public sector."[8]

The relationship between African beliefs and Congregationalism is ambiguous for the late nineteenth and early twentieth centuries. The number of Congregationalists in the colony was not specified in the census returns until 1931, and even then it is not possible to relate birth place to religion. Africans constituted a tiny group, which was diminishing by the turn of the century (the last Africans having arrived in the colony in the 1860s and considered elderly by the early 1890s), and the proportion of them belonging to the BGCU (itself not excessively

numerous, totaling 4,996 members in 1901) in the later post-emancipation period is uncertain. Whether African cultural patterns continued to influence Congregationalism or popular responses to it in the absence of new African immigration is difficult to establish.[9]

Congregationalism's opposition can be seen more obviously in the self-
conscious public statements of its ministers who vocally opposed the status quo.
Some Congregationalist pastors testified before government inquiries on behalf
of popular concerns; others attended such gatherings as the 1905 public meeting
held to inaugurate the People's Association—a loose collection of individuals
fired by opposition to the colonial government and advocating, among other
objects, an extension of the franchise and a reduction of the property qualifica-
tion for a seat in government. Individual ministers publicly condemned policies
they perceived as harmful to the Afro-Guianese laboring population.[10] Thus, Joseph Ketley decried state-supported immigration of indentured East Indians,
regarding it as "a scheme for reducing wages," and H. R. Shirley called for British
Guiana's laborers to organize a trade union to protect their interests. Shirley took
his advocacy a step further, founding and editing the *People,* a small newspaper
that articulated popular positions.[11] Perhaps the nature of its ministry—tar-
geting largely poor Afro-Guianese—made Congregationalist ministers sensitive
to the problems of British Guiana's laboring population, encouraging them to
articulate opposition to the status quo and to support the colony's workers.

Congregationalism's oppositional possibilities, though, can also be seen in the
actions of church members themselves as they manipulated their membership
to confront the systems oppressing them: in 1823, slaves "appropriated the missionaries' language and symbols," using church affiliation to facilitate participation in the 1823 Demerara slave uprising, and somewhat later, apprentices
manipulated LMS principles.[12] This willingness to turn a system against itself
is addressed by Richard Burton in *Afro-Creole: Power, Opposition, and Play in the
Caribbean.* He contrasts opposition to resistance, arguing (courtesy of Michel de
Certeau) that opposition, unlike resistance, emerges from the interstices within
a system and manipulates "the means and materials the system offers to outwit
and subvert it." Yet, Burton maintains, this kind of opposition tends to replicate
the system it counters, suggesting its inherent conservatism.[13]

In the later post-emancipation period, Afro-Guianese Congregationalists manipulated the principles of the church for their own purposes, attempting to
secure spiritual and social ends, and in the process articulated an alternative to
the dominant order. Yet, as Burton suggests, this opposition contained a conservative element, one which seemed to uphold elite ideological structures.

The very composition of Congregationalism contained the possibility of social
opposition. Congregationalism allowed for a counter social vision that saw, in the
face of white European hegemony, a black African suzerainty. Thus, in contrast to
a white, European power structure, Congregationalism provided more employment and social opportunities for Afro-Guianese than did the colony's other de-

nominations. Walter Rodney argues that the BGCU led the colony in appointing "Native Pastors," and indeed a difference can be seen with both the Methodist and the Presbyterian churches in British Guiana; in 1883, the BGCU had four Afro-Guianese pastors of a total of ten, and by 1911, six of seven. The Union encouraged this development, frequently educating its future Afro-Guianese ministers, both in British Guiana and abroad.[14]

Yet the very openness of Congregationalism could be manipulated by its members. Ambitious Afro-Guianese men could acquire a foreign education and a position of some respect and stature in British Guiana. Though such training was ideally directed toward producing ministers for the colony, young Afro-Guianese men at times exploited it to secure personal goals. Thus, some young men seized the opportunity of church-supported education in the United States to remain there, much to the dismay of Guianese Congregationalist officials and the congregations themselves.[15] In 1877, Congregationalist minister John London took advantage of a visit to England to begin medical studies. Despite some resistance from the BGCU, London got his way; he became a medical doctor and ultimately one of the leading Congregationalist ministers in British Guiana.[16]

Congregationalism also offered opportunity for other Afro-Guianese adherents. This may have been due, in part, to the small number of ministers in the BGCU. In 1895, for example, the Union had only eight pastors ministering to fifteen main churches and twenty-nine mission stations, with the likely result that church members were responsible for much of the work. In each of three years 1916, 1917, and 1918, the forty-five churches and outstations had a total of over one hundred catechists and lay ministers.[17] Church members led Bible classes, and deacons partly administered their churches, assisting ministers with financial and religious operations.[18]

Deacons could manipulate their positions to amass a certain amount of local power. A Misson Chapel deacon, Mr. Pitt, was described as having gathered too much power into his hands and as having the other deacons under his influence. The BGCU treasurer felt pressed to respond by placing four "intelligent active" men on the finance committee "as a sort of counter balance" to Pitt and was pleased when two of them became deacons.[19] Yet power, though limited, could result in conflicts between minister and deacons as each tried to preserve their bailiwick. Ministers who tried to have catechists or deacons removed or disciplined could face "serious opposition," as did those who tried to deny the deacons their traditional role. When Hopetown Chapel's Congregationalist minister, Reverend Issacs—who had been "almost at open strife" with his deacons—sent his son, a religious student, to preach in his place, some of the deacons objected.[20] The deacons at the Canal II chapel, having been without a settled minister for some fifty years, were upset by the arrival of a new minister, Reverend J. T. Issacs. The deacons had always managed the church's finances and paid the pastor a salary but had never kept books, leading one observer to suspect they "found a salary for themselves." Issacs's attempt to rationalize their financial practices was resented by the deacons. Other disagreements followed, and finally, Issacs had to leave.[21]

Yet Congregationalism provided more than temporal opportunities for ambitious individuals. Its ministers and buildings served a social and spiritual purpose. Churches were important recreational places; the frequent cake walks, pink teas, concerts, "excursions [and] ice-cream banquets," and the like originated as fundraising strategies but doubtless also functioned as significant social occasions. In a "cake walk," for example, individuals gathered in their best clothes could win a cake.[22]

Ministers constituted a key component of Congregationalist churches' spiritual and social life. They gave communion, doled out advice, comforted sick members, and buried the dead. Pastors had other important and recognized functions. Good ministers facilitated fundraising—money that could be used for the church and its members—and large congregations—which ensured state aid for the church school. Ministers and their wives ran the church schools and organized Bible classes for adults and young people.[23] Indeed, Congregationalist minister Reverend Woods argued that the "parson" was a central figure to the people, consulted on every matter. A mother brought her almost grown son to see Reverend Woods, to have the parson speak to him "severely" as he had become "a bit of a scapegrace" lately; estranged wives and husbands regularly applied to have the parson settle their disputes.[24]

Though such minister-produced accounts are no doubt self-serving, they suggest Congregationalism's popular significance on both religious and social grounds. When some members of Berbice's Lonsdale church expressed dissatisfaction with the Union ministers and the intention to call another, these individuals were articulating their assessment of the key duties ministers performed. The complaints largely centered on the irregular provision of communion. The congregation had not received communion from a Congregational minister for six months, and though it had asked a Presbyterian minister to administer communion, this state of affairs was unsatisfactory as he could not come once a month. The congregation seemed to want more than the regular communion; it wanted a minister who could visit when the congregation wanted him. Reverend T. B. Glasgow, the minister in charge of Lonsdale, was, according to the congregation, "80 miles distant" and had eight churches in his care. The congregation maintained it was "impossible for any minister living so far away from his members to do any good to them [as h]e [could not] visit them when sick and [could not] bury them when dead." The congregation thus called a nearby minister, Reverend Frank, as its pastor.[25]

Popular recognition of the importance of ministers and their ability to revitalize communities emerged particularly when new pastors appeared. Their arrival could energize communities and attract larger congregations and more money to individual churches. Thus, church communities responded enthusiastically to the arrival of new ministers. Even allowing for the possibility of newcomers' exaggerating the warmth of their reception, the similarity of descriptions suggests the church members were genuinely happy. The English Congregationalist minister Reverend Green was surprised at the enthusiastic public reception greeting his arrival. The church was crowded and became more so, "almost crowded out," for his inaugural sermon the following Sunday evening; "[s]eats in the aisles, gallery, stairs, and porches [were] all full." When Green arrived at his new church, he found close to nine hundred people present for the service and afterward shook the hands, so he believed, of all nine hundred, including those of an old woman who, after grabbing both his hands, fell to her knees before him from sheer joy.[26]

Congregationalism also provided a significant physical locus for Afro-Guianese spirituality. The Congregationalist system—"a standing protest against State patronage and endowment"—and the rapid decay of wooden buildings in a tropical climate placed considerable financial demands upon individual congregations to maintain and repair buildings. Alone of British Guiana's churches, Congregationalism remained aloof from government aid. Indeed, this independence was a point of pride for ministers and members of the church hierarchy alike. Prior to the late 1890s, the colonial government supported the clergy of the Church of England and the Church of Scotland, paying their salaries and providing for their accommodation. It also tendered an annual amount for the salaries of Roman Catholic and dissenting clergy. In the late 1890s, however, the colonial government initiated the slow reduction of grants to these churches and the gradual disestablishment of the Scotch and English churches, a process estimated to take some twenty years.[27]

As a consequence, late-nineteenth- and early-twentieth-century BGCU churches were chronically penurious. Contemporaries posited a halcyon age of Guianese Congregationalism, an early period following emancipation when the churches prospered from members' donations. Some observers blamed the moral failings of the later generation of Afro-Guianese for the churches' subsequent poverty, condemning them for not working sufficiently hard.[28] However, more charitable and perhaps less biased commentators cited instead the generally poor state of British Guiana's economy. A depression in the sugar industry continued from the 1880s through the 1890s and into the first years of the twentieth century, not easing appreciably until an international agreement to end subsidies for European beet sugar was established. The consequent hard times for British Guiana's working population were no doubt reflected in their inability to dig deep. Thus, in 1885, Reverend Downer of Betervenwating blamed the sugar depression and high unemployment for his congregation's meager donations, points repeated periodically by his colleagues.[29]

Though the BGCU received financial support from the LMS in England, primarily subsidies for salaries and building repairs, these funds were never adequate. As a result, BGCU congregations were responsible for maintaining church buildings and paying their ministers' salaries, a task to which even the poorest seemed able to rise.[30] With this responsibility came a degree of power and ownership.[31] Though most church buildings were vested in the BGCU, congregations expressed a moral right to the buildings.[32] Thus, when the congregation at Lonsdale threatened to leave the Union, it wanted to take the church buildings to which it had a right, "moral and otherwise."[33]

The significance of Congregationalism in the lives of its Afro-Guianese congregations—temporally and spiritually—saw disputes emerge as church members struggled to defend the restricted autonomy they exercised within this religious sphere. The opportunity Congregationalism provided to some individuals to amass a degree of power and prestige contributed to the passionate battles over calling ministers. The fervor with which such disagreements were articulated suggests some of the tensions existing within a colonial society, where the Afro-Guianese masses had few opportunities to exercise power and where those not born to wealthy families had as few chances to advance socially. It also hints at the different visions of Congregationalism in British Guiana. Whereas some members of the church hierarchy could equivocate on the right of congregations to call their ministers, congregations were often adamant on this prerogative. The author of a 1901 report into Congregationalism in British Guiana believed that it *"ought* not to rest solely with an individual church or group of churches to call [new ministers] to the Pastorate. . . . Congregationalism pure and simple . . . does not seem . . . to be the best form of church government for [the] people here."[34]

Though the process of calling a minister could vary, essentially it consisted of a dialogue between church and Union. Congregations could appeal to the Union's hierarchy to provide a minister, but they could also take matters into their own hands. Both approaches worked. Thus, following the death of Reverend Dalgliesh, minister of Mission Chapel, the deacons wanted to know what the Union was "going to do about getting a minister for [them]." With the approval of the church members and Reverend J. Foreman, the secretary and treasurer of the Guiana District Committee, the deacons wrote the BGCU, appealing for a new pastor "to preside over [them] in the work of the Lord." The Union forwarded the letter, along with a resolution by the BGCU Committee approving its being sent, to the secretary of the LMS.[35] Thus, the members of Mission Chapel placed the search for a new minister in the hands of the Union and the LMS.

At other times, church members solicited particular individuals for the pastorship of their churches, a procedure that, although "irregular," achieved the desired results. For example, when S. B. Blean finished studying for the ministry in England, a friend wrote him about a position at Smith Church. Though the offer was transmitted in a "singular" fashion—"by a private member of the Church, and not by the Deacons themselves" or by a member of the Union's hierarchy—a meeting between Blean, the deacons, and a Union official saw a firm offer made to Blean.[36]

Within this context, the controversy around the attempts of Reverend Frank to attain his own church is illuminating. The "Frank scandal" divided congregations, pitted Union officials against one minister and his supporters, and demonstrated the passion with which a minister and church members would fight for principles and livelihood, revealing in the process some of the fissures within colonial society.

When Congregationalist minister Reverend Frank returned to British Guiana after studying for the ministry in England, he was ready to lead a church. However, the decision of the BGCU that he be employed as a reserve pastor for ministerless churches offended Frank, who wanted a church of his own. Though two members of New Amsterdam's Mission Chapel requested that Frank be allowed to act as pastor for this church while its minister—Union secretary Reverend Glasgow—was absent, Glasgow refused permission. Frank's determination to confront the Union hierarchy, the willingness of church members to "call" him, and the adamant opposition of the BGCU suggest the importance of religion in the lives of Afro-Guianese as an area to exercise a degree of autonomy.

Frank disregarded the rejection and began a young people's improvement society at Mission Chapel. The Union responded by having its chairman write Frank a "strong letter"; in turn, Frank made the dispute public by giving the letter—he described it as "most unchristian"—to a Berbice newspaper and permitting himself to be interviewed by the colony's main newspapers (which consequently became the media for a "violent and vulgar attack" upon several Union officials). When the Union's executive eventually banned Frank from preaching in its churches, he ignored the prohibition, continuing to preach in several Congregationalist churches, sometimes at the invitation of other Congregationalist ministers or congregations themselves. Eventually, Frank began a new denomination, "In defence of Congregationalism."[37]

The "Frank scandal" emerged out of a clash between three parties: the BGCU, the Reverend Frank, and individual congregations. Union officials tended to emphasize Frank's machinations and to assume he was manipulating those churches that supported him. To one minister, Reverend Wilson, Frank's actions were part of a long-standing plan to "smash the union" and manipulate the vacancy at Mission Chapel to Frank's advantage.[38] Yet church members were clearly equal participants. The members of New Amsterdam's Mission Church criticized the Union's handling of the entire affair and defended their right to chose their own minister. They objected to the Union's decision to appoint Glasgow temporary minister of their church instead of Frank, rejecting Glasgow's position that "the people had no right to call an acting minister." They pointed out that "according to Congregational principles every church ha[d] the right of calling its own minister."[39]

The members of Berbice's Lonsdale Chapel expressed a similar independence and a willingness to exercise what autonomy they possessed. They asked Glasgow, their acting minister, to preach one weekend when he was in New Amsterdam. They responded to his refusal—he had pleaded a previous commitment to preach elsewhere that day—by declaring their intention to make their own arrangements; they invited Frank to preach to them. A division within Lonsdale soon developed. A majority called Frank to be the church's minister—he accepted—but a minority refused to have anything to do with the scheme, opting for Glasgow. The members of other Congregational churches seemed to have done much the same. Their actions, and that of the Lonsdale congregation, made the BGCU determined to decide matters; it applied to the colony's Supreme Court for an injunction to prevent Frank from preaching in any church building vested in the Union.[40] The members of Lonsdale chapel regarded the Union's actions as an attempt to take away their right to call their own minister "according to Congregational principle." As a result, the members began to consider leaving the BGCU.[41]

Though the Frank scandal demonstrates the opposition that limited religious autonomy allowed, it also reveals a vein of popular conservatism, a willingness to accept or to appear to accept the status quo. Union officials, Frank, and congregations appealed to British practice and principle as their ultimate defense. Union officials condemned the reluctance of individual ministers and congregations to be controlled, a response seemingly informed by a racialism that denigrated Afro-Guianese. During a time when individuals of African descent were moving into the professions and entering the government, beginning to exercise a more prominent leadership role in the colony as a whole, Reverend Wilson, for one, represented the Frank affair as demonstrating the "risks" of Afro-Guianese "rule." He adduced the dispute as evidence that salvation for Congregationalism lay outside British Guiana, with English men and financing. Native churches, he believed, were unfit for responsibility and the people "innately" quarrelsome and "divisive by nature." Though Congregationalism suited "English people of a certain class," it did not suit the Guianese.[42] The Union "would be all the better in every respect if [it] had a few Englishmen in the Union."[43] Though his rhetoric was extreme, Wilson was not the only BGCU minister to believe a Briton alone could solve local problems. Other Union officials did not waver in their determination to acquire a British minister, even a temporary one, to look after the churches in crisis. The offer of the LMS to mediate the dispute was thus accepted on condition it send to British Guiana a minister to act as a "special commissioner" as well as acting pastor of Mission Chapel and "superintendiary minister" of the vacant Berbice churches.[44]

Ironically, Frank, though not echoing such sentiments, also articulated a belief in "English" values. He defended his right to have his own church on the basis of his training and Congregationalist principles. He was, he argued, a fully trained minister, not a "catechist" or a "local preacher," and he wondered why he should be "denied the rights exercised by other ministers who [had] had an English training." Frank argued not only for himself—for his right to have his own church—but also for the right of the members of Congregational churches to call their own ministers—a right that, he argued, "all Congregational churches claim[ed]."[45] Indeed, he believed that the letter written him by Reverend Glasgow would not have been written by an "English minister."[46] Church members expressed their concerns in similar language. The Mission Chapel deacons wanted a relationship such as obtained in Congregational churches in England, where the churches did as they thought fit and the Union had no power over them.[47] (However, the sincerity of such statements is uncertain, and perhaps they represented a further attempt to manipulate members of the LMS and BGCU hierarchy.)

Congregationalism in British Guiana provided a site for poor Afro-Guianese to exercise a degree of local autonomy and constituted opposition to the status quo. Church members demonstrated a willingness to exploit the limited power they possessed in an attempt to control religious space in British Guiana. Yet this brief examination of LMS documents suggests the possibility for further research for scholars of colonial Guianese history. This rich material illuminates racial and class conflict in British Guiana and describes popular and elite attitudes, which in turn casts light upon the struggles to control colonial Guianese society in the crucial years of the late nineteenth and early twentieth centuries, a time when an Afro-Guianese middle class was attempting to exercise more political power and when the Afro-Guianese masses were beginning to organize as workers through trade unions and strike actions.

ABBREVIATIONS

CO	Colonial Office
CSL	Commonwealth Studies Library
DC	*Daily Chronicle*
LMS	London Missionary Society
MCC	Minutes of the Combined Court
PRO	Public Record Office
SOAS	School of Oriental and African Studies

Notes

In this chapter I rely mainly on contemporary accounts and London Missionary Society archival documents at the School of Oriental and African Studies in London.

1. Henry Kirke, *Twenty-Five Years in British Guiana* (Westport: Negro Universities Press, 1970), 42.

2. Woodville K. Marshall, "'We be wise to many more tings': Blacks' Hopes and Expectations of Emancipation," *Social and Economic Studies* 17 (1968). Reprinted in *Caribbean Freedom: Economy and Society from Emancipation to the Present,* eds. Hilary Beckles and Verene Shepherd (Kingston: Ian Randle Publishers, 1993), 15, 16; Mary Turner, *Slaves and Missionaries: The Disintegration of Jamaican Slave Society, 1787–1834* (Urbana: University of Illinois Press, 1982), 47, 93, 94, 143, 154.

3. H. V. P. Bronkhurst, *Among the Hindus and Creoles of British Guiana* (London: 1888), 9; Emilia Viotti Da Costa, *Crowns of Glory, Tears of Blood: The Demerara Slave Rebellion of 1823* (New York: Oxford University Press, 1994), 89, 114, 140; Joseph Ketley, *Historical*

Notices of the Congregational Church at Providence Chapel, Georgetown, Demerara, British Guiana (London: n.d.), West Indies—Odds—Box 3, LMS, 5, 6, 7, 9, 10, LMS, SOAS.

4. Foreman to Whitehouse, 23 August 1883, LMS Incoming letters—British Guiana—Demerara, Box 11 1883–1894, folder 1 1883–84, LMS, SOAS; Glasgow to Cousins, 26 July 1907, LMS Incoming letters—West Indies (with British Guiana) 1900–1908, Box 2, folder West Indies 1907, LMS, SOAS; encl. Thos. Glasgow to LMS and CMS Directors and the Executive Committee of the Congregational Union of England and Wales, 23 July 1907; James Rodway, *The Story of Georgetown* (Demerara: Argosy, 1920), 105.

5. See Da Costa; also see Monica Schuler, "Plantation Labourers, The London Missionary Society," *Journal of Caribbean History* 22, no. 1–2 (1988): 94, 91, 93, 95.

6. Dale Bisnauth, *History of Religions in the Caribbean* (Trenton: Africa World Press, 1996), 120, 121.

7. Brian Moore, *Cultural Power, Resistance and Pluralism: Colonial Guyana, 1838–1900* (Montreal: McGill-Queen's University Press, 1995), 125, 137, 138, 142, 153.

8. Schuler, 89, 91.

9. See L. Crookall, ed., *Manual of the Congregational Union for 1894* (New Amsterdam: 1894); L. Crookall, ed., *Manual of the Congregational Union for 1895* (New Amsterdam: 1895); *Congregational Union of British Guiana, Part I. Proceedings of the Annual Assembly, Summary of Reports, &c., &c. (1916)* (Georgetown: Daily Chronicle, 1916); *Congregational Union of British Guiana. Part I. Proceedings of the Annual Assembly, Summary of Reports, &c., &c. (1917)* (Georgetown: Daily Chronicle, 1917); *Manual of the Congregational Union of British Guiana. The Report of the Thirty-Fourth Annual Assembly. 1918* (n.p., 1918), West Indies—Odds—Box 3, LMS, SOAS; British Guiana Statistics 1901, LMS Reports West Indies Box 1 1866–1901, LMS, SOAS; see also the census reports for 1891, 1911, 1921, and 1931.

10. See, for example, Walter Rodney, *A History of the Guyanese Working People, 1881–1905* (Baltimore: Johns Hopkins University Press, 1981), 171, and MCC, *Report of the Commission Appointed to Enquire into and Report upon the General and Infantile Mortality; Together with Minutes of the Sittings, Evidence of Witnesses, Etc.* (No. 334, 1906) (Georgetown: Argosy, 1906), CSL.

11. *DC*, 4 April 1905, 4; *Creole*, 19 May 1906, 5; CO 111/522, Confidential 39787, 16 November 1900; quoted in Rodney, 171; see also, for example, Rodway, 95, 103; see also Wilson to Thompson, 19 February 1911, LMS Incoming letters—West Indies (with British Guiana) 1909–1923, Box 3, folder West Indies 1911, SOAS; encl. *DC*; see also Shirley to Cousins, LMS Incoming letters—West Indies (with British Guiana) 1900–1908, Box 2, folder West Indies 1900, LMS, SOAS.; encl. Shirley to the editor, "A Plea from British Guiana"; Wilson to Cousins, 23 March 1903, LMS Incoming letters—West Indies (with British Guiana) 1900–1908, Box 2, folder West Indies 1903, LMS, 5, SOAS.

12. See Da Costa, vii, 78; see also Schuler.

13. Richard Burton, *Afro-Creole: Power, Opposition, and Play in the Caribbean* (Ithaca: Cornell University Press, 1997), 8, 50, 51.

14. Minutes of District Committee, 27 February 1883; Foreman to Whitehouse, 23 August 1883, LMS Incoming letters—British Guiana—Demerara, Box 11 1883–1894, folder 1 1883–84, LMS, SOAS; Wilson to Currie Martin, 6 February 1911, 2nd letter, LMS Incoming letters—West Indies (with British Guiana) 1888–1899, Box 1, folder Demerara A. W. Wilson 1903/06/09/09–10/10/13/14/15, 26 LMS; Rodney 114; see also British Guiana Report 1901, 40, 53; Wilson to Cousins, 20 November 1888, LMS Incoming letters—West Indies (with British Guiana) 1888–1899, Box 1, folder 1895–99, LMS, SOAS.

15. Wilson to Thompson, 4 June 1913, LMS Incoming letters—West Indies (with Brit-

ish Guiana) 1909–1923, Box 3, folder West Indies 1913, LMS, 5, SOAS; *DC*, 13 June 1922, 5.

16. *DC*, 13 June 1922, 5; Mullent to Foreman, 28 September 1877, LMS Outgoing letters—West Indies 1 April 1876–16 November 1887, Box 9 LMS, SOAS; see also British Guiana Report 1901, LMS Reports West Indies Box 1 1866–1901, LMS, 17, SOAS.

17. Crookall, *Manual* (1895), 30; see also Crookall, *Manual* (1894); British Guiana Statistics 1901, LMS Reports West Indies Box 1 1866–1901, LMS, SOAS; *Congregational Union of British Guiana. Part I. Proceedings of the Annual Assembly, Summary of Reports, &c., &c. (1916); (1917); Manual of the Congregational Union of British Guiana. The Report of the Thirty-Fourth Annual Assembly. 1918* (n.p., 1918), West Indies—Odds—Box 3, LMS, SOAS.

18. See, for example, Weeks to Lenwood, 19 March 1915, LMS Incoming letters—West Indies (with British Guiana) 1909–1923, Box 3, folder West Indies 1915, 2, LMS, SOAS; Foreman to Thompson, 4 June 1884; Ketley to Whitehouse, 23 April 1884, LMS Incoming letters—British Guiana—Demerara, Box 11 1883–1894, folder 1 1883–84, LMS, SOAS; encl. questionnaires; Wilson to Cousins, 14 August 1901, LMS Incoming letters—West Indies (with British Guiana) 1900–1908, Box 2, folder West Indies 1901, LMS, 3, SOAS.

19. Foreman to Thompson, 1 February 1887, LMS Incoming letters—British Guiana—Demerara, Box 11 1883–1894, folder 2 1884–87, 1893–4, LMS, SOAS.

20. Algernon to Thompson 26 September 1913, LMS Incoming letters—West Indies (with British Guiana) 1909–1923, Box 3, folder West Indies 1913, LMS, 1, SOAS; Foreman to Whitehouse, 23 April 1884, LMS Incoming letters—British Guiana—Demerara, Box 11 1883–1894, folder 1 1883–84, LMS, SOAS.

21. Wilson to Cousins, 29 March 1904, LMS Incoming letters—West Indies (with British Guiana) 1888–1899, Box 1, folder Demerara A. W. Wilson 1903/06/09/09–10/10/13/14/15, LMS, 4, SOAS.

22. Kirke 43, 44; Wilson to Thompson, 30 August 1913, LMS Incoming letters—West Indies (with British Guiana) 1909–1923, Box 3, folder West Indies 1913, LMS, 3, 4, SOAS.

23. See, for example, Weeks to Lenwood, 19 March 1915, LMS Incoming letters—West Indies (with British Guiana) 1909–1923, Box 3, folder West Indies 1915, LMS, 2, SOAS.

24. Wood to Lenwood, 10 April 1917, LMS Incoming letters—West Indies (with British Guiana) 1909–1923, Box 3, folder West Indies 1917/1918, LMS, SOAS.

25. Beaton and others (Lonsdale) to Cousins, 23 January 1909, LMS Incoming letters—West Indies (with British Guiana) 1909–1923, Box 3, folder West Indies 1909, LMS, SOAS.

26. Green to Thompson, 27 March 1889; for example, see also Green to Thompson, 6 December 1887, LMS Incoming letters—West Indies (with British Guiana) 1888–1899, Box 1, folder 1888–1894, LMS, SOAS.

27. Alleyne Leechman, ed., *The British Guiana Handbook 1913* (Georgetown: Argosy, n.d.), 121, 122; Rodway, 96.

28. See Rodway, 102, 103; see also, for example, Wilson to Cousins, 29 March 1904, LMS Incoming letters—West Indies (with British Guiana) 1888–1899, Box 1, folder Demerara A. W. Wilson 1903/06/09/09–10/10/13/14/15, LMS, SOAS; Wilson to Thompson, 25 October 1912, LMS Incoming letters—West Indies (with British Guiana) 1909–1923, Box 3, folder West Indies 1912, LMS, 1, 2, SOAS.

29. Downer to Thompson, 22 July 1885, LMS Incoming letters—British Guiana—Demerara, Box 11 1883–1894, folder 2 1884–87, 1893–4, LMS, SOAS; see, for example, British Guiana Report 1901, LMS Reports West Indies Box 1 1866–1901, LMS, 39, SOAS.; Wilson to Thompson, 9 March 1904, LMS Incoming letters—West Indies (with British Guiana) 1888–1899, Box 1, folder Demerara A. W. Wilson 1903/06/09/09–10/10/13/14/

15, LMS, 1, 2, SOAS; Glasgow to Cousins, 26 July 1907, LMS Incoming letters—West Indies (with British Guiana) 1900–1908, Box 2, folder West Indies 1907, LMS, SOAS; encl. Glasgow to Directors.

30. See, for example, Green to Thompson, 20 February 1894, LMS Incoming letters—West Indies (with British Guiana) 1888–1899, Box 1, folder 1888–94, LMS, SOAS; Ketley to Whitehouse, 23 April 1884, LMS Incoming letters—British Guiana—Demerara, Box 11 1883–1894, folder 1 1883–84, LMS, SOAS.

31. Glasgow to Cousins, 26 July 1907, LMS Incoming letters—West Indies (with British Guiana) 1900–1908, Box 2, folder West Indies 1907, LMS, SOAS; encl. Glasgow to Directors of the LMS.

32. Wilson to Thompson, 5 March 1915, LMS Incoming letters—West Indies (with British Guiana) 1888–1899, Box 1, folder Demerara A. W. Wilson 1903/06/09/09–10/10/13/14/15, LMS, 5, SOAS; Wilson to Lenwood, 14 August 1914, LMS Incoming letters—West Indies (with British Guiana) 1909–1923, Box 3, folder West Indies 1914, LMS, 6, SOAS. Mary Turner makes a similar point for Jamaica during the period of slavery. She points out that Christian slaves contributed financially to their churches, helping pay for building repairs and the like, and argues that the slaves' donations "meant that mission development was partly their own creation; they could identify the chapel they attended as their own." Turner, 85, 86.

33. The members of Lonsdale Church to the LMS, Nov. 1908, LMS Incoming letters—West Indies (with British Guiana) 1900–1908, Box 2, folder West Indies 1908, LMS, SOAS; H. Dow and others, Lonsdale to Cousins, 8 January 1909, LMS Incoming letters—West Indies (with British Guiana) 1909–1923, Box 3, folder West Indies 1909, LMS, SOAS.

34. British Guiana Report 1901, 57.

35. Foreman to Whitehouse, 23 April, 1884; see also Foreman to Thompson, 4 June, 1884; see also Deacons of Mission Church, New Amsterdam to the BGCU, 18 May 1884, LMS Incoming letters—British Guiana—Demerara, Box 11 1883–1894, folder 1 1883–84, LMS, SOAS.

36. Foreman to Thompson, 23 July, 1885; see also Foreman to Thompson, 15 September 1885; Wilson to Lenwood, 5 March, 1915, LMS Incoming letters—West Indies (with British Guiana) 1888–1899, Box 1, folder Demerara A. W. Wilson 1903/06/09/09–10/10/13/14/15, LMS, 5, 6, SOAS; for a similar situation at New Amsterdam's Mission Church, see Foreman to Thompson, 25 November 1885; Foreman to Thompson, 1 Feb 1886, LMS Incoming letters—British Guiana—Demerara, Box 11 1883–1894, folder 2 1884–87, 1893–94, LMS, SOAS.

37. Frank to Cousins, 8 January 1909, LMS Incoming letters—West Indies (with British Guiana) 1909–1923, Box 3, folder West Indies 1909, LMS, 2, SOAS; London to Cousins, 29 May 1908, 7, 8, 9, 10; Wilson to Cousins, 10 July 1908, LMS Incoming letters—West Indies (with British Guiana) 1900–1908, Box 2, folder West Indies 1908 LMS, 2, SOAS.

38. Wilson to Cousins, 31 October 1908; Wilson to Cousins, 1 June 1908, LMS Incoming letters—West Indies (with British Guiana) 1900–1908, Box 2, folder West Indies 1908 LMS, 9, 10, 11, 12, SOAS.

39. Drainer and others to Thompson, 16 October 1908, LMS Incoming letters—West Indies (with British Guiana) 1900–1908, Box 2, folder West Indies 1908 LMS, 1, 3, 4, SOAS.

40. London to Cousins, 17 October 1908; Wilson to Cousins, 31 October 1908; encl. newspaper clipping "Congregationalism in the Law Courts"; see also Glasgow to Cousins, 11 November 1908, LMS Incoming letters—West Indies (with British Guiana) 1900–1908, Box 2, folder West Indies 1908, LMS, 1, SOAS.

41. The members of Lonsdale Church to the LMS, Nov. 1908, LMS Incoming letters—West Indies (with British Guiana) 1900–1908, Box 2, folder West Indies 1908, LMS, SOAS; H. Dow and others, Lonsdale to Cousins, 8 January 1909, LMS Incoming letters—West Indies (with British Guiana) 1909–1923, Box 3, folder West Indies 1909, LMS, SOAS.

42. Wilson to Cousins, 1 June 1908, 14; Wilson to Cousins, 2 October 1908, LMS Incoming letters—West Indies (with British Guiana) 1900–1908, Box 2, folder West Indies 1908 LMS, 2, 3, SOAS; Wilson to Cousins, 9 January 1909, 5, 6; see also Wilson to Thompson, 3 September 1909, LMS Incoming letters—West Indies (with British Guiana) 1909–1923, Box 3, folder West Indies 1909 LMS, 2, SOAS.

43. Wilson to Cousins, 23 March 1903, LMS Incoming letters—West Indies (with British Guiana) 1900–1908, Box 2, folder West Indies 1903, LMS, 3, SOAS.

44. London to Cousins, 22 January 1909, LMS Incoming letters—West Indies (with British Guiana) 1909–1923, Box 3, folder West Indies 1909 LMS, 1, 2, SOAS; encl. London to Cousins, Resolution of Committee, 23 January 1909.

45. London to Cousins, 29 May 1908, 11, SOAS; see also encl. Frank to Union Executive 22/3/08; Wilson to Cousins, 10 July 1908, LMS Incoming letters—West Indies (with British Guiana) 1900–1908, Box 2, folder West Indies 1908 LMS, 2, SOAS.

46. Frank to Cousins, 8 January 1909, LMS Incoming letters—West Indies (with British Guiana) 1909–1923, Box 3, folder West Indies 1909, LMS, 2, SOAS.

47. Drainer and others to Thompson, 16 October 1908, LMS Incoming letters—West Indies (with British Guiana) 1900–1908, Box 2, folder West Indies 1908 LMS, 1, 3, 4, SOAS.

Works Cited

ARCHIVAL SOURCES—LONDON MISSIONARY SOCIETY DOCUMENTS

Congregational Union of British Guiana. Part I. Proceedings of the Annual Assembly, Summary of Reports, &c., &c. (1916). Georgetown: Daily Chronicle, 1916. LMS, West Indies—Odds—Box 3. SOAS.

Congregational Union of British Guiana. Part I. Proceedings of the Annual Assembly, Summary of Reports, &c., &c. (1917). Georgetown: Daily Chronicle, 1917. LMS, West Indies—Odds—Box 3. SOAS.

Manual of the Congregational Union of British Guiana. The Report of the Thirty-Fourth Annual Assembly. 1918. N. p., 1918. LMS, West Indies—Odds—Box 3. SOAS.

Crookall, L., ed. 1894. *Manual of the Congregational Union for 1894.* New Amsterdam. LMS, West Indies—Odds—Box 3. SOAS.

———. *Manual of the Congregational Union for 1895.* New Amsterdam: 1895. LMS, West Indies—Odds-Box 3. SOAS.

Ketley, Joseph. *Historical Notices of the Congregational Church at Providence Chapel, Georgetown, Demerara, British Guiana.* London: n.d. LMS (CWM). West Indies—Odds—Box 3, SOAS.

LMS. British Guiana Report 1901. SOAS.

———. Incoming letters—British Guiana—Demerara, Box 11 1883–1894, folder 1 1883–84; folder 2 1884–87, 1893–4. SOAS.

———. Incoming letters—West Indies (with British Guiana) 1888–1899, Box 1, folder 1888–94; folder 1895; folder Demerara A. W. Wilson 1903/06/09/09–10/10/13/14/15. SOAS.

————. Incoming letters—West Indies (with British Guiana) 1900–1908, Box 2, folder West Indies 1900; folder West Indies 1903; folder West Indies 1907. SOAS.

————. Incoming letters—West Indies (with British Guiana) 1909–1923, Box 3, folder West Indies 1911; folder West Indies 1912; folder West Indies 1914. SOAS.

————. Outgoing letters—West Indies 1 April 1876–16 November 1887, Box 9. LMS. SOAS.

————. Reports West Indies Box 1 1866–1901. SOAS.

CONTEMPORARY PRINTED ACCOUNTS

Report on the Census Results, 1891. Georgetown: 1891.
Report on the Results of the Census of the Population, 1911. Georgetown: Argosy, 1912.
Report on the Results of the Census of the Population, 1921. Georgetown: Argosy, 1921.
Report on the Results of the Census of the Population, 1931. Georgetown: Argosy, 1932.
British Guiana. Minutes of the Combined Court. 1906. *Report of the Commission Appointed to Enquire into and Report upon the General and Infantile Mortality; Together with Minutes of the Sittings, Evidence of Witnesses, Etc. (No. 334, 1906).* Georgetown: Argosy. CSL.
Bronkhurst, H. V. P. 1888. *Among the Hindus and Creoles of British Guiana.* London.
Kirke, Henry. 1970. *Twenty-five Years in British Guiana.* Westport: Negro Universities Press.
Leechman, Alleyne, ed. *The British Guiana Handbook 1913.* Georgetown: Argosy, n.d.
Rodway, James. 1920. *The Story of Georgetown.* Demerara: Argosy.

NEWSPAPERS

Creole, 19 May 1906, 5.
Demerara Chronicle, 4 April 1905, 4.

SECONDARY ACCOUNTS

Bisnauth, Dale. 1996. *History of Religions in the Caribbean.* Kingston, Jamaica: Kingston Publishers, 1989. Reprint, Trenton, N.J.: Africa World Press.
Burton, Richard. 1997. *Afro-Creole: Power, Opposition, and Play in the Caribbean.* Ithaca: Cornell University Press.
Da Costa, Emilia Viotti. 1994. *Crowns of Glory, Tears of Blood: The Demerara Slave Rebellion of 1823.* New York: Oxford University Press.
Marshall, Woodville K. 1993. "'We be wise to many more tings': Blacks' Hopes and Expectations of Emancipation." *Social and Economic Studies* 17 (1968). Reprint, in *Caribbean Freedom: Economy and Society from Emancipation to the Present,* edited by Hilary Beckles and Verene Shepherd, Kingston: Ian Randle Publishers.
Moore, Brian. 1995. *Cultural Power, Resistance and Pluralism: Colonial Guyana, 1838–1900.* Montreal and Kingston, Jamaica: McGill-Queen's University Press and Press University of the West Indies.
Rodney, Walter. 1981. *A History of the Guyanese Working People, 1881–1905.* Baltimore: Johns Hopkins University Press.
Schuler, Monica. 1988. "Plantation Labourers, The London Missionary Society and Emancipation in West Demerara, Guyana." *Journal of Caribbean Studies* 22 (1–2): 88–115.
Turner, Mary. 1982. *Slaves and Missionaries: The Disintegration of Jamaican Slave Society, 1787–1834.* Urbana: University of Illinois Press.

9

Eden after Eve

Christian Fundamentalism and Women in Barbados

JUDITH SOARES

Too often, Caribbean feminists and women's activists, while recognizing the power of women in popular movements, have ignored the role of religion and Christian theology in women's lives and the spirituality of their quotidian existence. In a formal sense, therefore, women's organizations and feminist groups have been mainly concerned with the socio-economic and political aspects of women's lives. Their main concerns have centered on women's participation in politics, women at the level of decision making, women and poverty, women and domestic violence, women's role in the media, and women's reproductive rights, to name a few well-aired areas of concern. While they hold patriarchy and patriarchal relations and expressions responsible for women's social and political lot, little or no attention has been paid to understanding, in a fundamental way, women's religious experience in both a Christian and a social context.

In regions where religion and Christianity have historically played an important spiritual, ideological, social, and political role in the lives of the marginalized, the exploited, and the oppressed, it is foolhardy to ignore such a powerful social influence. Within the liberal churches, the relations of patriarchy have forced women theologians in Latin America, Africa, and Asia to move to the center of theological discourse, affirming their rootedness in a theology of liberation that challenges all sources that have denied and/or ignored the rights of women. Reconstructing "basic theological affirmations,"[1] women are raising their voices worldwide for new visions of hope and liberation. In this respect, feminist and womanist theologians continue to challenge the rigid structures of the church in their research efforts in theological reflection, biblical hermeneutics, and "creative liturgical experiences" (Ortega 1995: ix). At the heart of this theological reflection and theological movement is the demand for social justice for all women and all people.

However, while the words of these Christian women are being recorded in a well-developed recognized school of thought, feminist/womanist theology, there are those other Christian women, who form the majority of membership of the fundamentalist churches in the Caribbean and Latin America region, who are dismissed as embodying a "backward religion." While one can argue that religion, as ideology, is at the same time an oppressive and a liberating force and that fundamentalism represents the conservative wing of Protestantism, we need to temper our understanding of women in Christian fundamentalism, because in the final analysis the mobilization of all women is necessary to confront the patriarchal structures of gender, class, and race domination.

This chapter attempts to delineate emerging ideological strands in fundamentalism and their social expression in that religious community in Barbados. Based predominantly on primary research, it is to be seen as a preliminary piece requiring further research. This work, then, will examine fundamentalism both as an oppressive ideology, justifying or legitimating positions of the hegemony of men as they relate to the concept and practice of patriarchy, and as a potential liberating force for women. It will do so by discussing the unnoticed paradigm shift that has taken place in the 1990s in the context of a reinterpretation of biblical doctrine that challenges both traditional fundamentalism and its own interpretation of the Scriptures, and the structures of patriarchy in the Church and society. Up for discussion, therefore, are the non-denominational churches and their ideological location in the religious landscape of fundamentalism.

The non-denominational churches that are in the tradition of Pentecostalism operate within the theological context of fundamentalism. The respective pastors found and build their own ministries, establishing themselves independently of all denominations and basing their ministries on organizations of elders and/or deacons and team ministries. While they have international linkages, there are no connections with headquarters, whether locally or overseas. In a loose sense, then, they can be termed "indigenous." In this presentation, a distinction will be made between traditional fundamentalist thinking and that of non-denominationalism.

THE CONCEPT OF FUNDAMENTALISM

Fundamentalism and the corresponding fundamentalist movement are not native to the English-speaking Caribbean, although these religious experiences have become indigenized in the course of history. An offshoot of American fundamentalism, this religious movement began its exodus to the Caribbean from as early as the turn of the century, a period that coincided with the emergence of monopoly capitalism in the United States and the spread of imperialism in the Caribbean. While other denominations are in decline in the Caribbean, Pentecostalism is growing steadily (Austin-Broos 1997; Gmelch and Bohn 1997: 158).

In the United States, fundamentalism emerged simultaneously as a distinct religious theology and an ideology in post-revolutionary America. It responded to modernity, modernism in biblical interpretation, critical theology, and social Darwinism, which accompanied the rise of industrial capitalism following the 1776 Revolutionary War. A protracted debate within American evangelical Protestantism in this period resulted in a bisection of traditional Protestantism into conservative Protestantism and liberal Protestantism. The latter was favorably disposed to the growing development of industrial capitalism, while the former emerged as a hostile force against secularization, social change, modernity, and modernism in biblical interpretation.

The word "fundamentalism" was coined in 1920 to describe the conservative wing of North American Protestantism. Fundamentalists who were bent on protecting the "old time gospel" and who "would do battle for the Lord" against enemies of the Kingdom were described by Marsden as evangelical Christians bent on driving modernism out of church and culture (Marsden 1980). Fundamentalism and fundamentalists insist on biblical infallibility, a literal interpretation of the Scriptures, personal experience of religious conversion, the virgin birth, and the Bible as the only source or explanation of the origin of life and humanity. With the concept of millenarianism at its core, the *sine qua non* of fundamentalism can be enumerated as: (1) the inerrancy of the Scriptures; (2) the virgin birth of Jesus; (3) the resurrection of Christ; (4) the substitutionary atonement of Christ; and (5) the second coming of Christ (see Soares 1992).

For fundamentalists, therefore, the Bible is the sole and absolute authority on all life. It is the infallible word of God and the biblical message is regarded as clear and unchanging and unchangeable. For them, all aspects of human life are subject to religious laws, which are based on biblical text and, consequently, believed to be of divine origin. It is this belief that the Bible is an unquestionable authority that does not require interpretation that has implications for women and their role and status in the family, marriage, and Church ministry and, indeed, society.

ANDROCENTRISM AND PATRIARCHY IN FUNDAMENTALIST THEOLOGY

The creation narrative of Genesis 1 provides the basis for the concept of an androcentric God and is critical to an understanding of the fundamentalists' view on women and their relations with men: "And God said, let us make man in our image, after our likeness: and let them have dominion over the fish of the sea, and over the fowl of the air, and over the cattle, and over all the earth, and over every creeping thing that creepeth upon the earth. And God created man in his own image, in the image of God created he him; male and female created he them" (Gen. 1: 26).[2] God had created an order based on a hierarchy of beings, humans and animals. This becomes clearer in the Genesis 2 narrative, which presents for fundamentalists the creation hierarchy:

> And the Lord God said, It is not good that man should be alone; I will make him an help meet for him. And out of the ground the Lord God formed every beast of the field, and every fowl of the air; and brought them unto the man to see what he would call them: and whatsoever the man called every living creature, that was the name thereof. And the man gave names to all cattle, and to the fowl of the air, and to every beast of the field; but for man there was not found an help meet for him. And the Lord caused a deep sleep to fall upon the man, and he slept; and he took one of his ribs, and closed up the flesh instead thereof: and the rib, which the Lord God had taken from the man, made he a woman, and brought her unto the man. And the man said, This is now bone of my bones, and flesh of my flesh: she shall be called Woman, because she was taken out of Man. Therefore shall a man leave his father

and his mother, and shall cleave unto his wife: and they shall be one flesh. (Gen. 2:18–24)

Woman (Eve) was created after and from man (Adam) to serve as a helpmate. This divine creation of woman has given her an auxiliary role to man. This interpretation, according to theologian Maria Clara Bingemer, "makes for the ontological, biological and sociological dependence of women on men" (1989: 58), a view that fundamentalists hold dear. This is substantiated by their stated position that there is a hierarchy in the creation of man and woman: man is the head and has the final say. This in fundamentalist theology is divine law, as reflected in the account of creation. It is the combination of these two traditions that supports an androcentric and patriarchal understanding of social life. Bingemer further comments on the above Scriptures: "Throughout Biblical tradition in the economy of the covenant, that which is divine (God, Jesus Christ) is represented with masculine elements and that which is human (Israel, the Church) with feminine elements. Androcentrism and theocentrism are parallel. . . . [T]he male gender symbolizes the excellence of the divine image" (1989: 58).

The status and function of women in fundamentalist thinking is strongly influenced by the Judeo-Christian patriarchal family form, which prevailed among Jews and which is recorded in biblical doctrine. Fundamentalism and fundamentalists, therefore, in accepting the ideology and practice of patriarchy as the norm for family relationships, accept the view that the role of woman is first and foremost as wife and mother. So while a wife should enjoy the love and honor of her husband, she is essentially the bearer of children and a provider of sexual pleasure to her husband and is subject to his authority as defined in the book of Genesis. Theologian Rosemary Ruether aptly summarizes this view:

> The first subjugation of woman is the subjugation of her womb, the subjugation of access to her body, so that she should not choose her own beloved or explore the pleasures of her own body but that her body and its fruits should belong first to her father who would sell or trade her to her husband. She must be delivered as undamaged goods, duly inspected, any signs of previous use punished by death. Only the male to whom she has been legally handed over may put his seed in her body, so that he can be sure that the children which emerge from her body belong to him, pass on his name, inherit his property. (Quoted in Bisnauth 1986: 4–5)

Here one finds an assumption that all women will marry and bear children. However, once a marriage takes place, the Book of Ephesians governs this relationship, in which there must be submission of the wife to the husband and by extension of all women to all men. The submissiveness of women was, indeed, God's intention at creation. Here "submission" is intended to mean "humility," "meekness," and, very critically, "obedience," one ruling and the other obeying: "Wives, be in subjection unto your own husbands, as unto the Lord. For the husband is the head of the wife, as Christ also is the head of the church, being himself the saviour of the body. But as the Church is subject to Christ, so let the wives also be to their husbands in everything. Husbands, love your wives, even as Christ also loved the church, and gave himself up for it" (Eph. 5:22–25).

The comments of fundamentalists Rekers and Braun in respect to this area of Pauline doctrine are noteworthy. They argue that Paul revisited the creation story in order to reflect on "the principles of proper leadership that are expressed in human sexuality . . . God does not act arbitrarily. God didn't flip a cosmic coin in eternity and say, 'Heads, I'll make man first.' There was a plan to it. And when under the pressure of satanic assault, that order of leadership was reversed and Eve initiated action, the result was catastrophic. . . . It is no wonder that Satan assaulted Eve first; she was woman, made by God to be ever so sensitive to spiritual input. She was made to respond, and Satan lured her to take independent initiative" (quoted in Bisnauth 1986: 5). It is this thinking that is also responsible for the exclusion of women from pastoral functions and Church leadership, since the argument is that man was created first and woman was first in the Edenic fall.

REINTERPRETATIONS OF TRADITIONAL FUNDAMENTALISM

An interesting observation here is that there are those sections of the fundamentalist leadership of the non-denominational churches in Barbados who relax the rigidity of traditional fundamentalism. While advocating the core elements of traditional fundamentalism, they do not wholly subscribe to this thinking on the role and function of women. They agree with the notion that God's creation was intended to be hierarchical. However, they feel that the interpretation of traditional fundamentalism on women's roles and responsibilities in the family is too narrow. They agree that in a family context there are "things" women cannot do because of physical and emotional limitations. For example, women lack physical strength, and at another level are not able to handle stress like men. That is precisely why men were created to cover and shield them. However, while women are strong in child rearing, one finds that they have adapted to certain aspects of family life that could be seen as outside their intellectual realm and domestically defined roles and responsibilities. This includes making leadership decisions and exercising joint initiative. Pastor Fitzroy Wilson of the Kingdom First International Church states, "A woman's role in the family is not just for procreation and submission. Women are sometimes involved with children's education, instilling values, making joint decisions, and so on. That she can have children is a practical thing" (interview).

This strand of non-denominationalism agrees that the book of Genesis provides an understanding of the origin and order of society as they relate specifically to women's positions, roles, and functions. Therefore, woman and man were created with a divine mandate. This means that man was created first to represent headship, rulership, leadership, and authority. A further meaning, therefore, is that man must protect and shield woman, who was second in the creation project. In this view, there is an "equal" partnership between man and woman, but their roles are clearly defined. This concept of "equality" is explained by two pastors of the non-denominational churches. Pastor Fitzroy Wilson explains, "Men represent headship, which means they are leaders in a family context although they are in partnership with their women. The partnership is equal but with defined roles" (interview). Pastor Claude Brooks of the Love and Faith World Outreach International puts it this way: "Men and women were created equal, but there is a hierarchy; man has the final say because he is the head. They plan together, build visions together, but man is the head and the woman functions like a cabinet. So while there is plurality, there is no coequality between men and women; that is, they are one but not equal because the man is always the head" (interview). This viewpoint also influences women's roles and positions in the Church. Although there are usually more women than men in these churches, women can become local leaders in prayer or counseling, but they can never become head of the Church. The only way a woman can become head of the Church is in the unlikely situation that there are no men present in the ministry.

Traditional fundamentalism does not support positions of social change, and therefore, feminism and its programs of social change are an anathema. Within the variant of non-denominationalism under review, feminism and the feminist movement are recognized as injustices to both men and women. This is based on the notion that the movement, in its desire to encourage women to control their own destiny and to work toward their own independence, emasculates men and exposes women to harm by removing the covering they should have from their men. When this covering, this protection, is removed, women become vulnerable to society's destructive forces that place them in a position inferior to men, such as being underpaid in the labor market.

Furthermore, feminism and its associated movement lead to "disrespect for men in a subliminal way" by overstepping the boundaries in a relationship that are set by God, who has the final say. A relationship is a plan of God: "Traditionally, men went out to work and women stayed home. Now both women and men work. Some men are capable of taking care of their wives, but because feminism encourages this idea of the career woman, women have given up the care of their children to daycare centers and nannies. Feminism dismantles the headship and sets up a matriarchy. This goes against God's divine will" (Brooks interview). While these fundamentalist variants are not against fighting for women's rights, this should not be done at the expense of breaking down the divine order of God: "The challenge of women needs to be encouraged because of the Genesis mandate. But the guidelines need to be observed. Feminism steps over biblical boundaries. The concerns of women need to be heard because Jesus, the great liberator, exalted women. But the issues must be discussed within the boundaries set by God and the Bible. We must work within the parameters of those boundaries to find a solution" (Brooks interview). It is interesting to note that in addressing the concerns of women, single women, who seem to be deemed incapable of speaking for themselves, should be represented by men in the Church and, implicitly, wives by their husbands. It would seem that what these non-denominational Church leaders give to women with one hand they take away with the other.

Within the non-denominational churches, there is another emerging trend among some women, who now question the concept and practice of patriarchy. In this view, it is argued that in order to understand the relationship between men and women, one must first appreciate the relationship between the Church, biblical text, and the Kingdom of God. The Kingdom of God is defined as the broad context over which God rules. It is God's political rule on earth and encompasses all spheres of life—social, political, economic, and cultural. With a vision similar to that of liberation theology,[3] the Kingdom of God is interwoven into the daily lives of people and implies a society in which justice and dignity would prevail for all, a society that would correspond to Christian principles and biblical and doctrinal reflection. Simply put, the meaning of the Kingdom of God is making society a better place. This view of society conflicts with the Church's, for the Church is now seen as an agent of the Kingdom of God with the responsibility of establishing God on earth. In other words, the patriarchal views of the Church are incongruent to those of the Kingdom. The Scriptures, for their part, provide the ideological, theoretical, and religious guide for social behavior.

The Kingdom of God has always had implications for gender relations: "There can be neither Jew nor Greek . . . no male and female: for ye are all one man in Christ Jesus." (Gal. 3:28). But the Church has always maintained a parochial view on gender relations. According to Roslyn Henry-Wilson, wife of Pastor Fitzroy Wilson, "The Kingdom of God is broader than the Church. Christians do not have a concept of the Kingdom of God as a regime with philosophies" (interview). The politics and ideology of the Church are critical aspects of the status quo, which exists on the basis of elitist power—domination and subordination of the marginalized and the exploited. In this context, the Church is intended to inculcate ideas of the inferiority of women, which is a far cry from God's will and plan for humanity. For the Church understands God's intention only in the context of the fall and Adam's sin, which, in fact, is a distortion of God's program for social life. "God's intention is to be in life intimately, but the program was distorted when Adam sinned. So God is now trying to get us back on track" (Henry-Wilson interview).

So while God is trying to get humans back on track, the Church continues to hold fast to an intention that was never God's. For the fall did not eradicate the dignity and leadership of man and woman as stated in the creation narrative, nor did the fall change man's and woman's original equality. That the Church uses Adam's role in the fall is a corruption of biblical text and divine intention.

It would seem, then, that the conclusions drawn from Adam's role in what is seen primarily as Eve's sin arise external to biblical information. Nonetheless, it is Adam's sin that is used by the Church to justify gender inequalities and male dominance: "The oppression of women is seen as a consequence of the fall. But God's original intent for the sexes was different. God created man and woman and commanded them to subdue the earth. What is important is the pre-fall account of the position of man and woman from God's perspective in which there is no superiority or inferiority. Men interpreted the Bible to support the subjugation of women. . . . [T]he revelation of the Church does not focus on God's original and ultimate purpose. The Kingdom does" (Henry-Wilson interview). This variant in fundamentalism affirms that the Scriptures support the centrality of both women and men. The concept of a patriarchal divine law is not borne out by the Scriptures, for "before the fall God created woman and man equally" (interview). Hence, the question of submission as obedience and meekness does not arise.

Traditional fundamentalists hold that divine law dictates that wives should submit themselves to their husbands as reflected in Ephesians 5:22–25. Although this passage is usually cited as evidence to support the submissiveness of women, Henry-Wilson argues that this is a misinterpretation of Paul's message and a distortion of the concept of submission. Paul was in no way advocating that all men are heads and all women are subjugated to all men or that there is a rigid hierarchy in the family, the church, and society. For her, submission in a family context "is supposed to be mutual, and the wife is accountable to the husband, who is also accountable to the wife" (interview). This means that the woman does not always have to give in to the man but that decisions, for example, are better taken by the partner who has the greater expertise in the issue under discussion: "Submission is a conscious active choice to give way, recognizing ultimately that if a team is going to work, someone has to take responsibility for the ultimate decision. This does not mean that the woman will always have to give way to the man. Submission is supposed to be mutual. Within submission, there is room for leadership" (interview). In a broader societal context, women have a recognized place, and, therefore, the issue of women's subjugation to all men is really a non-issue.

This nascent theological and ideological trend does not reject feminist theories as explanations of women's position in society. Nor are its supporters averse to agitating for women's rights. This is necessary, they point out, because the Church has not been promoting a women's agenda because of its own distortion of women's rights. However, feminism is accepted with reservations because feminists are extreme in their views on God when they argue that God is female. For God transcends gender and is, therefore, neither male nor female, but both male and female. This understanding of social change finds support in an understanding of the Kingdom of God. As Henry-Wilson states, "If one understands the Kingdom of God, then they understand that Jesus' mandate was to 'disciple to the nations.' This in itself is a charge to social change and social transformation. This is the vision of the Kingdom" (interview).[4]

Perhaps the greatest challenge to fundamentalism and fundamentalists in Barbados—traditional Pentecostalism and other non-denominational churches—and even to the "liberal" church, is the ongoing effort of the Apostolic Teaching Centre (ATC) to create a woman-centered, gender-sensitive ministry based on a radical reinterpretation of biblical text. This ministry, described by its founder and pastor, Eliseus Joseph, as a "gender egalitarian" ministry, is an attempt to undermine the ideology and practice of patriarchy, male dominance, and women's subordination. This woman-centered ministry "follows the example set by prayer and dispensation, for the biblical paradigm recognizes women as equal partners in leadership, ministry, and social and political life" (Joseph interview).

With this understanding of biblical doctrine, Joseph's wife Marcia is a co-pastor of the ATC. That the co-pastor is a woman is an attempt by the ATC to indicate to women, in that particular ministry and beyond, that there is equal opportunity in the ministry for women to serve. In this new interpretation, women have equal rights to speak, to prophesy, to lead, to govern, and to administer communion. This is based on the strong belief that women and men are equal, having been created in the image of God. Such a ministry, then, is well placed to respect the rights of women: "Traditionally, in the Church [denominational and non-denominational] women played a marginal role although they were the majority. They held no leadership positions. They were always under the shadow of men and always compared with the patriarch. Therefore, women's gifts were suppressed. Placing my wife as a co-pastor is symbolic to say to women, 'There is equal opportunity'" (Joseph interview).

The ATC's example is not out of keeping with Christ's ministry, which was strongly supported by women. Mary Magdalene, Joanna, Susanna, and many other women played a financial and foundational role in allowing Jesus to perform his spiritual and social functions. The Gospel of Luke gives substance to this view when it speaks of the women who traveled with Jesus as he preached the good news of the Kingdom of God. Joseph points to a major shifting of social and spiritual paradigms in the biblical text to explain the need to be woman-centered: One woman, a Canaanite, asked Jesus to save her daughter, who had a demon and was in a terrible condition. Jesus, impressed by the faith of this woman, ignored the protestations of his disciples and located her at the center of his mission, extolling her as a woman of great faith. Jesus reframed His idea, His message, and His words in response to her. This, according to Joseph, is a "powerful" example of the dispensation of grace. It is this dispensation coupled with prayer (the power of a woman) as expressed in Luke 8 that serves to undermine the ideology and practice of patriarchy in the ATC's ministry.

Furthermore, the New and Old Testaments record a number of prominent women leaders who were active in the spiritual and social movement of the day and who by force of example present for the ATC models of faith, authority, and power. Besancon Spencer provides a summary: "[J]unia is called an apostle. Mary Magdalene, Joanna, Mary mother of Jesus, Mary mother of James and Salome mother of James and John were 'apostles' by definition. Anna is called a prophet, as were Miriam, Huldah, the wife of Isaiah and Deborah. Phillip's four daughters prophesied as did the women at Corinth. Priscilla and the women at Crete were teachers. The women at Crete were elders. Priscilla as well was a coworker and church overseer" (1985: 119–20). Like the New Testament, Old Testament doctrine supports the centrality of women in the social history of the Bible. A close reading of these Scriptures clearly shows that women played a dominant role in the different epochs of the movement of the Israelites. The book of Exodus records the revolutionary role women played in liberating Israel. Women were central to the deliverance of the Israelites from Egyptian bondage. In many respects, it was the women who liberated Israel. An early act of civil disobedience by women occurs when the "midwives" refused to murder all sons in keeping with the dictates of the King of Egypt, for "the midwives feared God, and did not as the King of Egypt commanded them, but saved the men children alive" (Exodus 1:17). It was the women who refused to give up Moses. Miriam, his mother, hid him for three months, after which she put him in a basket on the river, where he was found by the daughter of Pharaoh, who, in defiance of national decree, ensured that the young Moses was cared for by his own mother. Other powerful women stand out in Old Testament text: Sara, Rebekah, Ruth, and Naomi, to name a few. It is the example set by all these women that guides the ATC to break "religious, psychological and social impositions" in establishing "Christ-filled models of behaviour, relationships, family, work and leadership" (ATC 1998: 1).

Essentially, however, the basis for the ATC's radical posture is to be found in a reinterpretation of the Genesis narrative, which, according to Joseph, is not patriarchal since patriarchy and hierarchy were never the will or intention of God. "To say the Bible is patriarchal is incorrect" (interview). For patriarchy is a "social construction" and not a biblical construction or perspective. In this view, it is the Church that is patriarchal, having determined that patriarchal relations are a consequence of sin as expressed in the "fall." It is an interpretation that finds in Eve's curse a rationale for all men to rule over all women. It is the means used by the Church to legitimize male hegemony and women's inferiority in support of the status quo.

According to this ideological strand, both men and women represent God and were created equally to have equal partnership and participation in marriage, the family, and the ministry. Men and women together reflect God's image and nature (Gen. 1, 2). Men and women not only reflect the image of God, but also reflect leadership, authority, and equality in work. To understand this is in keeping with God's will and command. One relevant example is to be found in the Book of Joel, where the point is made that in the last days men and women would be treated equally, performing similar prophetic tasks: "And it shall come to pass afterward, that I will pour out my spirit upon all flesh; and your sons and your daughters shall prophesy" (Joel 2:28). Therefore, the view that man and woman were created with a divine mandate but with the man representing headship in a hierarchical "partnership" with defined roles finds no support in the theological and social reinterpretation offered by the ATC. For it, nowhere does the text of Genesis clearly state or imply that Eve's duties, roles, and responsibilities were different from Adam's. The contradictory expression of hierarchy within partnership is indicative of a parochial understanding of the creation story and its implications for an understanding of social life: "Man and woman are not opposite or separate sexes, they are complementary sexes. We should not deal with them separately but together. The social construction [of gender] polarizes men and women. This is not biblical text or God's intention. Man and the Church have warped God's intention. Woman is a divine partner. This undermines the concept of hierarchy based on divine law" (Joseph interview). The ground rules for marriage, family, and the ministry that were established by God in the pre-fall period were not altered after the fall. The rules of the game did not change. God continues to advocate joint leadership and rulership and to call women to minister; it is the Church that does not. Therefore, Christ's redemption after the curse and beyond is critical since Christ had ensured that the social construction of patriarchy never was and is no more.

It is against this background that the ATC's leadership challenges the traditional notion of "submission," in which it is argued that wives should submit themselves to their husbands and by extension to all men. For the ATC, traditional "submission" is unconditional and negates knowledge, talent, and creativity. In its view: "Submission starts with the principle of mutual submission. Within a societal system, there must be mutual submission. In this sense, mutual submission is systemic, that is, submit one to the other and submit to the system. Within the context of family and marriage it is a different concept. A reinterpretation of Ephesians 5:22 calls on women to submit to their *own*. A woman does not have to submit to any man with whom she is not in a relationship. This undermines traditional thinking that all women should submit to all men in the family, work, and the Church" (Joseph interview, his emphasis). However, in the process of mutual submission, both men and women, who should be "Christians," must recognize that they have to submit to the Lord because "the Lord is who constructs the relational system between man and woman, and without the Lord there is no Christian relationship" (Joseph interview). The concept of the Lord pervades all relationships.

Feminism is interpreted in the ATC's social and theological context as both positive and negative. It is positive in an ideological sense since it has forced women's issues onto the social and political agenda in a central way. Women are now in a position to understand the theoretical and ideological underpinnings of their allocated position in marriage, the family, the ministry, and the workplace and, generally, in society. It seeks to redefine women and to address gender imbalances and male hegemony. Additionally, feminism has made masculinity visible, and in so doing has forced men to examine themselves in the context of patriarchy and their own social context. Hitherto, men held hegemony without an understanding of themselves and their social context. Feminism, then, in presenting gender-specific demands for equality and justice allows for more than an appreciation of the need for movement toward social transformation and social justice.

However, this movement toward social transformation must take place at two levels: divine intervention and the social movements, which should be complementary in effort. For a social movement without prayer is tantamount to a fundamentalist, orthodox Marxism that is rigid and out of keeping with reality. Here we find an attempt at a conceptualization of a unity of body and soul. This view on social change is not in accord with traditional fundamentalism and fundamentalist thinking, which are opposed to social change. Traditional fundamentalism embodies an individualistic and pessimistic view of society based on personal salvation and the concept of millenarianism as the basis of societal change. This theological/ideological trend holds fast to "Christ's mandate of winning souls and saving sinners." Traditional fundamentalism, therefore, calls for a separation of body and soul: "[T]he curing of social ills is not the primary task of the church. The marching orders that Christ left the church was to evangelize—to go into all the world and win souls. And souls involve numbers. The Church must be concerned with numbers" (Jamaica Association of Evangelical Churches 1969: 7).

At the same time, however, feminism and the feminist movement are seen by the ATC as negative social influences since feminists create a social reality that does not recognize men as social partners. It is a situation in which men are not seen as important and hence, "women can do without them" (Joseph interview). This thinking only serves to place humans in discrete categories opposed to each other and does not augur well for addressing issues of social justice in a situation where there is continuous exploitation based primarily on gender, race, class, and age. Therefore, unless women and men are seen as complementary, issues of social justice and gender imbalances will continue to dog society since one of the "greatest social reconciliations" must be the "gender reconciliation": "The greatest reconciliation that needs to be made is the gender reconciliation because of society's agenda to create gender division for exploitative purposes. A 'gender egalitarian' society is what guarantees us, in part, social justice" (Joseph interview).

The ATC, in reading the Bible with "gender-sensitive" eyes and implementing its reinterpreted doctrine in a radical way, represents a significant shift in the current thinking of those fundamentalists who claim the theology and the movement. If the goal is a "gender egalitarian" society and by extension a society free of exploitation, then the ATC, given its mission to create a national church and a national program "bringing spiritual renewal and reform to the nation," will have a critical role to play in the forward movement of Barbados.

Some preliminary conclusions can be drawn from this essay. Christian fundamentalism with its dual ideological manifestations has served as a justification and legitimation of male dominance and the subordination of women. At the same time, it has been reinterpreted by both women and men of that faith as an ideology of social change. In this same vein, it is becoming evident that positions in fundamentalist churches are changing, and a rethinking of fundamentalism as a guiding theological principle is taking place among sections of the Church. Leaders and members are now more open to social movements and in this context are rethinking positions on women and their roles and functions in society. This is due, in part, to the dynamism of social and church life, the ongoing agitation for women's rights by women's organizations and feminist groups, and women's increasing visibility in the family (also as single mothers), the church, and the workplace. Women have made great strides in business, law, medicine, media, and other areas that were previously the domain of men. Added to this, women's reflection on their status and condition is experiential, that is, their experiences in a situation where they face discrimination has served to heighten their social consciousness.

This "shift in paradigm" is not to be overstated or to be seen as too radical a shift, but it must be recognized for its being a process of reflection on the nature of fundamentalism and for the implications it has for creating a just society, in which human dignity is respected and the aspirations of the people, both women and men, are satisfied. At another level, women who advocate fundamentalism should not be wholly dismissed as "backward," as some feminists are wont to do. Those who are open to ideas should be encouraged to raise their voices for a new vision for women.

Notes

1. The "liberal" churches are defined as those non-fundamentalist churches such as the Anglican, Roman Catholic, Methodist, Moravian, and others in similar traditions that subscribe to a hermeneutical understanding of the Scriptures. The "Church" as used in this paper refers to the fundamentalist church.

2. All biblical references are to *The Holy Bible,* King James Version (1964).

3. This reference to liberation theology is significant since fundamentalists believe liberation theology to be a subversion of biblical doctrine and tantamount to demonology. It is seen as an evil ideology intended to mislead.

4. Again, it is significant that mention is made of social change; traditional fundamental-

ist thinking sees societal change as an exercise in futility since the world is already doomed to destruction, divine intervention is the only cure for this world, and people should not control their destiny.

Works Cited

ATC. 1998. *Apostolic Teaching Centre.* Barbados.

Austin-Broos, Diane. 1997. *Jamaica Genesis: Religion and the Politics of Moral Orders.* Chicago: University of Chicago Press.

Besancon Spencer, Aida. 1985. *Beyond the Curse: Women Called to Ministry.* New York: Thomas Nelson Publishers.

Bingemer, Maria Clara. 1989. "Reflections on the Trinity." In *Through Her Eyes: Women's Theology from Latin America,* edited by Elsa Tamez. Maryknoll, N.Y.: Orbis Books.

Bisnauth, Dale. 1986. "Religious Fundamentalism and Its Implications for Women in the Caribbean." Paper presented at UNESCO/ISER(EC) Seminar on Changing Family Patterns and Women's Role in the Caribbean. Cave Hill, Barbados: University of the West Indies, 24–26 November 1986.

Brooks, Claude. Personal interview. 1 May 1998.

Gmelch, George, and Sharon Bohn. 1997. *The Parish behind God's Back: The Changing Culture of Rural Barbados.* Ann Arbor: University of Michigan Press.

Henry-Wilson, Roslyn. Personal interview. 13 May 1998.

The Holy Bible. 1964. King James Version. London: British Bible Society.

Jamaica Association of Evangelical Churches. 1969. *Why the Association of Evangelical Churches?* Jamaica.

Joseph, Eliseus. Personal interview. 22 May 1998.

Marsden, George. 1980. *Fundamentalism and the American Culture: The Shaping of Twentieth Century Evangelism, 1870–1925.* New York: Oxford University Press.

Ortega, Ofelia. 1995. *Women's Visions: Theological Reflection, Celebration, Action.* Geneva: WCC Publications.

Soares, Judith. 1992. "New Churches, Old Ideology: The Role of Fundamentalism in Jamaican Politics 1980–1988." Dissertation, Queen's University, Kingston, Ontario.

Stewart Van Leeuwen, Mary. 1990. *Gender and Grace: Love, Work and Parenting in a Changing World.* Downers Grove, Ill.: Intervarsity Press.

Tamez, Elsa, ed. 1989. *Through Her Eyes: Women's Theology from Latin America.* Maryknoll, N.Y.: Orbis Books.

Wilson, Fitzroy. Personal interview. 1 May 1998.

10

Current Evolution of Relations between Religion and Politics in Haiti

LAËNNEC HURBON

Sociological research on religion and politics in Haiti usually takes into consideration only the Catholic Church because it is the most visible, best known, and dominant system of worship. However, Protestantism and Vodou are as important as Catholicism in the Haitian political field. Protestantism, with its innumerable religious denominations, is reaching not only the popular classes of the suburbs but also the peasantry, with the result that Catholicism sometimes seems to be practiced by a minority. Vodou, often the first thing that comes to mind when Haiti is mentioned, is the set of practices and beliefs that have the deepest influence on the daily life of the Haitian people. It is no simple matter to speak about religion and politics in Haiti.

To understand the current evolution of relations between religion and politics in Haiti we need to look at two key moments: the point where Catholicism, Protestantism, and Vodou broke with the Duvalier dictatorship and the point at which the Catholic Church withdrew from politics in general and from the popularly based democratic movement in particular. At both points the democratic experience modified the status of each religious system and introduced or, if you like, revealed a deep cultural crisis in Haitian society.

RELIGION AND THE COLLAPSE OF THE DUVALIER DICTATORSHIP

During the early 1980s the Haitian Conference of Religious opposed the Duvalier dictatorship when political parties were banned. As the dominant religious institution in Haiti since the Concordat of 1860, the Catholic Church assumed a leadership role in the struggle to overthrow the dictatorship.[1] The Church's political opposition to Duvalier represented a radical change from its traditional pastoral role, which had revolved around an anti-Vodou strategy for at least a century. From the 1970s on, the Church had begun to link social development to evangelization. Up to that time, the Church had been the place where the social and cultural divide in Haitian society had found its ideological justification. The principal characteristic of Haitian society was a kind of social apartheid derived from slavery, which kept the majority of the people deprived of rights. In this context, the Church guarded its own privileges, interests, and power. In contrast, popular Catholic practice rested on a vision of the Church as a foreign institution, one that permitted access to the symbols of the civilized world, in opposition to Vodou, which represented the roots of a particular national culture.

Following the Second Vatican Council, the language of the Haitian popular classes could be incorporated into church liturgy. Creole, the vernacular language, was used, and the rhythms of Vodou ceremonies were brought into Catholic songs so that people would feel at home in church. The creolization of the liturgy meant that the popular classes could participate in church for the first time since the age of slavery. The consequences were enormous: the Episcopal Conference was obliged to take the experiences of the popular classes and the peasantry into account, including problems of civil rights, health, access to schools, poverty, and more. People were no longer considered objects of charity and compassion, and they started to feel responsible for their own political destinies. However, this liberation only appeared within the Church, because only there could Haitians claim their rights and realize what Michel de Certeau calls *la prise de parole*. Christianity was no longer a religion from abroad; it would henceforth be appropriated and reworked in accordance with the perspectives and interests of the popular classes. This would mean, in turn, that the Catholic hierarchy would lose its authority. By the time the Duvalier regime became aware of the shift, it was too late. The people were ready to face the dictatorship. What is known today as *dechoukaj* (uprooting) is the direct result of this mental and symbolic preparation inside the Church. This is the originality of the social and political movement in Haiti during the 1980s.

Protestantism and Vodou already were closer to the experiences lived by the people. However, the new orientation of the Catholic Church was more focused on politics, particularly because the theology of liberation inspired the pastoral practice of many priests and religious. This pastoral practice had an important impact on Protestantism and Vodou. How was this possible? I don't know if one can observe the same phenomenon in Brazil or in Latin America with the theology of liberation and its application to the *comunidades de base* (base communities), but in Haiti, those involved in the *comunidades de base* played an active role in community life and succeeded in creating a tendency to contest religious power whatever its form, whether Catholic, Protestant, or Vodou. In any case, the way was open for a politicization of religious practice in general. Very little is known about the role that Protestantism and Vodou played in the struggle against the dictatorship, but it was very important. The democratic experience succeeded in reaching all social classes and every sector and institution in Haiti.

THE CRISIS OF RELIGIOUS SYSTEMS

Just after the collapse of the Duvalier dictatorship, the hierarchy of the Catholic Church withdrew from the popular democratic movement because of the difficulty of controlling the democratic process in Haiti. (The Vatican was also moving to stop the participation of Catholic priests in political life.) This resulted in a wide split between the Catholic hierarchy and members of the Church led by priests who had adopted the theology of liberation. The context was set for Jean-Bertrand Aristide to assume a leadership role.

If we focus on the principal characteristics of the political struggle in Haiti, it is noticeable that the moral and religious connotations of that struggle had the greatest impact. It was also necessary to manifest an absolute will to win in order to overthrow the dictatorship. The foundations of the society had to radically change if people were to pass from a *régime* of arbitrary rule to one founded on right and law. The traditional state was obsolete, and people lived in a political vacuum. We have evidence of this in the practice of *dechoukaj* when many *tonton macoutes* were considered "witches" or *loup-garous* (werewolves) and therefore lynched. Both Catholics and Protestants (Evangelicals, Baptists, Pentecostalists, Adventists, and so on) engaged in *dechoukaj*. The target was not Vodou as such; it was a matter of reaching the origin of evil and recreating the society from new foundations. The same tendency can be noted after the first *coup d'état* against Aristide, which was organized by the former chief of the *tonton macoutes,* Roger Lafontant: people did not hesitate to destroy and burn the old cathedral, the Episcopal Conference Centre, and the papal nuncio's residence. How can we explain such a religious investment in politics, and what are its effects?

The religious investment in politics was efficient and maybe even necessary in the dictatorial context. The same situation was observed in Poland. But when it is a matter of governing, politics becomes routinized, and this is followed by disenchantment on the part of the people. At that moment the status of religion in the society begins to change. This is the actual problematic of religion in Haiti.

At the political level, institutions have to be founded on rational norms that everybody can discuss, which means that there must be a separation between politics and religion. It is clear that the democratic experience implies such a separation. There has to be a new foundation to the social bond, and it cannot be religious. It is not easy for religious systems to accept this and to give up their pretensions to organize all sectors of life and society. That is why populism seemed to be a solution, but it was a solution that delayed real movement to a democratic system. In a sense, to live in Haiti today is to live in a double bind, where, on the one hand, the state is becoming institutionalized, and, on the other, populism is feeding religion's investment in politics.

One can certainly speak about a conflict between tradition and modernity as the key factor for explaining the political situation in Haiti. However, it is important to reverse the traditional sociological and philosophical ways of understanding the opposition between tradition and modernity. It used to be assumed that the popular classes and the peasantry had a natural inclination to be attached to traditional practices where the sense of community outweighed that of individual autonomy, where ancestral authority was more important than law and rights, and where there was a religious interpretation of the world and of society. Such a perspective implied that the cultural system was not adapted to democracy and that people were not yet mature enough for democracy. In the case of Haiti, the upper class and the political class are more attached to the traditional functioning of Haitian society than are the popular classes, not only in their commitment to the extended family, but also in their preference for the despotism that maintained a social situation comparable to a kind of a social apartheid. The reconstruction of a social bond that would permit the consolidation of the democratic process appears to be a new beginning for Haitian society. However, this implies that religion can no longer play its traditional role, not only for the upper class and the political class, but also for the popular classes and the peasantry.[2]

At the religious level, we must distinguish the political position of the Catholic hierarchy from that of the Catholic popular classes. The hierarchy's withdrawal from politics after the collapse of the dictatorship did not signify a disinterest in politics; on the contrary, the official Catholic Church tried to regain its power and lead the democratic process. However, its target was not political; it was a matter of the Church remaining the official and preeminent religion of the state in order to preserve its privileges. Its open struggle against the theology of liberation a little while after the collapse of the dictatorship and against the rise of the leadership of Aristide meant precisely that it wanted to guide the political choices of the Catholic popular classes. Such a position certainly corresponds to the new orientation of the Vatican in its moves to reestablish its power over Latin American churches in general and to break the growing success of the theology of liberation.

If we consider the political orientation of the Catholic popular classes, we see that although they lose their traditional symbolical references because of the experience of the democratic process, they continue to express social and economic claims in their religious practices. Social claims explode in an anarchic way. On one hand, the new state cannot reply to those claims; on the other hand, Catholicism is unable to satisfy practicing Catholics. There results a division at the level of consciousness itself. No authority has sufficient legitimacy any longer. This psycho-sociological situation will not be overcome without a transformation of the status of the religious systems.

One sign of the religious and political confusion seems to be the successful charismatic movement, which reaches not only members of the upper middle class but also Catholics and Protestants of the popular classes. This recent phenomenon is worth analyzing. The social content of religious practice remains, but each individual in the movement believes he or she is responsible for his or her afflictions. This could be the beginning of a change in how Haitians interpret the country's social and political problems. Inside Protestant denominations like the Pentecostalists or the Baptists, the popular classes are seeking the amelioration of social and economic life through an inner, spiritual change. It is clear that people, whether they are Catholic or Protestant, do not know yet what place religion is to occupy in the new state which is being built in Haiti.

Both Catholics and Protestants in the charismatic movement experience a particular difficulty in having explicit or open recourse to Vodou, while, paradoxically, Vodou continues to be the matrix for interpreting social and political problems. The matter is somewhat complex. Vodou does not imply a sense of the interiorization of individual culpability; it supposes on the contrary that the

Gods and the invisible world are responsible for resolving any social and political problems. However, in the charismatic movement, as in Haitian Protestantism in general, Vodou beliefs are maintained through a new interpretation, which makes Vodou into a diabolical cult. Vodou is considered unable to satisfy social and economic claims and is then transformed into a cult of the devil. The charismatic movement is successful because of a crisis in Catholicism and a crisis in Vodou.

The practice of Vodou as it relates to politics has been transformed. After having been persecuted for at least a century by the Catholic Church and by the state, Vodou was used by the dictator François Duvalier, who was an ethnologist. That aspect of the recent history of Vodou in relation to politics is well known. In the context of the democratic experience, followers of Vodou participated in the popular movement against the dictatorship, with the result that a division was produced inside some *ounfo* (temples). One can no longer speak about a unanimity of Vodou priests in relation to politics. During the *dechoukaj* directed against many Vodou priests identified as "witches," it was not a matter of destroying Vodou as such, as we have already explained. But with the irruption of the people onto the political scene in Haiti, Vodou had to relinquish its clandestine nature and seek a legitimacy to be practiced openly. The new Constitution of 1987 depenalized the religion and acknowledged the right of Haitians to be Vodouists. Clearly, the struggle for freedom of religion and freedom of conscience will benefit Vodou. Catholic and Protestant churches are not going to be in favor of the freedom of Vodou if they continue to identify that religion with Satan or with superstition. But Haiti has no other recourse than to accept religious pluralism; otherwise we have to renounce the democratic process.

FREEDOM OF RELIGION

I would like now to be more explicit about the position I am defending by making two critical remarks based on recent research on the evolution of Vodou in the current Haitian cultural and political context. In a scientific study in the suburbs of Port-au-Prince, 3.5 percent of the persons interviewed openly admitted practicing Vodou, while 49.6 percent acknowledged being Catholic and 39.0 percent Protestant (Houtart and Rémy 1997). Without a doubt, Protestant denominations have grown significantly in Port-au-Prince. However, it is noteworthy that many Haitians fear, even now, declaring that they practice Vodou. This means that social and ideological control over the population is still strong, with the result that Vodou continues to be unacceptable. To move Vodou out from underground, we need to accept rules of democracy, which assume principles of freedom of religion and freedom of conscience. It is not easy, however, for the Catholic Church in Haiti to accept these freedoms, as it has been accustomed to being the official religion of the country from the time of the Concordat; nor is it easy to have in Haiti a *régime* that recognizes the neutrality of the state in matters of religion. We are probably beginning a new stage in the struggle for democracy in Haiti and for the consolidation of the right to practice Vodou.

To defend Vodou is not to make every Haitian practice Vodou. This would be a dangerous reaction to the traditional denial of Vodou. It would mean that there is an essential particularity about Haitians, namely Vodou, and such an opinion could lead to a new kind of religious fundamentalism, based on the idea of an authentic "Haitianity" that could justify religious and cultural fanaticism. Vodou is far from supporting any kind of fanaticism; it is not a religion of conquest, but above all a system of tolerance, almost exactly like the religion of the ancient Greeks. Vodou remains a heritage and could never become a religion that sought to impose its beliefs and practices on anyone.

The second remark I would like to make concerns a recent qualitative study involving a conversation with a *mambo* (a Vodou priestess). It reminded me that studies such as that done by Karen McCarthy Brown (1991) are very useful for understanding Vodou. Because of the long persecution and the long silencing of Vodou, it is important to let the practitioner speak. The *mambo* with whom I recently discussed these issues told me that conditions for the development of Vodou had changed since the installation of a democratic *régime;* she did not have the impression that the religion was being repressed in any way. Despite anti-Vodou proselytizing by Protestant denominations, freedom of religion must be protected by the rule of law in a democratic state. In this respect, the religious problem in Haiti clearly becomes a political problem. If we do not accept this, I wonder if we will not go once again into a dead end with regard to the development and modernization of our country. The neutrality of the state, what Europeans call *laïcité* (secularity), appears to be a problem in the present political situation. This means we should at least open the debate at every level in Haitian society on how to obtain respect for the freedom of different religions, notwithstanding the Concordat between the state and the Catholic Church.

The middle and upper classes are ideologically and culturally prepared for this. In Catholic theology, under the influence of the Second Vatican Council, the arguments for the persecution of Vodou disappeared. At the cultural level, in general, and especially in painting, Vodou became a matrix for interpreting Haitian society and history. It is the same with recent Haitian music, which openly and decisively utilizes the rhythms of Vodou. Many musical *gwoup-rasi-n* ("roots-groups") bring aspects of Vodou into public view, such as "trance" and "possession" by the *lwa* (spirits or deities). This situation is absolutely new in Haitian society. Until now, a Haitian Vodouist was supposed to be "possessed" by a *lwa* only within the context of a ceremony taking place in an *ounfo*. Moving that important aspect of Vodou into public view implies a transformation of Vodou's meaning.

Although this may mean a loss of the sense of the sacred, it offers a way to use religion as a cultural force, as a way of affirming an identity. The status of Vodou is transformed: it becomes the place where the peasantry and suburban population as well as the Haitian Diaspora, especially those who live somewhat uprooted in the United States, can affirm their personality. Taking Vodou onto the public scene expresses perhaps an inclination to end the social apartheid that was one of the principal characteristics of Haitian society. But the cultural situation remains ambiguous because of the uncertainty of the strength of the new social bond. It cannot be a question of either Christianity or Vodou. Maybe the country is now undergoing a new period of transition, a consolidation of a state of law that is really modern.

In closing, I would like to call attention to the fragility of the democratic experience in Haiti as revealed by the religious crisis, a crisis that affects at the same time the status of three religious systems and consciousness itself. Can one say that the situation is similar to that of religion and politics in Latin America? I do not think so, for at least two reasons: first, because of the important role of Vodou, which was persecuted as symbolic of the primitive and the barbaric, and which is now recognized as being full of meaning; second, because the country is moving out of a long period of stagnation and by virtue of the democratic experience is living through a real transformation of its foundations. Political events in Haiti during these last ten years appear to be somewhat exemplary.

Notes

1. See Hurbon 1987, 1989, 1995, 1997, and forthcoming. On the evolution of the Church in Haiti since 1986 see also Nérestant 1994, Toussaint 1992, Midy 1989, and Dominique 1996.

2. For further discussion of the political crisis in Haiti see among others Delince 1993, Corten 1989, Hurbon 1994, and Hurbon 1998.

Works Cited

Brown, Karen McCarthy. 1991. *Mama Lola: A Vodou Priestess in Brooklyn.* Berkeley: University of California Press.

Corten, A. 1989. *L'État faible: Haïti et la République dominicaine.* Montréal: CIDIHCA.

Delince, K. 1993. *Les forces politiques en Haïti: Manuel d'histoire contemporaine.* Paris: Karthala; Plantation, Fla.: Pegasus Books.

Dominique, M. 1996. "Rôle de la théologie de la libération dans la transition démocratique en Haïti." In *Les transitions démocratiques,* edited by L. Hurbon. Paris: Syros.

Houtart, F., and A. Rémy. 1997. *Les référents culturels à Port-au-Prince: Etude des mentalités face aux réalités économiques, sociales et politiques.* Port-au-Prince: Centre de recherche et de formation économique et sociale pour le développement (CRESFED).

Hurbon, L. 1987. *Comprendre Haïti, Essai sur l'état, la nation, la culture.* Paris: Karthala.

Hurbon, L. 1989. "Enjeu politique de la crise actuelle de l'Église." *Chemins critiques, revue haïtiano-caraïbéenne* 1 (1): 11–22.

Hurbon, L. 1994. "Nationalisme et démocratie en Haïti." *Chemins critiques, revue haïtiano-caraïbéenne* 3 (1–2): 7–30.

Hurbon, L. 1995. "Haïti et la politique du St.-Siège." In *Tous les chemins ne mènent plus à Rome,* edited by R. Luneau and P. Michel. Paris: Albin Michel.

Hurbon, L. 1997. "Rôle et statut du religieux dans les luttes haïtiennes de sortie de la dictature." In *Religion et démocratie,* edited by P. Michel. Paris: Albin Michel.

Hurbon, L. 1998. "Gnadenlose Liebe zum Volk. Irrwege der Demokratie." *DU, die Zeitschrift der Kultur* 2 (Feb.): 68–72.

Midy, F. 1989. "Haïti; La religion sur les chemins de la démocratie, L'affaire Aristide en perspective; Histoire de la formation et du rejet d'une vocation prophétique." *Chemins critiques, revue haïtiano-caraïbéenne* 1 (1): 23–44.

Nérestant, M. 1994. *Religions et politique en Haïti.* Paris: Karthala.

Toussaint, H. 1992. "Église catholique et démocratie en Haïti." *Problèmes d'Amérique latine* 4 (Jan.–Mar.): 43–60.

Religion, Identity, and Diaspora

11

Jamaican Diasporic Identity
The Metaphor of Yaad

BARRY CHEVANNES

To name is to summarize. It is to plot as onto a single point all the references of an identity. He, or she, who is without name is without summary, and therefore without reference, lost and confused, like Kamau Brathwaite, who describes his catastrophic experience of Hurricane Gilbert: "as if I have been blinded in my metaphors; cosmology totally disordered, my personal contribution to the culture . . . is almost irrevocably eradicated and destroyed, my name no longer Kamau—but almost back to little naked Eddie on the unverberating hillside" (1997: 62). Or, I would imagine, like Ben Johnson, one of whose very critical references the morning after that infamous dash changed from *Canadian* to *Jamaican-born Canadian,* and the day after that to simply *Jamaican.* If Donovan Bailey may have restored the tarnished glory of Canada at the 1996 Summer Games in Atlanta, Jamaicans did not watch this Olympian with dispassion, since they know him as *Jamaican-born,* as if to remind the Canadians to whom they, the Canadians, owe their present fortune, even though we did not quite take blame for, and tried not to share in, that earlier shame.

Being and defining Jamaican, being and defining Canadian, being and defining anything is a necessary and urgent task. The more we are subjected to globalization, the more that necessity. The relationship between the necessity for self-definition and globalization need not, indeed should not, be construed as oppositional or dialectical. As Stuart Hall states, the London-based global ethnic traverses the world, or does not think it out of his or her stride, on his or her mobile telephone, but is more self-conscious about being Jamaican than his or her own parents who, unlike the global ethnic, were born and grew up in Jamaica (1997: 28).

Being Jamaican for Hall's global ethnic means language and idioms and style and the creation/invention of a memory of loss. For to be Jamaican *a farin*[1] is to have a diasporic memory, that is to say, the memory of a particular reference point, a land, with which there are primordial ties of sentiment but to which there may be no real or enduring return.

It is the memory of *Yaad,*[2] and it is on this that I focus. Among the young people in the Jamaican diaspora, *Yaad* has become metaphor for home. The yard, as Sidney Mintz (1974: 233–47) more than any other Caribbean anthropologist, or Erna Brodber (1975; 1980: 1–3) more than any other Caribbean intellectual/artist, understands, is a central reference point of self-definition among the

African-Caribbean peoples. Long before the dream of freedom became the act of emancipation, the yard was personalized space, set apart from the nakedness of the plantation, as Waddell, the nineteenth-century English missionary to Jamaica, found. With a characteristic Manicheanism that viewed sex as belonging to the baser instincts, if not downright sinful, and the dance of the Africans, with its characteristic pelvic thrust and stirring, as sexual debauchery, the missionaries were very watchful over their congregations on the eve of the coming emancipation. On the pretext that "a company of loose and disorderly people" were disturbing the neighborhood with their "singing, and drumming, and dancing" in celebration, Waddell, with a confident air of pastoral (and probably racial) superiority, boldly barged without permission into the yard of the host and began remonstrating with him. This is what he reported this "wild fellow" told him in reply:

> I had no right to come into his yard; for he might do what he liked in his own place, and have what company he pleased. Because he had a black face and I a white one made me do so, but when the first of August arrived, he would see who would meddle with him or his dance. He would be as good as me then, and would split my head if I came into his yard that way again. (Waddell 1970: 147)

That a man's home is his castle was clearly not meant only for the Englishman. It applied equally well to those transported from continental Africa with the intention of stripping them naked, baptizing and clothing them with a new and non-threatening identity.[3] But the Africans in plotting their identity restored the most basic element in their graph of references, the personal space, the yard.[4]

The development of the peasant communities across the Caribbean was actualized on the basis of individualist settlement patterns. As M. G. Smith (1965: 176–95) noted for Jamaica, the people of a village live not in clusters but spatially distant, each family on its own piece of bought, rented, or captured land, each in its own yard. Ownership of land could be male, could be female, but over "the house-yard complex, providing the nucleus of the peasant culture and community" (Besson 1995: 55) presides not the man as in his castle but the woman as mother, guardian, and transmitter of the cultural values of the art and artifice of survival. Knowledge of Kwaaku Ananse, the vulnerable spider god, hero of brain over brawn, becomes almost immanent, reproduced through transference without rational thought, instinctively, in the face of greater power. But that bit of space behind the decorative shrubs and hedges, signaling identity and summary, became for the once-enslaved, the now-free, the summary of memory, life, and hope—of memory because it hosts the ancestors, who are buried and tombed within its confines, in what is commonly referred to as "family plot" (Besson and Chevannes 1996); of hope, because the *navel string,* the umbilical cord, of each newborn is buried there and a tree planted on top of it, two gifts of nature twinned in the struggle for survival and the richness of possibilities together, forever; of life, because the yard is the focal point of nurturing and sustenance, of discipline and healing, of growth and transition, of connectedness and integrity. *Yaad* thus becomes that space where lineage identity is constructed and maintained, where the circle of life opens with birth, matures with living, and closes with the burial and tombing.

The African-Caribbean people have always understood this, and for this reason women have always occupied a position of reverence in the family structure, and indeed, in the wider community. For as they presided over birth, so too they presided over growth, and over death. A respected man is called *Taata,* or *Faada* (Father); respected woman, *Mada* (Mother). The archetypal Mada is the charismatic healer, whose touch restores what other powers destroy. Most parsons and bishops are male (see Austin-Broos 1997), as are most practitioners of the destructive power of *obya,* but most healers are women (Wedenoja 1980). Their healing space is the *balm yard.*

From a tempting psychoanalytical point of view, the diasporic yearning for *Yaad* among the *Yardies* could be interpreted as the quest for the security of the womb. However, this does not necessarily signal regression. To the contrary. It is a necessary aspect of diasporic being, for, as Stuart Hall (1997) argues, without this memory, without this "narrative of loss," we, whoever we are, in whatever diaspora, could never begin to reconfigure the contexts in which we find ourselves, since we would not know where to begin, for we would not know who we are. It is a distinct characteristic of diasporic culture, to paraphrase Hall, to look back in order to look forward. We thus may say that the Yardies need to define themselves in relation to the archetypal *Yaad*, Jamaica, in order to confront and negotiate their way in the a bigger and more complex world. Many bring to this bigger world, as Gunst (1995) and Small (1995) will tell you, a history and a tradition, as well as years of schooling in the urban ghettoes of Kingston. The ghetto, Jamaican-style, is an enclave, whose ethnicity is its poverty. The typical urban ghetto is a criss-crossing and interweaving of access streets, lanes, and footpaths to yards separated from the outside view by zinc fences. The yards are called tenement yards. Some, like Bob Marley's "government yard in Trench Town" (1974), were built by the government for poor people. Most, however, are the results of the spatial reconfiguration of the city when the affluent people moved out, taking with them their status symbols of residence and social class, and the poor people moved in, bringing with them their rural but changing worldview. Inside a small tenement yard will live ten to fifteen people; inside a large one, over forty. Over time they pay no rent, as rent collection is sometimes hazardous for the landlord who, if he/she has not already migrated, now lives in the hills—Red Hills, Beverly Hills, Jacks Hill, Stony Hill, looking down.

The two most socially significant characteristics of the tenement yard are its ritualized privacy and its cooperation. As private space, the yard is enclosed from public view and commerce. Its gate is always closed, and none but the most familiar may push and enter without calling or knocking, seeking permission. Entering this private space, the stranger is made to feel unwelcome until his or her *bona fides* is established. Then there is also the privacy of the occupants. Each room or apartment is secured from the intruding eyes and familiarity of the other occupants. Meals are usually served and eaten inside. From a functionalist point of view it hides the time of shame when a "lot of people have no supper tonight,"[5] for *daag swet bot tek ier kiba i* ("a dog's thick hair hides the fact that it perspires"). Your shame is your own. So also is your pride. As Harry Belafonte's mother drilled into him, "Poverty is no excuse for lack of class."[6]

Second, the urban yard is a shared space of cooperation. They cooperate in the use of the domestic facilities, the kitchen, bathroom, and standpipe, and in common security against strangers. They cooperate, too, for mutual security against the state, the police. The yard, as Brodber (1975) found, is also a problem-solving space for its occupants, particularly the women who cooperate in dealing with the problems of children. Such cooperation, however, assumes respect for each other. People who cannot get along with others are usually forced out by protracted quarreling, body language, singing,[7] facial expressions that are the common legacy of the African-Caribbean people.

As in the rural communities, so also in the Kingston ghetto, it is the women who are the guardians of the enculturating privacy of the yard, home. The rearing of the children, particularly the girls right through adolescence, boys up to puberty, is the responsibility of the women, whether or not a man provides (Cumper 1958; Davenport 1961; R. T. Smith 1960; Wilson 1973). Like working mothers just about everywhere, they carry the burden of domestic work as well, under the threat of wife beating and gender-based humiliation. But on top of that, the ghetto woman is engaged in daily combat against the forces outside the yard that relentlessly seek to contaminate and steal the souls of her children. Girls are carefully protected. Their proper domain, therefore, is the yard. Seen outside, they are either going or coming from somewhere—the shop, the school, a neighbor, but never aimless. When they do play outside, it is under the watchful eye of mother, grandmother, or brother.

The outside is another world altogether, the streets. It is the world of the males: the street corner with its blaring music on a Friday night, or any night; the rum bars and clubs with their night life, their middle-of-the-day life, where the uptown Camrys and BMWs frequent and the *sketel* hang out, those girls of easy virtue; the gambling dens and corners; the coke-peddling runners; where the gun is only fingertips or a quick dash away; an acid-throwing, badword-spilling, uncontrollable, untamed world.

Of significance is the sense of community, which the yard and the street combine in a sort of creative tension to generate in this young, lovable, but disturbing city. This is not Toronto or New York. Kingston has nothing of the anonymity of Harvey Cox's *Secular City* (1966). Not only is it not secular (it is, in fact, a city of a multiplicity of religious denominational activism, where every public function, from a youth club meeting to a state activity, begins with a prayer), but its vibrancy rests on a geographically based spirit of community. This sense of community generates youth and sports clubs and corners all over the city; brings out thousands to support their football teams; prompts the street murals, clean-up campaigns, and sidewalk gardening of the young people. In other words, Kingston is an overlapping congeries of communities.

And each ghetto community has a name, a summary of references and experiences that serves as a rallying point for identification. The name *Tivoli* means intense and unswerving Jamaica Labour Party affiliation, excellent football, dance, and Kumina[8] cultural expression, control of the largest market in the city, a safe and secure garrison,[9] great dynasties of Don Dadas, of which Jim Brown's is the latest, and an urban seat of the spiritual power of Revival (see Besson and Chevannes 1996). The name *Jungle* means intense and unswerving People's National Party affiliation, excellent football, popular dance, Peter Metro, a safe and secure garrison. These two ghettos are models of the garrison community, but they are communities, like hundreds of others where people live in daily face-to-face, primary relationships of trust and social control: Maxfield, Tower Hill, Waterhouse, Balcombe, Payne Land, Dunkirk, Southside, Tel Aviv, Hermitage, August Town, Tavern, Flats, Cassava Piece, Black Ants Lane, Maverly, Stan' Pipe, Swallofield, Back Bush, and so on.

The word *ghetto,* as in *mi baan an gruo iina di ghetto* (I was born and grown in the ghetto), signifies toughness and fearlessness. The ghetto dweller has earned a degree in survival, through hustling and juggling (Gayle 1997)—hustling being the ingenious, illegal, and criminal ways of earning a living, from *picking pocket* to *ray-ray* (the art of reconditioning old clothes and passing them off in the market as new); juggling being the hard-working management of several legitimate occupations. It is the world of raw, *ital*[10] sexuality, where uptown men go to get *di wickedest slam,* which they apparently do not get in the constraints of the uptown bedroom; where women make fashion statements about their sexuality, at dance hall sessions, at funerals; where well-to-do higglers *upkeep* their young male lovers in the latest fashion and discipline them when they stray.[11] It is the world of the DJs, the world where the power of the word is revealed in a changing lexicon: the *concord,* for the new $500 bills; a *bills,* for the $100; *bups,* for a "sugar daddy"; *sketel,* for a loose girl; in two hundred new singles produced in the music studios every week; a world where young men sing their improvisations as they walk along in the street, dreaming of some studio, and fame; where the bogle was born and later the butterfly, where, in some yard, or perhaps in some studio, first ska, then rock steady, then reggae were not only born, but referenced and named. For reggae was created not to satisfy an international market, but to satisfy a ready market of believers, who heard in the new beat the memory of loss and at the same time the new context of rhythm and blues, and with great self-conscious wit and irony called it *reggae-reggae* (see Cassidy and LePage 1980: 380) because it came from the ghetto—profane and uncultured. It is the world of the Friday night street corner sound system, of chicken-foot soup and boiled corn, and boiled crab; of the ganja splif, if one wants to smoke by himself, or Bongo Iri's yard if one wants to *lik a chalis and praise Jah.*[12]

This is *Yaad*. This is home. This is the metaphorical celebration by *les damnés de la terre* of their damnation, of the triumph of the human spirit over its desecration (see Fanon 1961). This was the essence of Maurice Bishop's reminder to Barbadian Prime Minister Tom Adams that he was a *yard fowl* after all. But this is also the place where most of the eight hundred people in 1980 were killed, where most of the nine hundred were murdered in 1996, where schools are forced to close, so intense and so violent the war, where the Dons rule, whence emanate the Showers and the Spanglers and the Vikings, posses that controlled the drug trade in many North American cities.

Of course, there is more to being Yardie than a wild, aggressive, and ruthless member of a gun-toting gang. Every posse member, or Yardie, is some mother's child and the likely father of children. It goes even further, in a case like that of Jim Brown, whose death and funeral not only received coverage in the international press but whose funeral was attended by an estimated twenty thousand mourners and a "catalogue of Jamaican dignitaries" (Small 1995: 2). For this nationally and internationally notorious Don of the Shower Posse was in fact not just Don but Don Dada—the respected protector, father, patron, dispenser of justice, and enforcer, their hero.

But the achievements of the Yardies and posses in the ruthless competitive underworld of the North Atlantic are viewed with secret satisfaction by some members of the diaspora, who, in the face of a hostile, racially constructed world, identify with the Yardie's Number One status, no matter that he is number one in fear-inspiring aggression and violence. But for the extraordinarily wanton and indiscriminate quality of that violence, this is most similar to the sentiments of returned migrants from the UK, who in my interviews with them[13] credit Jamaican aggressiveness for their ability and the ability of other Anglophone islanders and continental Africans to stand up to British racism as they experienced it in the 1950s, 1960s, and 1970s. Declaring oneself Jamaican was the same as saying: "Don't mess with me!"

The sense of being Yardie, Jamaican, is not confined only to one's sense of identity, but on it depend sometimes whole communities for the material support of a barrel of cargo at Christmas time, or visas obtained through means that still baffle the FBI. The sense of community was the strength of the Jamaican posses, a circumstance known by the United States law enforcement agents to make them difficult to penetrate.[14]

But as the Jamaican diaspora negotiates its understanding of what it means to be Jamaican, the African diaspora in Jamaica attempts to do the same. This, as we all know, is the major significance of the Rastafari—who in actual fact sometimes refer to Africa as *Yaad*, in particular Ethiopia, Zion, where Jah dwells— and before the appearance of Rastafari in the early 1930s, of the Garvey movement. This rich heritage nearly a century old is even older, the legatee of a long tradition of Ethiopianism, which I prefer to call the idealization of Africa (Chevannes 1994). For it is an idea that sprang from what Rex Nettleford (1993: 39–

40) calls the creative imagination, to become a self-defining affirmation. Black Jamaicans may be more than their ancestors, the Africans, were, but only by starting there can they really begin to have hope, to create, and to live. The point of that affirmation is to effect not so much a physical return (though there are many who have made it back) but a spiritual return, a point of beginning, a point of departure, in what is an existence of many layers.

Only when that definition is made will the work begin. In traditional Ghana, there is no mourning for the child who dies before the naming ceremony. Only they count who have a name, a point of reference in family, lineage, tribe, and nation. Only they count who have a *Yaad*.

Notes

1. *A farin* (in foreign) refers to anywhere in that vast space outside Jamaica; it is a term used when the speaker chooses not, or is unable, to identify the particular country.

2. I have used this spelling for "yard" throughout as a way of conveying the broad sound that in the Jamaican patois communicates such rich feelings.

3. See Alex Haley (1976: 214–18, 255–56) for Kunta Kinte's awareness of an imposed name change and his rage at this threat to his identity. Africans were the only people systematically stripped of their names on coming to the new world.

4. From as early as the mid-eighteenth century, the yard was clearly of symbolic importance. In his diary entry, Thomas Thistlewood recorded that Abba buried her son "near her house" (quoted in Douglas Hall 1989: 185). This tradition of burial on family land remains as the most widespread pattern of burial in rural Jamaica. See Besson (1995: 54).

5. From the popular song *Armagideon* by the little-known artist Willie Williams.

6. Harry Belafonte in his address at a special convocation to confer on him the doctor of letters (*honoris causa*) by the University of the West Indies, 5 March 1996.

7. A woman will replace verbal communication with singing to herself in order to signal criticism or displeasure.

8. Kumina is an ancestral religious cult of BaKongo origin found in the eastern parish of St. Thomas.

9. The name "garrison community" was coined by the late Carl Stone (1980) to describe those communities of monolithic allegiance to a political party. Garrison communities are defended by paramilitary gangs led by a don or superdon (Don Dada). They do not entertain opposition and are given to overvoting.

10. *Ital* is the Rastafari term for "natural." Here it denotes sex without restraint, especially that of the condom.

11. Higglers are traders in foodstuff grown in the countryside and marketed in the city. Usually women, they are the backbone of the internal marketing system (see Katzin 1959; Mintz 1974; Witter 1989). Extending their trade abroad, these women have developed a lucrative niche, and as a result many have become quite well-off. Hence their ability to keep male lovers, providing them with the latest in designer clothes and jewelry. Their wealth makes it possible for them to buy protection or enforce their will. Called Informal Commercial Importers, or ICIs, since the 1980s, this subset of higglers has not been much studied. A recent attempt, which focuses on their sexuality, is Wyatt et al. 1995.

12. The term *lik a chalis* refers to the Rastafari mode of smoking marijuana as a means of communing with Jah in a circle of believers. The *chalis* (chalice or cup) is the *huka,* or water pipe, through which the substance is consumed.

13. A project on ethnic identity undertaken in September–October 1988 for the Smithsonian, Washington, D.C.

14. See Chevannes 1994 for a discussion of a study commissioned by the New York Police Department.

Works Cited

Austin-Broos, Diane. 1997. *Jamaica Genesis: Religion and the Politics of Moral Orders.* Chicago: University of Chicago Press.

Besson, Jean. 1995. "Religion as Resistance in Jamaican Peasant Life: The Baptist Church, Revival Worldview and Rastafari Movement." In *Rastafari and Other African-Caribbean Worldviews,* edited by Barry Chevannes. London: Macmillan.

Besson, Jean, and Barry Chevannes. 1996. "The Continuity-Creativity Debate: The Case of Revival." *New West Indian Guide* 70 (3–4): 209–28.

Brathwaite, Kamau. 1997. "Rex Nettleford and the Renaissance of Caribbean Culture." *Caribbean Quarterly* 43 (1–2): 34–69.

Brodber, Erna. 1975. "Yards in the City of Kingston." Working Paper 9. University of the West Indies (Mona)/Institute of Social and Economic Research.

Brodber, Erna. 1980. "Life in Jamaica in the Early Twentieth Century: A Presentation of Ninety Oral Accounts—Some Notes on Its Purpose and Contents." Unpublished. University of the West Indies (Mona)/Institute of Social and Economic Research.

Cassidy, Frederic, and R. B. LePage, eds. 1980. *Dictionary of Jamaican English.* 2nd ed. Cambridge: Cambridge University Press.

Chevannes, Barry. 1994. *Rastafari: Roots and Ideology.* Syracuse: Syracuse University Press.

Cox, Harvey Gallagher. 1966. *The Secular City: Secularization and Urbanization in Theological Perspective.* Rev. ed. New York: Macmillan.

Cumper, George. 1958. "The Jamaican Family: Village and Estate." *Social and Economic Studies* 7 (1): 76–108.

Davenport, William. 1961. "The Family System of Jamaica." *Social and Economic Studies* 10 (4): 420–54.

Fanon, Frantz. *Les damnés de la terre.* 1961. Paris: François Maspero.

Gayle, Herbert. 1997. "Hustling and Juggling in Jamaica." Dissertation, University of the West Indies (Mona).

Gunst, Laurie. 1995. *Born Fi' Dead: A Journey through the Jamaican Posse Underworld.* New York: Henry Holt and Company.

Haley, Alex. 1976. *Roots.* New York: Doubleday.

Hall, Douglas. 1989. *In Miserable Slavery: Thomas Thistlewood in Jamaica, 1750–1786.* London: Macmillan.

Hall, Stuart. 1997. "Caribbean Culture: Future Trends." *Caribbean Quarterly* 43 (1–2): 25–33.

Katzin, Margaret. 1959. "The Jamaican Country Higgler." *Social and Economic Studies* 8 (4): 421–35.

Marley, Bob, and the Wailers. 1974. "No Woman No Cry." *Natty Dread.* LP. Island.

Mintz, Sidney W. 1974. *Caribbean Transformations*. Baltimore: Johns Hopkins University Press.

Nettleford, Rex. 1993. *Inward Stretch, Outward Reach: A Voice from the Caribbean*. London: Macmillan.

Small, Geof. 1995. *Ruthless: The Global Rise of the Yardies*. London: Warner Books.

Smith, M. G. 1965. *The Plural Society in the British West Indies*. Kingston: Sangster's Book Stores; Berkeley: University of California Press.

Smith, R. T. 1960. *The Negro Family in British Guiana: Family Structure and Social Status in Villages*. London: Routledge and Paul.

Stone, Carl. 1980. *Democracy and Clientelism in Jamaica*. New Brunswick: Transaction Books.

Waddell, Hope Masterton. [1863] 1970. *Twenty-Nine Years in the West Indies and Central Africa: A Review of Missionary Work and Adventure, 1829–1858*. 2nd ed. London: Frank Cass.

Wedenoja, William. 1980. "Religion and Adaptation in Rural Jamaica." Dissertation, University of California.

Wilson, Peter J. 1973. *Crab Antics: The Social Anthropology of English-Speaking Negro Societies of the Caribbean*. New Haven: Yale University Press.

Witter, Michael. 1989. "The Role of Higglers/Sidewalk Vendors/Informal Commercial Traders in the Development of the Jamaican Economy." In *Higglering/Sidewalk Vending/Informal Commercial Trading in the Jamaican Economy: Proceedings of a Symposium,* edited by Michael Witter. Mona, Jamaica: University of the West Indies.

Wyatt, Gail, M. B. Tucker, D. Eldermire, B. Bain, E. LeFranc, and C. Chambers. 1995. "Female Low Income Workers and AIDS in Jamaica." Research Report Series 14, International Centre for Research on Women. Washington, D.C.

12

Identity, Personhood, and Religion in Caribbean Context

ABRAHIM H. KHAN

One of the preoccupations of contemporary Caribbean literature is to define a postcolonial vision of the future with a social philosophy for people of the Caribbean region. Discourse for that purpose frequently employs the term "identity," and more specifically the idiom "Caribbean identity." In the zeal to redefine and eulogize a vision, sometimes ordinary terms can have their meanings stretched to the point of semantic and conceptual confusion. This seems to be the case with the term "identity" in discourse and meta-discourse[1] promoting the idea of a Caribbean culture, or consciousness, or person. Even the literature[2] on socio-economic and political aspects of the region reflects confusion about Caribbean identity and its representation.

To have to propose through literature an identity, however, creates suspicion about it as an ideological invention by those frustrated in their search for lost fragments of cultural roots deemed necessary for the formation of a person. An imagined and internalized identity would offer relief from psychic despair that such frustration occasions, but at the same time it posits a difference or otherness. That difference, in an energized socio-political milieu, can become translated by popular feelings into an incentive for hegemonic power instead of an incentive for critical self-understanding, without which there is no sound economic and cultural development, no peace and security for the ethnically diverse 30 million people[3] of the Caribbean region. Though there are other possible reasons[4] for the proposal of such an identity, the one stated here is significant for the task at hand insofar as it implicitly recognizes that the connection between one's cultural identity and personhood formation is complex. The task is to inquire about conceptual coherence, the extent to which Caribbean identity and personhood conceptually cohere, and more specifically whether the concept "Caribbean identity" is an internally consistent one.

My basic contention is that the notion of Caribbean identity does not conceptually cohere with notions of personhood for culturally diverse groups[5] of people forming the socio-historical reality of the geographical region, and therefore is suspect. Furthermore, "Caribbean identity" is in itself an internally incoherent expression that appears to be intelligible in ordinary speech. Its apparent intelligibility rests on a confusion of at least two types of identity and on a misconstrual in language or a category mistake. In short, the notion is problematic, much more than might be suspected on a surface inspection. Its treatment here is intended to shed some light on its problematic aspects.

To focus sharply the contention, I pose the following simple question: Is a Caribbean identity a challenge or threat to personhood formation for the culturally and religiously diverse peoples of the region? Not easily answered, the question has at least two terms of which each has an intricate meaning complex: identity and personhood. Each of them therefore requires glossing to shed light on aspects of the meaning complex relevant to the question, and consequently to establishing plausibility for the case that an invented Caribbean identity is more a threat than a challenge.

Of the two terms, *personhood* is the more intricate one.[6] It is a cognate of the word *person* and refers to the quality of becoming a person. However, the concept of person has a meaning complex whose core has at least two aspects. One of them is designated by the Latin *persona* (person), which is a composite of *per/sonare* meaning to sound through, as in the case of a mask through (*per*) which resounds (*sonare*) the voice of the actor. There is some doubt as to whether the origin of the word is Latin, since one view is that it is of Etruscan origin *phersu* (mask), and another is that *phersu* is borrowed from the Greek *prosopon*, which means primarily mask and secondarily the role played in a drama. Either way, the institution of mask is a characteristic of each of these civilizations and suggests the notion of role (*personage*), type, or character when *persona* is used. That is, persona is understood as the image or mask superimposed on the individual. Among classical Greek and Latin moralists (for example, Cicero and Panaetius), the meaning of *persona* takes on a moral tone, a sense of being conscious, free, and responsible. From this extended sense, the step is a short one to the juridical meaning of *persona* as an individual human with both legal and moral rights. This latter meaning component has in recent years become entrenched in everyday speech as referring to the word *person*.

The other aspect of the meaning complex is designated also by *persona* and signifies the human and even divine personality (*personnalité*). The idea characterizing this aspect is that of tearing away superimposed layers. The objective is to lay bare the nature of the role-player, or to reach through to that which is one in itself (*per se una*), which is whole. That the human substance is open to the possibility of divinity is an idea that gained prominence when *persona* was used in fourth- and fifth-century theological controversies on the three "persons" in the Trinity. Boethius, a theological thinker of that period, added on the idea of rationality to the formation of an indivisible and whole substance to yield our classical definition of a person. Boethius was in fact rendering in Latin terms what is expressed in Greek by Neoplatonism. Plotinus, whose name is connected with Neoplatonism, was convinced that personality as such must have its ground in a transcendent order. He provided a metaphysical foundation for the notion of person. On that foundation, Christianity developed a philosophy of personality. It was then borrowed and altered by modern philosophy.

One of the accomplishments of modern philosophy is that it defined the concept of personality in accordance with psychological knowledge. Its reason for doing this was to preserve humanity's distinctive position in the face of tendencies to speak of a general uniform order in the world. Descartes, for example, emphasized human consciousness, Leibniz placed the true essence of human personality in self-consciousness, and Kant deepened the ethical view of personality by defining it in terms of freedom and independence from the mechanism of the whole of nature. In Fichte, the notion underwent further transformation to become the category of self (*moi*), which is already a primordial category in the Pietist tradition but becomes a central category in contemporary philosophy.

The social sciences followed the lead of modern philosophy by redefining personality in terms of observable behavior and emotional tendencies. That is, personality came to have for its reference a socially perceived individual, or the organized stimulus and response characteristics of an individual dynamically involved in social situations. Hence, the concept of personality came to imply an inference from behavior, and it is this meaning of the concept that gained ascendancy in ordinary language.[7] Such a meaning does not tally with, or is far removed from, that of personhood understood as the opening up of oneself to transcendence in order to become fully a self.

Different religious traditions, in addition to Christianity, tend to understand the person as consciously opening up to transcendence. Each tradition offers its adherents strategies—symbols, myths, and rituals—intended to form the human in conformity with a vision of becoming a person. The strategies are not a hodgepodge of practices—actions, utterances, and narratives—but in fact a shorthand representation of a metaphysics of the person or self. They presuppose that something is awry with human existence and has to be put right, or straight, for a human individual to become fully a person.

To illustrate, take Islam, whose population is significantly large in some countries[8] of the Caribbean region. Its vision is informed by the Qur'ān, or divine word addressed to humankind. On Qur'ānic accounts, humanity is a unique reality, created out of matter and God's own spirit. Sealed within the human breast is a covenant or mission, according to which humankind took upon itself to become God's representative on earth to create a moral social order. The Qur'ān describes humankind as being unjust or foolish to volunteer for such a mission and as tending to forget the responsibility it accepted. Qur'ānic report indicates further that the primordial nature of humankind is endowed with the ability to excel in knowledge and virtue with respect to the mission and to act counter to its own instinctive nature. An individual, therefore, conceivably could rebel against its creature-creator relationship, could defy its own spiritual or physiological needs, or could even choose to turn away from engaging in moral struggle. For the individual to become a person, however, would mean having to sustain the creature-creator relationship through moral struggle. Tersely put, the vision is that existential remembrance of God occasions formation of personhood.[9]

The Islamic religious tradition offers strategies for existentially remembering God. One set of strategies is the five pillars of Islam: *Shahāda* (repetition of the creed), *Ṣalāt* (daily prayers), *Zakāt* (giving alms), *Ṣawm* (fasting), and *Ḥajj* (making the pilgrimage to Mecca). Fulfilling them prevents seduction from the straight path or deters one from forgetting the relationship to the Creator. The *Sharī'a*, or Divine Law, with its injunctions is another set of strategies. Really an expansion of the five pillars, *Sharī'a* offers an ideal for human living by regulating human life to guarantee in the here and now harmonious existence, and in the hereafter felicity. The life of Prophet Muhammad provides yet more strategies. It exemplifies a human form that is perfectly oriented toward divine essence, or qualities by which one becomes attached to God: piety, combativeness, and magnanimity. They are in effect the characteristics of personhood. Through reverencing Muhammad's specialness that makes him Exemplar, or model for good conduct, a Muslim acquires moral strength to resolve the conflict between good and evil within him/her and absorbs divine blessings. In effect, Muhammad's spiritual personality is a gateway to becoming open to transcendence, a widely and readily available instrument in the formation of personhood.

In Hinduism, whose following in the Caribbean is much larger than that of Islam, the strategies are different, but the understanding of person as occasioned through realizing one's spiritual nature hardly varies. Rabindranath Tagore, artist and literary voice of modern Hinduism, articulates the vision of becoming a person in this way:

> At one pole of my being I am with stocks [sic] and stones. There I have to acknowledge the rule of universal law. That is where the foundation of my existence lies. . . . Its strength lies in its being held firm . . . in the fullness of its community with all things. But at the other pole of my being I am separate from all. There I have broken through the cordon of equality and stand alone as an individual. I am absolutely unique, I am I, I am incomparable. (1972: 69)

Tagore continues a few lines later, "So we must know that the meaning of our self is not to be found in its separateness from God and others, but in ceaseless realisation of *yoga,* of union; not on the side of the canvas where it is blank, but on the side where the picture is being painted" (79).

An aspect of Indian thought, this vision of becoming a person is informed by *śruti* and *smṛti* literature of Hinduism. It is lived out by medieval Hindu saints, recalled by Baul poets in the north of India, and passed on in the discourses of modern-day sages such as Ramana Maharishi in the south. According to that vision, the human situation is also marked by ignorance that has to be overcome. Ignorance makes an individual believe that separateness of self, as in the separateness of a material object, is precious. It is, in effect, an obstruction to the human self in its becoming a full or true self on the side of the canvas where the painting of the picture is occurring.

Strategies to remove ignorance and thus ceaselessly to realize *yoga,* or personhood, can be put in one of four categories. To one category belong Vedic sacrificial rituals performed to maintain the stability and welfare of the world. These strategies are available to a very small group of people. The devotional category has strategies appealing to a large number of Hindus. Devotion is directed to one of the manifestations of Brahman: Shiva, Vishnu, Rama, Krishna, or the Mahadevi in her different forms. It includes specific ritual performances, which range from *pūjā* to *havana* (hawan) to *kīrtana* (kirtan). A third set of strategies is available to the few whose temperament is suited for an ascetic form of life. They include ritual actions that employ mandalas, mantras, and yogic techniques, and require adepts to partake of five religious pollutants associated with Tantric Hinduism. Such strategies amount to a dramatic and radical attempt to shock one into realizing the truth about the nature of selfhood, or to break free from notions and prejudices that spawn the illusion of separateness of self. A fourth set of strategies characterizes folk Hinduism. It involves making pilgrimages to sacred sites, treating certain plants and objects as sacred, and observing certain signs, omens, and auspicious moments that are astrologically determined for life's undertaking.

It may appear that the different categories of strategies are inharmonious or impose different demands on the individual as a social being. To reconcile whatever tension their demands create, the Hindu tradition proposes a view of the human life as passing through four stages, or *āśrama*. Each stage has its set of strategies or rituals for passage of the self from one existential possibility or stage to another in its struggle to ceaselessly realize full selfhood. It is worth noting that the *āśrama* provide the basis for Erik H. Erikson's eight stages in his tracing of ego development in the human life cycle (see 1959).

Aspects of Muslim and Hindu traditions sketched here indicate that symbols are integral to the strategies that Islam and Hinduism make available. That is, symbols play an important role in the formation of personhood. However, religious symbols are strikingly distinctive in at least three ways for the purpose of this discussion. In the first place, they differ from ordinary symbols in that they represent the presence of an unconditioned transcendence in the empirical order. Their truth depends on their "inner necessity for a symbol-creating consciousness" (Tillich 1966: 29). They enable one to grasp the Unconditioned in its unconditionalness. Or, put differently, what distinguishes them from all other kinds of symbols is their power of expression and their immediacy. They speak to the soul, whether it be of the individual or of the culture. Soul, definitionally, has a relation to a transcendent source. Conversely, one might speak of a spiritualizing tendency among humankind to interpret reality symbolically. In short, symbols are considered to have a religious potentiality. Jacques Waardenberg, scholar of religion, distinguishes between those codified by the communities concerned, which are considered fixed or established, and those not yet sacralized, which are therefore free (1980: 47). Here, our concern is with those that are fixed, but not to the exclusion of those that might become fixed later.

In the second place, religious symbols have also a social dimension and function. They express values for those who are sensitive to them, and strengthen solidarities of a different kind. They might play a pedagogical role, or might help to integrate different human capacities. Though closely linked to society's life, religious symbols have their own "life," which is not the same as that of the society. As Waardenburg notes, the social dimension of symbols is less on solidarity that they bring about and more on "the kind of people they produce by the education they provide" (46).

Thirdly, a characteristic of symbols that orient one to opening up to transcendence is that they have a historicity or facticity for religious believers. In Islam, such symbols are few: Qur'ān, Muhammad as Prophet, and *Sharī'a,* employed variously in the strategies. Of the many Hindu symbols, the primary ones are the manifestations of Brahman: Shiva, Vishnu, Rama, and Krishna. The historicity of the symbols is warranted by their ties to places or events: at Mecca or Medina in Arabia, at Ayodha, Mathura, Vrindaban in India, and so on. Consequently, they can be subjectively appropriated or introjected by a believer so as to become a part of the existential life history of who that individual is. Personhood is clearly context-sensitive in that it requires the use of specific communal symbols with a historicity or facticity. Through the use of such symbols, one acquires an identity as well.

To gloss the second term, *identity,* any understanding of it is as elusive and as dynamic as the understanding of "person" or of "religious symbol." It has for its core meaning the idea of sameness, at least in generic characteristics, and is generally linked to the idea of consciousness or self-awareness. In his psychosocial studies, Erikson makes the term speak for itself, examining it from different angles. As he notes, it "connotes both a persistent sameness within oneself (selfsameness) and a persistent sharing of some kind of essential character with others" (1959: 102).

For the purpose of this study, a distinction[10] between two types of identity has to be observed. One type is the *fact* of identity and relates to a group situation. To speak of this type of identity relative to a group is to have in mind features that are shared by its members or marks by which a member is recognized as belonging to the group in question. In this usage designated here as fact of identity, bodily considerations play a role: how one behaves, carries oneself, or tends to select from among the many. The emphasis is clearly on objective attributes and behavior, by which one is recognized as belonging to a community, as sharing its ideals and values (which are indicative also of a historical continuity) and which are different from behavior and declaration of personal goals that are either fashionable, quotidian, or idiosyncratic.

In contrast, one might speak of a sense of identity, the second type. Its emphasis is on the *how,* that is, how one sees the world from a particular position and relative to what aspects, or how one experiences selfhood. Quite clearly, this second type of identity involves subjective and psychological matters such as memory, consciousness, a range of emotions, and so on. In sense of identity, bodily considerations may play a role, but the emphasis is on the acquisition or becoming of a *self* out of a *me.* Though the two types of identity or usages are distinct, it might be claimed that an individual develops sense of identity (second type) through social practices, and that social practices are tied to the fact of identity (first type). However, sense of identity depends largely on an inner psychological reordering, an experiential transcendence or oneness that underscores the quality of awareness of the social practices in which one is engaged. It is symbols of transcendence, embedded in certain social practices, that unify the psyche and occasion the quality of awareness correlating with sense of identity.[11] The relation between sense and practice that obtains for religious symbols might be understood on the analogy of the relation that obtains for self-worth. That is, self-worth, or how one feels about oneself, depends more on ego-strengths and their unity than on mere participation in or exclusion from social practices.

To speak about acquiring identity through symbols of religious traditions is to refer to both types of identity. To talk, however, about Caribbean identity, or any national cultural identity for that matter, is to refer to fact identity (first type) and not necessarily sense identity (second type). As the contemporary discourse indicates, the fact of identity implies approval and endorsement of a historical and ethnic experience at the center, from which flows social and political power; furthermore, the endorsement does not accommodate at the center the experiences of diverse cultural groups or ones with different symbols, as mentioned earlier. More specifically, it sees as the claimant for the center the experience of a single "numerical majority"[12] described by observable attributes: musical and dance forms, Creole languages. It does not consider the subjective factor or the sense of identity relative to actualizing personhood according to groups with different religious symbols. In short, there is no evidence that the espoused Caribbean identity correlates with specific symbols reflective of a metaphysics of self or related to becoming a person.

Further, in the idiom "Caribbean identity," the referent for the designator "Caribbean" is ordinarily ambiguous. We find at least three separate conceptions[13] of the Caribbean: (1) the English-speaking Caribbean; (2) the Caribbean archipelago and mainland extensions in South America and Central America; and (3) the Caribbean basin—a geopolitical concept that spans countries in the archipelago and littoral nations of Central and South America. The discourse promoting Caribbean identity, however, implies as its intended referent the English-speaking Caribbean primarily. By this intention, talk of Caribbean identity becomes problematic in a threefold way: (a) it precludes linguistically and culturally diverse peoples from sharing the center stage of the socio-political life it envisions for the Caribbean; (b) it implies a totality constituted by a single numerical majority of the region and in the direction of one cultural group as a diaspora people; and (c) it marginalizes even those from the creole color-class stratification that do not share in the experience of colonial oppression. Clearly, the Caribbean identity espoused by the literature is an invented or highly fictive one. To a large extent, cultural and personal self-representations are fictive.[14] However, this invented or highly fictive identity is unrepresentative of the multifaceted Caribbean ethos, and culturally marginalizes those who do not share in the power to generate the knowledge and requisite material productions necessary to energize or revitalize their cultural lives.

The two key terms clarified, we might now better perceive how the imagined and eulogized Caribbean identity is a threat to personhood. Simply put, it presumes a cultural center that is definable by the experience of the single numerical majority and occupiable through a hegemonic move.[15] Such a move is, in effect, a threat to culturally diverse peoples whose sense of identity involves symbols that are different from those whose class interests are to dominate and to become an emblem for the region. Hindus and Muslims in the Caribbean form two large groups that are culturally diverse, even though to outsiders the two may seem to be ethnically homogenous—similar aesthetic tastes, consumer habits, historical origins, and diasporic experiences. In fact, each as a socio-religious community is sensitive to a different set of symbols that indicate historical continuity, that determine the values it wishes to transmit from one generation to the next, and thus, that define for its members their sense of identity communally and individually. To foist on them an imagined identity, or one proffered as shaped in the crucible of experience of one ethno-cultural group, amounts to cultural hegemony, even against those whose identity and self-identification[16] are shaped by Afro-Christian or Afro-Islamic spirituality.

Not race, but cultural hegemony is the problematic factor that is implicit in the imperative of the eulogized Caribbean identity. It affects not just Muslim and Hindu communities, but also the Christian community with its missionary zeal. This latter community, another source of input to the region's cultural texture, expresses its ideals in the form of western or European values and social practices. Though it counts among its adherents a large percentage with African ancestry, its religious outlook no more provides, it seems, a framework for the desired Caribbean identity than does Islam or Hinduism. Its outlook too will have to give way in the contrived geopolitical cultural identity formation to an outlook that is reflective of "the people from below" and proffered by Rastafarianism (Nettleford 1993: 125–26, 168).[17] Christianity as a form of socio-cultural interaction is therefore subject to displacement even though it defines itself differently. It draws on a different network of symbols related to making human life bearable and has a different cultural matrix and history from the traditions of Islam and Hinduism in the Caribbean. Though constitutive of Caribbean ethos, these three religions represent diverse cultural worlds.

Cultural worlds are popularly depicted by consumer habits and preferential tastes: ethnic food, music, pictures, and ancestral costumes. These represent, however, only the material aspect of the foundation from which such worlds are constructed. Integral to their foundation is a psycho-social aspect[18] as well. A more adequate depiction, one that spans both aspects, is rendered in terms of religion, language, and customs. These three are developed to express natural impulses in a way that would maximize adaptation to the environment, materially and socially, for a satisfying life. They provide a framework for orienting behavior, thought, and feelings, or for resisting disorder. But the framework has to be appropriated subjectively, internalized by individuals, such that they become more self-conscious and reflective about how they live and think. In this way, individuals begin to acquire the sense of identity. Put differently, the sense of identity involves meanings, expectations, and understanding in which they find themselves or form their personhood. The subjective appropriation by which personhood is formed occurs at the inward level of one's being and correlates with employment of symbols in the sphere of religion.

By religion, the intended reference here is less to institutional forms, local rites, and images or artifacts made hallow through supposedly divine sanction. As a form of praxis, religion runs the risk of harboring idolatry, of accumulating cultural accretions that are extraneous to the opening up of oneself to transcendence or that are deleterious to the fabric of society. Accretions can reach a level at which reform within a religious tradition has to be undertaken. Reformers are in general adherents with ability to make judgments about the relationships of practices to larger aggregates of practices that characterize a religious tradition. Illustrations of this happening are the Wahabbi movement and the reconstructions of Muhammad Iqbal in Islam, the Brahmo Samaj and Arya Samaj movements in Hinduism, and Protestantism in European Christianity.

The proper reference to religion, therefore, is less to cultural forms and more to symbols. Specifically, it is to symbols of transcendence codified by traditions of a religious community and correlated with rituals and explanatory myths. In fact, each religion presents a view of the satisfying human life in the form of an algebra of symbols, rituals, and myths as received commentaries. The algebra is characterized further by a specific personalistic note or subjectivity. Tagore strikes that note in the following remark: "Gladness is the one criterion of truth, and we know when we have touched truth by the music it gives, by the joy of greeting it sends forth to the truth in us. This is the true foundation of all religions" (1966: 107). Itself a custom or practice, the algebra of symbols to a greater extent than history becomes important for peoples that lack a common state or constitution.

Caribbean peoples clearly constitute such an example. The Caribbean is not a single nation-state. At best, it is a cluster of nation-states that have culturally diverse groups of people. To take Caribbean identity as privileging the historical experience of a single numerical majority as a national cultural status, or even as a badge of where one originally hails from, is selectively to appropriate the inheritance of one ethnic group and thereby to exclude that of groups integral to the region's cultural matrix. Excluding other groups is part of a tradition of pigmentocracy[19] that belongs to Caribbean history and that appears even among the immigrant population from the Caribbean in Canada. According to a recent ethnographic study, "Caribbean diasporic identities in Toronto have become increasingly politicized around issues related to black representations . . . in the media, in school curricula. . . . These new identities also attempt to universalize blackness" (Yon 1995: 492). Whether in Toronto or the Caribbean, this privileging or selectivity is a form of politicizing that strikes at the heart of personhood formation. It amounts to a concocting of algebra that is unrepresentative of regional cultural diversity, and that is one step removed from the claim of right to rule in some nation-states.

Any proposal for a Caribbean identity would have to accommodate as much as possible the experiences of all who make up the cultural *chiaroscuro*—from the Aboriginal peoples to the latecomers[20] of the Caribbean region. This would not lessen the difficulty implicit in constructing such an identity,[21] since the taxing question for each cultural group would then be, if it is not already the case, which patches of experiences, symbols, and practices are most representative of who they are, or how they have become who they are. Such a question has, however, the merit of challenging some religio-cultural practices presumed to be strategies when in fact they burden or stifle the formation of personhood. The challenge, in effect, calls for a critical reexamination of communal judgments regarding the appropriate contextual use of certain symbols and strategies (when to use/do what, publicly or communally). It might even force a rethinking of the idea of identity as an explanatory cultural category in delimiting those who populate the Caribbean region. Not all the peoples share the lived experience shaped by a blue sea with corals and shipwrecks, or by mountains, valleys, and hurricane seasons. Geography, land mass, and environmental conditions can also have an impact on vision of life, dispositions, and traits—on the fact of identity. Furthermore, methodical and self-conscious choices, as shown by a comparative case study of Chinese communities in Jamaica and Guyana (Patterson 1977: 492), do not make any easier the challenge of constructing a single identity that spans all the peoples of the region.

Finally, a misleading analogy or category mistake creates an impression that the idiom "Caribbean identity" is conceptually meaningful. Considered as a linguistic form, "Caribbean identity" is by itself conceptually unclear and lacking conventional use. To see that this is in fact so, the temptation has to be resisted to treat it on the model of idioms that have concrete referents or count nouns: Caribbean islands, Caribbean leaders, or Caribbean products. The reason is that as an abstract noun, *identity* is a category of quality or whatness to which no spatial or regional position is ordinarily assigned. When modified by *Caribbean*, it yields a form of idiom that appears to belong to the same logical type as those either with count nouns just mentioned or with certain abstract nouns found in idioms such as "American citizenship," "British nationality," and "Canadian experience." The logical behavior of each of the three—citizenship, nationality, experience—in the forms just mentioned is circumscribed by indisputably clear or concrete ideas related to public policy development and practices, especially to making forecasts and determining trends.

In the case of "Caribbean identity," its logical behavior based on its use is very different. As this essay indicates, its use in recent literary discourse is choreographed to introduce a cluster of ideas related to neutralizing African denigration. Central to the cluster is the idea of privileging the socio-historical experience of one ethnic group and, by implication, marginalizing the experience of the others in the Caribbean. The choreographing canvasses the experience of that group as the cultural emblem of the Caribbean region. Thus, the use of the idiom is largely stipulative: to facilitate ethno-cultural domination. That usage notwithstanding, "Caribbean identity" remains internally incoherent, is linguistic nonsense in the guise of sense. It opens in the mind no new possibility for self-renewal or human dignity, perhaps because the term *Caribbean* is a positional reference to a particular land mass[22] that has people of many cultures, and not a reference to nationality, ethnicity, or culture.

In summary, the Caribbean identity espoused by this literature is problematic on five counts:

1. It correlates with no network of symbols to raise questions about meaning of life and to provide answers. It is not an algebra for a satisfying human life.

2. It does not accommodate various strategies for the formation of personhood associated with different religious communities and understood as the opening up of oneself to transcendence. In that respect, it is a threat to the formation of personhood, religiously understood.

3. It refers primarily to an experience forged in the crucible of selective memories of a single numerical majority in the region. It therefore implicitly nationalizes the experience of one cultural group and consequently marginalizes the historicity or experience of other cultural groups that share the same geographical space. Put differently, it assumes that the cultural *chiaroscuro* of the Caribbean has a hegemonic center that rightfully belongs to a particular ethnic group.

4. It is more likely to be a source of conflict than a source of inspiration to rethink judgments about appropriate contextual use of symbols and strategies in relation to identity and personhood formation.

5. Its apparent meaning rests on a category mistake, which, once exposed, makes the purported idea of Caribbean identity an internally incoherent one.

Notes

This is an augmented version of earlier publications by the same title in The David Rockefeller Center for Latin American Studies, *Working Papers on Latin America*, Paper 96, 1997–98, and in *'Ilu Revista de ciencias de las religiones* 2 (1997): 49–62.

1. For such discourses, see Nettleford 1993: 10, 57, 61, 65, 119, 123, 125, 126, *passim*. His book is a collection of essays presented on different occasions over the last dozen years. Other relevant materials include Premdas 1995; Zavala 1994; Thomas-Hope 1984; Clarke 1984; Worcester 1992: 119; and Toumson 1986.

2. See, for example, Bryan, Green and Shaw 1990; Bilby 1985; Boxhill 1993; and Demas 1974.

3. Estimate by Franklin W. Knight and Colin A. Palmer (1989: 3). They note that the estimate is slightly more than the population of the seven Central American states and give also a population profile and information on the social and cultural characteristics of the

region. Of course, how the region is defined depends on the purpose to be served. Knight and Palmer (3–4, 16–19) indicate some of the different ways, and at a later stage in this paper I address the definition of the Caribbean region. For a recent overview, see James 1997: 19–22.

4. Three reasons, at the least, are offered by Eric Hobsbawm (1983: 1–14).

5. For example: Mulattos, Mestizos, Europeans, Indians, Africans, Chinese, Aboriginal peoples, and recent arrivals. See also notes 3 above and 21 below.

6. Kenneth L. Schmitz gives a solid account of its network of meanings, especially the ambivalence between the hidden depth that the term implies and that exhibited by the term *personality*. See Schmitz 1967, 1986.

7. In cultures outside the West, *personality* as understood from a linguistic point of view does not exist, or exists in such a radically different way that it is senseless to claim any meaningful comparison. See the discussion in Erchak 1992: 8ff. Erchak notes in social sciences overlapping and competing definitions of *personality* and *self* and a shift in the use of *personality*. Generally, it now comes to refer to "a more 'inner' theoretical concept, inaccessible to direct observation, whereas the 'self' is conceptualized as something 'presented' to the community at large and thus accessible . . . through behavior observations, autobiographical accounts and so on," and psycho-cultural studies are now replacing it with *self* or talk of egocentric and socio-centric selves (9, 11).

8. Muslims in the Caribbean are primarily of Indian background, especially in Guyana, Trinidad, and Suriname, whose population consists of 45–51 percent East Indians. In Jamaica, Bermuda, and Martinique, they are roughly 5 percent of the population. However, in Cuba and other islands or territories of the region, we find that Muslims come also from the Middle East. For 1990 figures on ethnic and religious groups, see *Caribbean 1993: Basin Databook*. See also note 21 below.

9. For a fuller treatment, see my "Idea of Person with Reference to Islam" (Khan 1990).

10. This distinction is borrowed from Harré 1984: 203ff.

11. This position intimates insights by Erikson or by Robert Jay Lifton (1976: 145).

12. Nettleford claims that the African descendants are a unifying cultural influence Caribbean-wide and constitute a "numerical majority" (1993: 179, cf. xii, 128). That formulation of African descendants as a numerical majority, along with expressions such as "East Indian variable" and "struggle of the African presence," suggests that his is a discourse of race or ethnicity. For forms of observable attributes (language, dance, and music), see also 84–88. The tone of Nettleford connects him to the Black Arts Movement in America (1965–1973), which, as Skip Gates notes in one of his lectures on Afro-American literary tradition, is informed by the ideas of Janheinz Jahn. The idea of Nommo, according to Jahn, is at the heart of Black aesthetics, informing the work of neo-African poets such as Aimé Césaire, Senghor, Ortiz, and others who are politicians and exercise official function. See ch. 5 of Jahn 1961 and note 20 below.

13. See Demas 1979: vii; Pons 1979. Definitions of the region with its nearly 30 million inhabitants are taken up by Knight and Palmer (1989: 3, 19). They indicate that the most conventional definition refers to the islands spanning Bahamas to Trinidad and includes Belize, Guyana, Surinam, and French Guiana.

14. Owen Flanagan points out, as does Daniel Dennett, that the self is a useful fiction, meaning that it is different from a fictional self in that it is more answerable to facts, it plays a causal role in one's overall psychological economy or in the organizing and giving of "meaning to a life that will last on average three quarters of a century" (1992: 204, 207). An invented identity would be different from a fictive one in that it is self-representation

(for one's eyes) that does not have actual identity as its cognitive object, that is a far-fetched and deeply fictional account of the self, or that is hardly connected to actual identity. Flanagan, distinguishing between actual and self-represented identities, takes a middle position between realism and non-realism to insist on the legitimacy of these two identities that are interactive (195–96, 210). By an invented identity, then, I mean one in which the interaction is very minimal, incorrect, and massively deceptive.

15. Nettleford hints at Rastafarians and their philosophy as providing the ontological underpinnings for the artistic manifestations of such an identity (1993: 125). In contrast, the lyrics of the Trinidadian prize-winning calypso "Caribbean Man" are blunt to the point that it created controversy, a three-month public debate involving six of the seven national newspapers and prominent community leaders and columnists from Trinidad's major ethnic groups, in February 1979. Its singer, appearing in a television interview the following month, confirmed that the "Caribbean Man" was of African decent, "that Africans here were the ones who developed the Caribbean, and that they were the only ones concerned with Caribbean unity" (quoted in Deosaran 1987: 87).

16. The distinction between *identity* and *self-identification* was drawn to my attention by Frank Cunningham, a philosophy colleague, in an informal discussion about identity sparked by a printed version of this paper. I think that his *self-identification* approximates the *fact* of identity according to Harré's distinction or *self-represented identity* according to Flanagan. However, Cunningham does distinguish further between self-identification and quotidian identity or behavior by which individuals might be recognized as belonging to a specific group or collectivity.

17. See also note 15 above.

18. Erchak speaks of culture as having a tripartite foundation: material, mental, and social. I have collapsed the latter two into one for brevity: psycho-social. See Erchak 1992: 3ff.

19. In the latter part of the nineteenth century there emerged a group of Afro–West Indian intellectuals. According to Roberto Marquez, they saw themselves as representing the legitimate national majority, which they identified with the creole descendants of slaves, in the "struggle to advance their own alternatives in the assumption of white supremacy" (1989: 304). The sensitivity to pigmentation became one of the thematic foci of *négritude* for post-war Caribbean writers, among whom are C. L. R. James and Austin Clarke. It emerged as a leitmotif also for those Hispanic and Francophone writers of the region engaged in undermining a Eurocentric cultural perspective. See also note 13 above.

20. Some groups arrived as neither colonial adventurers or outcasts, nor slaves, nor indentured workers. Arabs, for example, constitute one such group. Their arrival, which began in the 1860s, became a major flow thirty years later. They are predominantly in countries such as Jamaica, Dominican Republic, and Haiti, making significant contributions to the economic, social, and political life of the Caribbean region. See Nicholls 1985. Jamaica Kincaid (1988: 62, 63) provides a perception of Syrians and Lebanese as "other" in Antigua.

21. This is not the same as a trans-Caribbean identity, which Ralph Premdas sees as "the highest form of nationalist fantasy" in his typology of Caribbean identities. As he notes, a trans-Caribbean identity does not exist in reality (1995: 79–80). An identity that incorporates patches of all different cultural experiences might also not exist, but constructing one might be a heuristic exercise for culturally diverse groups occupying the region.

22. The Caribbean as a land mass characterizes a clear spatial pattern and hence is a place concept. But spatial concepts, as J. Nicholas Entrikin indicates, can have a semantic

depth with respect to personal or group identity, that is, to understanding that humans are linked to specific cultural communities as moral agents. Stated differently: for a humanistic geographer, "seemingly concrete concepts have as their primary referent a set of abstract ideals" (1991: 9, 56). Consequently, it is quite conceivable that *Caribbean* as a spatial term has for inhabitants of that space referent primarily abstract ideals. But what is at stake here is whether the ideals are those to which Kwame Anthony Appiah (1992: 178) intimates: ones tied to advancing economic, political, and social goals that are in consonance with promoting plenitude of the human self. Such ideals, as this chapter contends, are not the ones associated with discourse that includes in its idiom "Caribbean identity/self."

Works Cited

Appiah, Kwame Anthony. 1992. *In My Father's House.* New York: Oxford University Press.

Bilby, Kenneth M. 1985. "The Caribbean as a Musical Region." In *Caribbean Contours,* edited by Sidney W. Mintz and Sally Price. Baltimore: Johns Hopkins University Press.

Boxhill, Ian. 1993. *Ideology and Caribbean Integration.* Mona, Jamaica: University of the West Indies.

Bryan, Anthony T., J. Edward Green, and Timothy M. Shaw, eds. 1990. *Peace, Development and Security in the Caribbean.* London: Macmillan.

Caribbean 1993: Basin Databook. 1993. Washington, D.C.: Caribbean/Latin American Action.

Clarke, Colin G. 1984. "Caribbean Consciousness." In *Perspectives on Caribbean Regional Identity,* edited by Elizabeth M. Thomas-Hope. Liverpool: University of Liverpool.

Demas, W. 1974. *West Indian Nationhood and Caribbean Integration.* Bridgetown, Barbados: CCC Publishing House.

Demas, W. 1979. "Forward." In *The Restless Caribbean,* edited by Richard Millet and W. Marvin Will. New York: Praeger.

Deosaran, Ramesh. 1987. "The 'Caribbean Man': A Study of the Psychology of Perception and the Media." In *India in the Caribbean,* edited by David Dabydeen and Brinsley Samaroo. London: Hansib.

Entrikin, J. Nicholas. 1991. *The Betweenness of Place.* Baltimore: Johns Hopkins University Press.

Erchak, Gerald M. 1992. *The Anthropology of Self and Behavior.* New Brunswick: Rutgers University Press.

Erikson, Erik H. 1959. *Identity and the Life Cycle.* Psychological Issues 1.1. New York: International Universities Press.

Flanagan, Owen. 1992. *Consciousness Reconsidered.* Cambridge, Mass.: MIT Press.

Harré, Rom. 1984. *Personal Being.* Cambridge, Mass.: Harvard University Press.

Hobsbawm, Eric. 1983. "Introduction: Inventing Traditions." In *The Invention of Tradition,* edited by Eric Hobsbawm and Terence Ranger. Cambridge: Cambridge University Press.

Jahn, Janheinz. 1961. *Muntu: An Outline of the New-African Culture.* Translated by Marjorie Grene. New York: Grove Press.

James, Canute. 1997. "The Caribbean: An Overview." *South America, Central America and the Caribbean.* 6th ed. London: Europa Publications.

Khan, Abrahim H. 1990. "Idea of Person with Reference to Islam." *Hamdard Islamicus* 13 (4): 17–29.

Kincaid, Jamaica. 1988. *A Small Place.* New York: Penguin.

Knight, Franklin W., and Colin A. Palmer. 1989. "The Caribbean: A Regional Overview." In *The Modern Caribbean,* edited by Franklin W. Knight and Colin A. Palmer. Chapel Hill: University of North Carolina Press.

Lifton, Robert Jay. 1976. *The Life of the Self.* New York: Simon and Schuster.

Marquez, Roberto. 1989. "Emergence of a Caribbean Literature." In *The Modern Caribbean,* edited by Franklin W. Knight and Colin A. Palmer. Chapel Hill: University of North Carolina Press.

Nettleford, Rex. 1993. *Inward Stretch, Outward Reach: A Voice from the Caribbean.* London: Macmillan.

Nicholls, David. 1985. *Arabs in the Greater Antilles.* Vol. 2 of *Caribbean Societies,* edited by Christopher Abel and Michael Twaddle. London: Institute of Commonwealth Studies/ University of London. 2 vols.

Patterson, Orlando. 1977. *Ethnic Chauvinism: The Reactionary Impulse.* New York: Stein and Day Publishers.

Pons, Frank Moya. 1979. "Is There a Caribbean Consciousness?" *Américas* 31 (8): 33–36.

Premdas, Ralph. 1995. *Ethnic Identity in the Caribbean: Decentering a Myth.* Lectures and Papers in Ethnicity Series 17. Toronto: University of Toronto.

Schmitz, Kenneth L. 1967. "Persons." In *The Encyclopedia of Philosophy.* New York: Macmillan.

Schmitz, Kenneth L. 1986. "The Geography of the Human Person." *Communio* 13 (Spring): 27–48.

Tagore, Rabindranath. 1966. *The Religion of Man.* Boston: Beacon Press.

Tagore, Rabindranath. 1972. *Sadhana: The Realization of Life.* Tucson: Omen Communications.

Thomas-Hope, Elizabeth M. 1984. "Caribbean Identity: A Matter of Perception." In *Perspectives on Caribbean Regional Identity,* edited by Elizabeth M. Thomas-Hope. Liverpool: University of Liverpool.

Tillich, Paul. 1966. "The Religious Symbol." In *Myth and Symbol,* edited by F. W. Dillistone. London: SPCK.

Toumson, Roger. 1986. "The Question of Identity in Caribbean Literature." *Journal of Caribbean Studies* 5 (3): 131–42.

Waardenberg, Jacques. 1980. "Symbolic Aspects of Myth." In *Myth, Symbol and Reality,* edited by Alan M. Olsen. Notre Dame: University of Notre Dame Press.

Worcester, Kent. 1992. "A Victorian with the Rebel Seed: C. L. R. James and the Politics of Intellectual Engagement." Vol. 1 of *Intellectuals in the Twentieth-Century Caribbean,* edited by Alistair Hennessy. London: Macmillan. 2 vols.

Yon, Daniel. 1995. "Identity and Differences in the Caribbean Diaspora: Case Study from Metropolitan Toronto." In *The Reordering of Culture,* edited by Alvina Ruprecht and Cecilia Taiana. Ottawa: Carleton University Press.

Zavala, Iris M. 1994. "A Caribbean Social Imagery; Redoubled Notes on Critical-Fiction against the Gaze of Ulysses." In *Latin American Identity and Constructions of Difference,* edited by Amaryll Chanady. Minneapolis: University of Minnesota Press.

13

Sanfancón

Orientalism, Self-Orientalization, and "Chinese Religion" in Cuba

FRANK F. SCHERER

Ellos dicen, a segun yo tengo entendido, que cuando ellos mueren, van directamente a China.

(They say, as far as I have understood, that when they die, they go directly to China.)

—Comment made in 1995 by a gravedigger of La Habana's Chinese cemetery

CHINESE DREAMS

Chinese dreams are being dreamt in the island of Cuba. There are, on the one hand, those dreams indulged in by a Cuban political elite that is willing to introduce economic change without allowing for social and political change. These efforts in trying to keep a traditional power base intact are reminiscent of Deng Xiaoping's precedent[1] and should be understood, additionally, in the context of the particular significance that the People's Republic of China holds—after the demise of the Soviet-Cuban alliance in 1991—for the only socialist state in the Western hemisphere. On the other hand, and intimately linked to the above, there is the announced "revitalization" of Cuba's Chinese community (Grupo Promotor 1995; Strubbe 1995), a project that includes not only the restoration of La Habana's Chinatown for tourist consumption, but, simultaneously, a not so subtle and rather unexpected return to notions of difference conceived in ethnic and cultural terms.

It is my contention that the recent revival of "Chinese" ethnicity in Cuba is based both on a number of Euro-American Orientalist assumptions of a distinctive and essential Chineseness, and on the "Oriental" use of Orientalist discourse, which perfectly illustrates the "indigenous" employment of what I call *strategic* Orientalism. While the former is being promoted, somewhat ambiguously, by the Cuban state and its intelligentsia, the latter is articulated by first- and second-generation Chinese Cubans. In this way, the very process of reintegrating, re-creating, and re-ethnicizing the Chinese Cuban "community" is marked by the peculiar practice of self-Orientalization (Ong 1993; 1997; Dirlik 1996). This complex discursive practice, complete with Confucian ideas and certain capitalist aspirations, facilitates the articulation of difference conceived in ethnic and cultural terms by first- and second-generation Chinese Cubans and allows—at least in Cuba—for the opening of alternative spaces, where the construction of identities other than those prescribed by the Cuban state can take place.

Furthermore, the phenomenon of self-Orientalization feeds, apparently, not only into familiar Euro-American Orientalist discursive formations, but also on the revival of "Chinese religion" in Cuba, and with it, on the recent remobilization of the Chinese-Cuban "saint" Sanfancón. In all, the overt reappearance of Orientalism, self-Orientalization, and "Chinese religion" in Cuba remain inextricably linked to the profound ideological, political, economic, social, and cultural transformations that the island is currently undergoing.

I shall begin with some reflections on a body of critical literature concerned with Edward Said's *Orientalism,* an influential study, which, though pointing to essentializations based on a fundamental distinction between "East" and "West," has itself largely ignored the responses and challenges of the peoples involved. The sharp criticism brought forth by Marxist scholars (for example, Aijaz Ahmad) will be interrogated and juxtaposed to those criticisms of Said's *Orientalism* that themselves come from "de-centered" and postcolonial perspectives, such as that of James Clifford. But, more importantly, I want to show how Sadik Jallal El-Azm, Aihwa Ong, and Xiaomei Chen were able to reach beyond Said's paradigmatic contribution, trying to expand the concept of Orientalism into a dialectical one so as to incorporate the part that "Orientals" may actually have in its making.

Thereafter, I want to discuss forms of modern Orientalism as expressed by the Cuban intelligentsia as well as by members of the Chinese Cuban community. I shall approach these discursive practices from three different angles: firstly, by exploring the history of Cuban Orientalism as well as the concurrent impact of Euro-American Orientalist discourse as promoted by Cuban officials, journalists, writers, and others; secondly, by examining the peculiar practice of self-Orientalization, and in the Cuban context, the links, imagined or real, that exist with the icon Confucius; and thirdly, by analyzing the contemporary presence and significance of "Chinese religion" in Cuba, and in particular the recent resuscitation of the Chinese Cuban "saint" Sanfancón.

HYBRID STRATEGIES

Edward Said's *Orientalism* (1979) stands out as a seminal work that, though confronted with harsh criticism, has nonetheless managed to maintain much of its paradigmatic stance. While we can recognize the significance of its political and academic positioning, the book has not succeeded in overcoming an array of logical, ontological, epistemological, and methodological shortcomings. Yet, *Orientalism* is forbidding and enabling at the same time: forbidding for the monolithic "Occidentalism" that emerges in its pages, and enabling for the critical potential that this text has unearthed. This enablement is one of the reasons why it was, and still is, so enthusiastically received by many scholars in the social sciences and humanities.

At the same time, the popular and academic usage that is sometimes made of Said's *Orientalism* appears to be uncritical and little aware of a number of contradictions that undermine the force of this founding contribution to the development of postcolonial theory. While Said's rather flexible theoretical positionings may be confounding to some, to others it is precisely this double-sidedness that constitutes the strength of Said's rethinking the concept and practice of Orientalism. However, what is at issue here is not Said's unfortunate failure to do away with essentialisms of the Occidental/Oriental kinds, but rather his reinforcement of those categories by entrenching them further into his own text and, most significantly, his complete oblivion and unreflexive erasure of those concerned, the "Orientals."

A closer look at *Orientalism* will help to explain why the contradictions, the double-sidedness, of this work are of so much importance. Hence, it is within the very first pages that Said offers three definitions of Orientalism:

[1. Orientalism is] a way of coming to terms with the Orient that is based on the Orient's special place in European Western experience. The Orient is not only adjacent to Europe; it is also the place of Europe's greatest and richest and oldest colonies, the source of its civilizations and languages, its cultural contestant, and one of its deepest and most recurring images of the Other. . . . The Orient is an integral part of European material civilization and culture. Orientalism expresses and represents that part culturally and even ideologically as a mode of discourse with supporting institutions, vocabulary, imagery, doctrines, even colonial bureaucracies and colonial style. . . .

[2.] Orientalism is a style of thought based upon an ontological and epistemological distinction made between "the Orient" and (most of the time) "the Occident." . . .

[3.] Taking the late eighteenth century as a very roughly defined starting point Orientalism can be discussed and analyzed as the corporate institution for dealing with the Orient—dealing with it by making statements about it, authorizing views of it, describing it, by teaching it, by settling it, ruling over it: in short, Orientalism as a Western style for dominating, restructuring, and having authority over the Orient. (1979: 1–3)

As indicated by Ahmad, we are facing here not just pressing ontological and epistemological problems, but an important issue of periodization. If there is an *uninterrupted* discursive history—as Said, notwithstanding his own arguments, claims on the same pages—that can be traced from Aeschylus to Dante to Marx to Lewis, then the post-Enlightenment eighteenth century can hardly figure as that "roughly defined starting point" of Orientalist discourse (see Ahmad 1994: 179–81). Another crucial issue is the relationship that exists between Orientalism and colonialism. Prioritizing textuality, Said argues that Orientalism "produced" (1979: 3) the Orient, which is to say that colonialism is a product of Orientalism itself. Ahmad opposes such views by pointing to the fact that this "narrative of convergence between colonial knowledges and colonial powers simply cannot be assembled within cultural studies itself, because histories of economic exploitation, political coercion, military conquest play the far more constitutive part; those other histories are the ones which provide the enabling conditions for the so-called 'Orientalist Discourse' as such" (1994: 164). In addition, there is Said's complete neglect, and thus the erasure, of the subaltern voice. As Ahmad states:

> A notable feature of *Orientalism* is that it examines the history of Western textualities about the non-West quite in isolation from how these textualities might have been received, accepted, modified, challenged, overthrown, or reproduced by the intelligentsias of the colonized countries; not as an undifferentiated mass but as situated social agents impelled by our own conflicts, contradictions, distinct social and political locations, of class, gender, region, religious affiliation, and so on. . . . (1994: 172)

The major theoretical as well as methodological influences apparent in Said's work are twofold, with the result that a typical quality of *Orientalism* is its "hybrid strategy." On the one hand there are Said's "humanist" claims, while on the other there is his introduction and use of Foucauldian discourse analysis, later taken up by cultural studies, postcolonial theory, and anthropology. Emerging from a formational background in comparative European literatures, Said seems to be inspired especially by German comparativists such as Auerbach, Curtius, and Spitzer, who had been busy in creating an aura of "High Humanism" around their academic endeavors (Ahmad 1994: 162). This humanist stance re-emerges in Said's *Orientalism* in the form of a totalized European history that traces its beginnings, and its "Orientalisms," all the way back to Greek classics. (This idea has been countered in sharply critical ways by many contemporary postcolonial theorists, including Bhabha [1994] and members of the Subaltern Studies Group [Prakash 1990; Spivak 1996].) How can Said reconcile conceptualizations of "High Humanism" with ideas of "anti-humanism," so rigorously observed in Foucault's work? Confirming this problem, Clifford makes an effort to reach beyond Said's ambiguous *lacunae*. He points out that "Said's humanist perspectives do not harmonize with his use of methods derived from Foucault, who is of course a radical critic of humanism. But however wary and inconsistent its appeals, *Orientalism* is a pioneering attempt to use Foucault systematically in an extended cultural analysis" (1988: 264). Said's text is hybrid as he depends for his strategy on a flexible positionality, continuously vacillating between humanist and anti-humanist paradigms.

ORIENTALISM AND BEYOND

We have, then, not only theoretical and methodological contradictions accompanied by hybrid strategies, but also an incisive obliteration, that is, the silence around those involved—"the Orientals"—which has confronted Said's *Orientalism* with the devastating charge of "Occidentalism." Said essentializes Europe and the West, the "Occident," as a self-identical, fixed being that has always had an essence and a project, an imagination and a will, and the "Orient" as no more than its silenced object. Accordingly, "Said's discourse analysis does not itself escape the all-inclusive 'Occidentalism' he specifically rejects as an alternative to Orientalism" (Clifford 1988: 271).

It is, in my view, this (reversed) charge of "Occidentalism" that has motivated other writers to look for ways to go beyond *Orientalism* and to find alternatives that may help to conceptualize, in the place of silence and neglect, a dialectic that would include those involved. Even Said himself, after revisiting *Orientalism,* felt prompted to think about "Resistance Culture" (1994: 209–20). But how is one to think of Orientalism as an expandable concept, one that takes into account the ways in which Orientalism is received, accepted, modified, rejected, or otherwise challenged by the subaltern? Moreover, how does one conceptualize a critique of Orientalism that includes the subaltern voice, and that can thus conceive of an Orientalism in terms of difference and differentiation? To reach beyond *Orientalism* means, then, to employ this critical tool in strategic ways while tapping its *enabling* potential, that is, the acknowledgment of a plurality of Orientalisms as well as the examination of Orientalist dialectics. In fact, a number of authors have made efforts toward a differentiation of Orientalism(s), not just in the sense of its "national" histories and conditions, but rather in terms of moving away from a monological, one-sided discourse to one of multiplicity and multivocality. This is of summary significance as such a move makes space for the subaltern voice by opening new terrains of struggle and contestation.

The pertinent literature reveals an impressive variety of refinements of Said's paradigmatic work. Yet, once again, Said himself set the precedent by introducing us to notions of *ontological/epistemological* and *manifest/latent* Orientalism(s): the former pair indicates *what* is distinguished and *how,* that is, the "Orient" from the "Occident" by way of essentializing; the latter pair points our attention to the recognizable and hidden elements of Orientalist discourse. However, the possibilities are far from exhausted. El-Azm (1981), for example, reiterates Said's *ontological/epistemological* types and adds two more sets, the *institutional/cultural academic* and the *proper/in-reverse.* The first of these is employed as in Said. The second indicates "a whole set of progressively expanding institutions, a created and cumulative body of theory and practice, a suitable ideological superstructure with an apparatus of complicated assumptions, beliefs, images, literary productions, and rationalizations" and, in a more restricted sense, "a developing tradition of disciplined learning whose main function is to 'scientifically research' the Orient" (5). The third, finally, opposes "Orientalism proper" to what El-Azm coins "Orientalism-in-Reverse." This last concept is used in the context of the essentialization of *the Orient* by secular Arab nationalists as well as by the movement of Islamic revival, reminding us of Said's early warning not to apply the readily available structures, styles, and ontological biases of Orientalism upon others or upon oneself (1979: 25).

Ong (1993) differentiates between *grand* and *petty* Orientalist discourses, where the former stands for "those which reached supreme authority under the British Empire," and which remain "dialectically linked" to the latter, described in terms of an alternative terrain that is "generated in the transnational context of corporate and media circulation and that rework Anglo-European academic concepts into confident pronouncements about Oriental labor, skills, deference, and mystery" (746). The *petty* type is then quite identical with her notion of a "self-Orientalizing discourse" (Ong 1997: 181), underlining two neglected elements of Orientalism. On the one hand we have a "dialectic" between *grand* and *petty* Orientalism(s), and on the other there is the "Oriental" self. This exemplifies an instance where differentiation acknowledges those who are involved, namely "the Orientals." But the main point is that the authoritarian Orientalist discourse that emanates from Western voices, be they institutional, intellectual, or popular, is always already adopted, modified, challenged, or rejected.

Another important differentiation is offered by Chen (1995), who explores different and divergent discursive levels, not of Orientalism but of its opposite, by using labels of *official/anti-official* Chinese "Occidentalism[s]." The *official* discourse is articulated by the Chinese government, "not for the purpose of dominating the West, but in order to discipline, and ultimately to dominate, the Chinese self at home" (5). In contrast and in response to the former, there is its counterpart, "which can be understood as a powerful *anti-official* discourse using the Western Other as a metaphor for a political liberation against ideological oppression within a totalitarian state" (8). But where the *official* Occidentalist discourse must still rely for its existence on Orientalist discursive formations, the *anti-official* Occidentalist does not necessarily.

Most interestingly, here, Chen goes a step further when she rejects mere binaries by highlighting their overlaps. In this way, she points to a third kind of discourse, in which "the anti-official Occidentalism overlapped with the official Occidentalism of the early post-Mao regime" (25). Clearly, Chen's emphasis rests with "the failure to recognize the indigenous use of Western discourse and the great variety of conditions that might provide the focus for its utterance" (15). This last point cannot be overemphasized and remains of essential importance to this essay. The insights gained from the works of El-Azm, Ong, and Chen are crucial for an evaluation of Cuban Orientalism, self-Orientalizing discourse, and "Chinese religion" in Cuba, to which we will now turn.

CUBAN ORIENTALISM

To Cuba's colonial inheritance of slavery and racism, one could add the historical Spanish obsession with the "Orient," an Orientalism that originated with "centuries of domination by the Moors from Northern Africa" (Kushigian 1991: 2) and that continued, after the *reconquista,* through sustained encounters with the Arabic Other. In stark contrast to these medieval adventures, modern Orientalism in Cuba finds its beginnings in the nineteenth-century transition from slave-labor to wage-labor and represents, indeed, a dark chapter that was opened just previous to the arrival of the first ship filled with contract workers, or "coolies," from southern China in 1847.

The century and a half of Cuban Orientalist discursive production that followed was shaped in particular by authors such as Ramón de la Sagra (1861), the utilitarian, who saw in Chinese "coolies" little more than a docile labor force for the insatiable needs of Cuban sugar mills; Gonzalo de Quesada (1896), once Cuba's ambassador in Berlin, and recognizably influenced by German Orientalists, who compiled the first scholastic and *sympathetic* study of "los chinos," thus marking an important discursive variation on the same theme; the renowned Cuban historian and anthropologist Fernando Ortiz (1995), whose blatantly racist views of "yellow Mongoloids" perfectly reflected the "scientific" discrimination against Chinese immigrants that was instilled during the period of U.S. domination; Juan Jiménez Pastrana (1983), whose "revolutionary" task it was to rewrite *their* history along (Communist) party lines; one could even add the contemporaries Baldomero Álvarez Ríos (1995), Jesús Guanche Perez (1996), and José Baltar Rodriguez (1997), all of whose sinological intimations about "Chinese" tradition, folklore, and ritual remain crucial to any serious historical reconstruction of the development of Orientalism in Cuba.[2]

Considering this incisive historical pattern, contemporary expressions of Cuban Orientalism often present themselves in disguise and may reach us from the most unexpected corners. To give but one striking and typical example, a newspaper article, published in the international edition of Cuba's party organ *Granma*, commented on the renowned Chinese-Cuban paintress Flora Fong on the occasion of her second trip to China. While the article begins and ends with citations from Miguel Barnet, celebrated author of *The Autobiography of a Runaway Slave*, the signing journalist must have been aware of the awkward contradiction that characterizes them. I shall offer both here, so as to illustrate how official Cuban pronouncements regarding "transculturation" and hybridity are lined up, and possibly even confused, with the racist essentialism inherent in Euro-American Orientalist discourse. The opening paragraph runs like this:

> It is impossible to separate in her art what is oriental from what is occidental. One is the result of the other and both come together in a legitimate process of transculturation. That is what fascinates me in Flora Fong's painting. (Barnet, quoted in *Granma*, 13 January 1991: 11, my translation)

This is, no doubt, a clear reminder of the fact that the Cuban nation, as well as the state it engendered, was constructed on the basis of a hybrid process of "transculturation," a notion originally formulated by Fernando Ortiz (1995: 97–103).[3] Thus, be one of Caribbean, European, African, or Asian descent, transculturation—or, as Roberto Fernández Retamar (1989: 4) would prefer, *mestizaje*—is what constitutes and supposedly unites all Cubans in a classless, raceless society. And yet, after dwelling for the most part on Flora Fong's felicitous encounter with members of her "extended" family in Canton, the article concludes, to no little surprise, with this paragraph:

"The blood that runs in Flora's veins marked her painting well before she made the voyage that would bring her to the soil of her ancestors, Taoist China, [the land of] the Roots of the Lotus, and the Imperial Jade" (Barnet, quoted in *Granma*, 13 January 1991: 11, my translation).

This sudden and unexpected turn from Caribbean hybridity to Orientalist essentialism reveals the extent to which even "revolutionary" authors may in fact slip back into antiquated Eurocentric discourses. Here, I chose the term "antiquated" so as to point to discursive formations that find their origins with nineteenth-century power relations where the "East" is represented as the inferior Other, and where the "West" takes the place of the dominant Self. Although this may have been the case in the past, it is no longer applicable to the present. As a result, the ambiguity and double-sidedness of Barnet's comments stand out as particularly characteristic of contemporary Cuban Orientalism, not just betraying the pitfalls of its revolutionary (un)consciousness, but indicating, rather, the persistence and longevity of its colonial burden.

Obviously, Orientalism is not a thing of the past, but alive and well in many places. Arif Dirlik, in this context, and to mimic E. P. Thompson, reverses the Eurocentric, and later Euro-American, perspective and poses the valuable question: "Is orientalism a thing or a relationship?" (1996: 99). An essential argument of this paper consists precisely in rejecting clear-cut distinctions between Euro-American and "Oriental" representations of Chineseness in Cuba, but, instead, viewing them in terms of dialectics. Thus, in sharp contrast to Said's *Orientalism* and the unfortunate failure to erase ontological distinctions between "Orient" and "Occident," Orientalism is here treated as a relationship and not as a monolithic construction that solely belongs to the "West."

But how is this relationship to be conceptualized? Simply by repeating binaries such as colonizer/colonized, oppressor/oppressed? Or, instead, is it by locating points of contact, encounter, even dialogue, that we might find some answers? In this sense, we will now discuss the topic of self-Orientalization and the complex dialectics that are at work in Chinese-Cuban Orientalist pronouncements. The term "self-Orientalization" is here understood as an emic category, rather than as a label of purely Western fabrication.

"SELF-ORIENTALIZATION" AND THE ICON CONFUCIUS

After considering the history of Cuban Orientalism, and after pointing to its present expressions, often hidden or in disguise, by using Miguel Barnet's ideas about Flora Fong's paintings, it might be worthwhile to consider Flora Fong's own ideas in this respect (for my representational concerns rest not so much with China-born immigrants as with their offspring, that is, first- and second-generation Chinese Cubans—such as Flora Fong). In regard to her artwork, she explains in her most recent catalog and artbook, *Nube de otoño*:

> In very ancient times, the Han nationality of China created pictographic characters inspired by the tracks left by birds and animals, which evolved in several aspects. In regard to style and form, brushstrokes slowly replaced drawings, symbols replaced pictographs, and simple forms replaced complex ones. . . . I consider this explanation necessary, in that Chinese characters were an essential part of my art since the early 1980s. (1997: 6)

Thus, the task of representing Chineseness begins in her first line, where she opts to evoke a timeless Chinese antiquity, the cultural inheritance of the Han period, as well as the exoticism and mystique that Chinese "brushstroked" characters continue to hold for Western audiences. Flora Fong emphasizes not only the notion of timelessness, but also the observation of nature (a known Confucian principle), as well as the "essential" importance of Chinese characters in her painting, all of which points to an understanding of Chineseness as essence. Is this, then, simply the reflection of Flora Fong's artistic sentiment and her striving for a personal style, or are we facing a vivid example of what Dirlik (1996) recognizes as the Orientalism of "Orientals"?

The use of self-Orientalizing discourses (that is, Chinese-Cuban articulations of an essential and distinctive Chineseness, which allow for conceiving of "difference" in ethnic and cultural terms) has (re)appeared in Cuba only very recently. Together with the need to improve official relations with the People's Republic of China (after the end of the Soviet-Cuban alliance in 1991) came also certain economic interests in the touristic redevelopment of La Habana's Chinatown. Thus, an officially promoted campaign of re-essentializing people ("the Chinese") and places ("Chinatown") is now in progress. This initiative is evidently based on Orientalist notions of a distinct "Chineseness," which have, as we noted above, a long history on the island. Although undertaken by the Cuban government within a larger, national framework of "touristifications," its modernizing policies are being implemented through the *Grupo Promotor del Barrio Chino,* a governmental agency that is run by first- and second-generation Chinese-Cuban professionals (see Grupo Promotor 1998; 1995).

In a transnational but mainly U.S.-informed context, Ong clearly rejects "Asian modernist imaginations that insist upon their cultural and spiritual distinctiveness," as she detects in them little more than "contradictory, self-Orientalizing moves" (1997: 194). Dirlik, in stark contrast, and in the attempt to further develop Said's *Orientalism,* suggests instead that contemporary tendencies of self-Orientalization among Asian intellectuals are "a manifestation not of powerlessness but of newly-acquired power" (1996: 97). This last point remains central to the developments in Cuba's Chinese-Cuban community.[4] In this context, it is interesting to observe how a series of interviews, conducted with Chinese Cubans in La Habana, Villa Clara, Camagüey, and Santiago de Cuba from 1995 to 1998, indicates some of the assumptions that are at the basis of self-Orientalizing discourses. Surprisingly, independent of age, gender, professional background, or location, the vast majority of interviewees emphasized the significance that certain "Chinese" values, such as honesty, courage, fidelity, perseverance, austerity, hard work, respect for the ancestors, filial piety, mutual aid, and beneficence, hold for them. These references to Confucian values are all the more remarkable when we consider that: "Today, the Chinese Cuban community, integrated by Chinese immigrants (now only a few hundred), but also by thousands of first- and second-generation Cubans, who were formed in the Revolution, and who are thus culturally and professionally capable, work to recuperate and to enrich the contributions made by the Chinese over a century and a half to Cuban patrimony and nationality" (Grupo Promotor 1995: 7, my translation).

What is the particular interest that "culturally and professionally capable" Chinese Cubans, who are, in addition, "formed in the Revolution," find with Confucian values and with representations of themselves that are formulated in terms of an essential "Chineseness"? How does this new, decontextualized "Confucianism" inform the practice of self-Orientalization in Cuba?

Clearly, the concept of "self-Orientalization" is a complex one that remains inextricably linked to Orientalism itself. That is, if we conceptualize Orientalism as an entirely Western construct, without accounting for the dialectics involved in a process that was shaped all along by both Westerners and "Orientals," then, in fact, we may conclude, erroneously, that Asians had simply no say in the making of Orientalism. However, it is by investigating the notion of "Confucian values" that we are enabled to reconceptualize our ideas of what constitutes a self-Orientalizing discourse.

Such a reconceptualization is offered by Jensen, who develops the idea that "East and West have become bound by commerce and communication and joined, more importantly, in imagination" (1997: 3). In his recent work, *Manufacturing Confucianism* (1997), he explains how the arrival of a detachment of Jesuits in Guangzhou (Canton) in 1579 resulted in the fact that "Confucianism is largely a Western invention, supposedly representing what is registered by the complex of terms *rujia* [*ru* family], *rujiao* [*ru* teaching], *ruxue* [*ru* learning] and *ruzhe* [the *ru*]. Presuming that the ancient Chinese philosopher Confucius (known to the Chinese as Kongzi) is the source of this complex, it takes his figure as its focus" (5). Jensen points out "that Confucius assumed his present familiar features as the result of a prolonged, deliberate process of manufacture in which European intellectuals took a leading role. Our Confucius is a product fashioned over several centuries by many hands, ecclesiastical and lay, Western and Chinese" (5).

Thus, in both the "West" and the "East," and owing to the untiring efforts of

Jesuits, sinologists, Chinese nationalists, and, not to be forgotten, the overseas-Chinese community, the icon Confucius soon became equated with "Chinese culture" in general, and with "Chinese religion" in particular. After the demise of the Qing dynasty in 1911, the icon offered itself as an ideal image of essential "Chineseness" to Chinese nationalists, who did not hesitate to appropriate this icon in their struggle to define culture, history, and identity, providing in this way "a conceptual vernacular that would unite the diverse cultural constituencies of a new nation" (Jensen 1997: 4). Obviously, there is a link between Chinese nationalism and the cultural nationalism of overseas-Chinese.

In the meantime, Confucius' significance has not lessened, but, on the contrary, Confucianism has been promoted throughout the last two decades by Southeast Asian nations, and in particular by Singapore's Lee Kwan Yew, as the ethico-spiritual "foundation" of their socio-economic success. This latest Confucian revival translates, therefore, not only into the complete reversal of Weber's Eurocentric pronouncements on Confucianism (1968: 142–70), but also into the articulation of an indigenous subjectivity that lends itself to be used as a counter-discourse to Euro-American Orientalist positionings. In fact:

> The Confucian revival of the past decade, I suggest, is an expression not of power-lessness, but of a newfound sense of power that has accompanied the economic success of East Asian societies who now reassert themselves against an earlier Euro-American domination. In this sense, the Confucian revival (and other cultural na-tionalisms) may be viewed as an articulation of native culture (and an indigenous subjectivity) against Euro-American cultural hegemony. (Dirlik 1996: 113)

At the same time, Dirlik does not ignore the self-defeating aspects of employing self-Orientalizing strategies:

> The part that self-orientalization may play in the struggle against internal and exter-nal hegemony, and its claims to alternative modernities, however, must not be exag-gerated. In the long run, self-orientalization serves to perpetuate, and even to con-solidate, existing forms of power. . . . Self-essentialization may serve the cause of mobilization against "Western" domination; but in the very process it also consoli-dates "Western" ideological hegemony by internalizing the historical assumptions of orientalism. At the same time, it contributes to internal hegemony by suppressing differences within the nation. (1996: 114)

But where he affirms that the use of self-Orientalizing discourse "contributes to internal hegemony by suppressing differences within the nation," he must have been thinking of the People's Republic of China, and not of the little-known situation of a "minority" in the Caribbean. The case of the Chinese-Cuban community in Cuba has produced a unique situation in which an Orientalist discourse of basically Eurocentric orientation cooperates and, at the same time, competes with a *strategic* "Oriental," or self-centered, one. Thus, the post-1991 battle for political and economic survival in Cuba appears to have opened up new discursive terrain (and there was very little during almost forty years of de-ethnicization), in which claims for ethnic and cultural difference can be articulated. These new discursive spaces are increasingly taken up by first- and second-generation Chinese Cubans who show, simultaneously, great interest in resuscitating "Chinese values," or a "new" Confucianism in Cuban attire. To explore these ethico-spiritual discourses a little further, we will now turn to "Chinese religion," the figure of the Chinese Cuban "saint" Sanfancón, and the "Chineseness" of Confucianism in Cuba.

"CHINESE RELIGION" IN CUBA

The question of religion in Cuba has been discussed mainly in terms of Spanish Christianity, African religions, and their "syncretic" expressions (see Ortiz 1975; Peréz Sarduy and Stubbs 1993). Contemporary ideas surrounding the concept of *cubania,* or Cubanity, rest on similar assumptions of, and even a certain fixation with, a Euro-African version of hybridity,[5] in which "the Chinese" hardly ever appear. Even though it is not just since the 1959 Cuban Revolution that Cuba has insisted on its *mestizo* character, which is supposedly based on four main groups, "Indio," Spanish, African, and Chinese, the disproportionate obsession with Afro-Cuban "cults," shown by historians, sociologists, and anthropologists alike, has left little space for the exploration of "Chinese religion" in Cuba.

One of the earliest commentators, Ramón de la Sagra, a Spaniard, Christian, and staunch defender of Cuba's "scientific revolution," noted how "[t]hese Chinese show no religious disposition whatsoever, but they like to go out on Sundays" (1861: 150, my translation). The white supremacist José Antonio Saco insisted that "the Chinese race [remains] different in its language and color, in its ideas and feelings, in its uses and customs, and in its religious opinions" (1881: 186, my translation). These descriptions of essential incomprehension and radical Otherness coincide with the Eurocentricity of many nineteenth-century Spanish and Cuban writers. The reason, then, for these descriptions' bias resides in the Eurocentric and Christian perspectives of observers who had obviously great difficulty in conceiving of religion in non-Christian terms.

In this sense, it is particularly revealing how the making of a syncretic Chinese-Cuban "saint," Sanfancón, remains inextricably linked to bringing "Chinese religion" into an orderly Hispanic pantheon, or at least into a mentality, occupied by "Christian" gods so as to become intelligible even to the non-Chinese mind. Eventually, Sanfancón entered a symbiosis with other saints and deities of Euro-African extraction. Thus, even followers of Santería continue to pay respects to Sanfancón in some of the remaining Chinese societies, and popular culture has it that Santa Barbara (Spanish) is Shango (African) is Sanfancón (Chinese).

According to Orientalist knowledge, the name Sanfancón, also San Fancon,[6] San-Fan-Con, or San Fang Kong, represents a Western corruption of Cuan Yu, who, after his death, became the "Venerated Ancestor Kuan Kong" and eventually the "patron" of all Chinese immigrants to Cuba. This mythical figure is traced to the Han period (ca. 220–280 C.E.), when a brotherhood was formed between three legendary ancestors/warriors/philosophers named Lau Pei, Cuan Yu, and Chiong Fei (here given in hierarchical order by age). These were later joined by a forth member, Chiu Chi Long. But it is the second of these, Cuan Yu/Kuan Kong, who became crucial to the Cuban invention of Sanfancón. Interestingly, the appearance of Sanfancón coincides with the establishment, in the year 1900, of the first clanic society on the island, the Lung Con Cun Sol. This society brought together members with the last names Lao, Chiong, Chiú, and Kuan (Baltar Rodriguez 1997: 180). But what kind of values does Sanfancón represent?

The type of "Chinese values" that are conveyed by Sanfancón have become accessible through Antonio Chuffat Latour's remarkable work *Apunte histórico de los chinos en Cuba* (1927). Chuffat Latour had been working between 1885 and 1892 for several Chinese consulates on the island, when, at the turn of the century, he became the secretary of the Chinese Nationalist Party, the Kuo Min Tang, in Cienfuegos. His study of "the Chinese in Cuba" represents a unique compilation and an outstanding testimony of the Chinese presence in Cuba. The author collected his data from numberless conversations held with Chinese immigrants to Cuba, be they workers, shopkeepers, or entrepreneurs. Recorded in Matanzas province, his rendering of "the legend of Kuan Kong in Cimarrones" (85–89), in which one Chung Si was sitting in his house when a powerful spirit entered his body and began speaking "Chinese" to him, contains a number of Confucian-style prescriptions:

1) God in Heaven will reward those who are virtuous, honest, hard working and just with your brothers.
2) Happiness and good fortune will accompany you if you do acts of charity. Share your rice with those in need.
3) Do not be violent in your acts and be very prudent so as to have no regrets.
4) If you appreciate friends, do not speak of their acts in ways that could offend them.
5) Do not believe in slander nor in lies. If you want to be happy, keep away from all evil [influence].
6) The Chinese have their God, the White, the Black, Indian, Malay, each has their God.
7) The true God is not White, Chinese, Black, Indian, nor Malay, it is God Almighty.
8) Do not despair [in this world]. Remember that you are in transit, you brought nothing and nothing you shall take.
9) You have no property, the only one, the real, is the one of your fall. Think well, and you are going to be convinced.
10) God Almighty asks us nothing, he wants no gold, no payments. It is God Almighty, great, just, good; he has no hate and no defect. If you believe in God, he is going to be with you; if you have faith, he is going to save you from all evil. (Chuffat Latour 1927: 87, my translation)

These Confucian[7] values show, indeed, a great concern with "God Almighty." Although "Chinese religion" consists not only of Confucianism but also of Taoism and Buddhism, forming what is known as the "Three Ways," it is difficult to find in any of these doctrines the monotheistic prevalence so characteristic for Christianity. Yet the Chinese-Cuban invention of Sanfancón, and especially the built-in flexibility of his triple function as sage, saint, or god, reflects the need to satisfy typically "Christian" preoccupations with monotheism. Thus, it is this "Western" reading (and writing) of Sanfancón that may explain Chuffat Latour's "Ten Commandment" version of Confucian values.

We may ask, finally, of what quality is the "Chineseness" of Confucius in Cuban garb, and how essentially and distinctively "Chinese" can Sanfancón possibly be? Apparently, as the Cuban historian and ethnographer Baltar Rodriguez found out—after consulting the available sources and after conducting a number of interviews with non-Cubans—the figure Sanfancón is not known in China or among members of its overseas community elsewhere (1997: 182). Clearly, Sanfancón is as Cuban as can be.

His being used in the name of an essential and distinctive Chineseness as well as being pressed into service by first- and second-generation Chinese Cubans (who were "formed in the Revolution") for the promotion of a "new" Confucianism reveals the *strategic* quality of his reappearance in Chinese societies and on the streets of La Habana's Chinatown. "Chinese religion" in Cuba today has less to do with long-standing "Chinese" traditions, or even a return to "religion" per se,[8] but everything to do with the subaltern employment of strategies that allow for the opening of alternative spaces in which the construction of identities other than those prescribed by the state takes place. It is, then, Cuba's "transition to somewhere" that explains the recent rearrangements of its ideological, political, economical, social, and cultural spheres.

IN LIEU OF CONCLUSION

Since 1994, the anniversary of the Chinese presence in Cuba had been celebrated again around June 3, the day of the arrival of the first ship to bring Chinese workers to the island in 1847. But the months of May and June do not fit in well with the tourist season, which is mainly from November to April, and so it was decided by a governmental agency, the *Grupo Promotor del Barrio Chino*, that from 1999 onward, it would be held in the first week of November, now coinciding with the anniversary of the People's Republic of China. Although this choice may not conform to the history of Chinese immigration to Cuba, its deliberate decontextualization perfectly illustrates the priorities, as well as the "Chinese Dreams," of the Cuban government and of first- and second-generation Chinese Cubans. Perhaps it is only a minor occurrence, but, in my view, this example makes quite clear how meanings, metaphors, and discursive formations are shifted, and even pushed, around so as to channel them into more or less convenient directions.

In our discussion of Orientalism, we have seen how the employment of "hybrid strategies" makes it possible to offer enabling perspectives, even though Said's *Orientalism* completely neglects the people involved, that is, the "Orientals." This opens space for a further exploration that leads us "beyond *Orientalism*" and toward more sophisticated developments of Said's precedent, in which we find an opening for the "indigenous" use of, and its complicity in, Orientalist discourse. In this way, we can identify both Euro-American and "Oriental" Orientalist discourses.

Cuban Orientalism not only consists of historical manifestations but is also found in contemporary discourse in Cuba. The apparent ambiguity and double-sidedness of these discourses reveals how even "revolutionary" writers succumb to their (un)conscious colonial burden of racism and Orientalism. By contrast, the Orientalism of "Orientals," particularly when seen in the context of Confucian thought, addresses precisely what Said's *Orientalism* leaves out: that Orientalism is not simply a monolithic construction of the "West," but rather is a dialectical relationship that includes the "East."

Our incursion into the intricacies of "Chinese Religion in Cuba" and, with it, into the figure of the Chinese-Cuban "saint" Sanfancón not only points to the contemporary uses of a decontextualized Confucianism, but also shows the extent to which first- and second-generation Chinese Cubans are willing to activate an essential and distinctive "Chineseness" in the service of a return to notions of difference in ethnic and cultural terms. These unexpected articulations, made within the confines of a socialist state, are indeed surprising, especially after almost forty years of revolutionary de-ethnicization in which Orientalist erasure dominated the picture. Contemporary Orientalist discourse in Cuba should, therefore, be grasped in the context of rearrangements of a Cuban society in "transition to somewhere."

Notes

1. Jorge I. Dominguez's interesting but largely conservative comments in his chapter "Cuba in the 1990s: The Transition to Somewhere" (1998: 173–202) speculate about possible scenarios that could be envisaged for Cuba's mid- and long-term future. See also *Informe central: Discurso de clausura. V congreso del Partido Comunista de Cuba* (Castro Ruz 1997: 149–51).

2. These works could be juxtaposed, for example, to a number of "Chinese" voices such as can be found in *The Cuba Commission Report* (Cuba Commission 1993), an oral history that comprises over a thousand interviews and individual petitions recorded from Chinese contract laborers near the end of Cuba's first national struggle, the Ten Years' War. Another significant emic view is reflected in Antonio Chuffat Latour's *Apunte histórico de los chinos en Cuba* (1927), a unique compilation that is based on the author's conversations with Chinese (that is, mainly Cantonese) workers and entrepreneurs resident in Cuba.

3. Curiously, the inventor of the concept of "transculturation," Fernando Ortiz, himself referred to Chinese immigrants in overtly racist terms: "And still other immigrant cultures of the most varying origins arrived, either in sporadic waves or a continuous flow, always

exerting an influence and being influenced in turn: Indians from the mainland, Jews, Portuguese, Anglo-Saxons, French, North Americans, even yellow Mongoloids from Macao, Canton, and other regions of the sometimes Celestial Kingdom" (1947: 113).

4. There are other such communities in South Florida, New York, and New Jersey (Garcia 1996: 43), but also in Mexico, Panama, Venezuela, Peru, Macao, and Hong Kong (Bastos da Silva 1994: 157–79).

5. Although both José Martí's *Our America* (1977) and Fernández Retamar's *Caliban and Other Essays* (1989) make place for the vanished American "Indian" (that is, Taino or Carib) in their arguments concerned with *mestizaje,* they consistently ignore, and thus continue to erase in proper Orientalist fashion, the presence of Chinese immigrants on the island.

6. Curiously, the linguistic Christianization of "Chinese religion" is already recognizable in the first three letters of the name San Fancón, that is, in the title *San,* which means three or three people in Mandarin, while also being used as an abbreviation for the Castillian term *santo,* or saint.

7. In regards to the complicity of Western intellectuals in *manufacturing* Chineseness and Confucian values, Jensen suggests that "[b]y the late eighteenth century, as Europe acquired an 'Enlightened' cultural self-consciousness, Confucius was firmly entrenched in contemporary Western culture as a sage, and his followers were called 'Confucians', a term that evoked a panoply of associations: deference, urbanity, wisdom, moral probity, reasoned and not slavish classicism, and a learned, paternal authoritarianism. These qualities, like the figure who embodied them, were the desiderata of Europeans doubtful of the institution of monarchy and despairing of religious war" (1997: 8).

8. I should mention that discussions of religious practices in the Chinese-Cuban community in Cuba often develop along lines of B.C./A.C., that is, Before Castro and After Castro, in as far as the Cuban Revolution marked a major change by building an atheistic state that was antithetical to religion. Its Marxist-Leninist conception of religion as "mystification" allowed for little religious tolerance until the Cuban Constitution was rewritten in 1992. Cuba is now a "secular" state, government and church are separated, religious freedom is constitutionally guaranteed, and even Pope John Paul II came to visit the island in January 1998 (see also *Constitución de la República de Cuba* [Cuba 1992: 5]).

Works Cited

Ahmad, Aijaz. 1994. *In Theory: Classes, Nations, Literatures.* New York: Verso.

Álvarez Ríos, Baldomero. 1995. *La inmigración china en la Cuba colonial: El barrio chino de La Habana.* La Habana: Publicigraf.

Baltar Rodriguez, José. 1997. *Los chinos de Cuba: Apuntes etnograficos.* Coleccion La Fuente Viva. La Habana: Fundación Fernando Ortiz.

Bastos da Silva, Beatriz. 1994. *Emigração de culés: Dossier Macau, 1851–1894.* Macau: Fundação Oriente.

Bhabha, Homi K. 1994. *The Location of Culture.* New York: Routledge.

Castro Ruz, Fidel. 1997. *Informe central: Discurso de clausura. V congreso del Partido Comunista de Cuba.* La Habana: Ediciones Politicas.

Chen, Xiaomei. 1995. *Occidentalism: A Theory of Counter-Discourse in Post-Mao China.* New York: Oxford University Press.

Chuffat Latour, Antonio. 1927. *Apunte histórico de los chinos en Cuba.* La Habana: Molina y Cia.

Clifford, James. 1988. *The Predicament of Culture: Twentieth-Century Ethnography, Literature, and Art.* Cambridge, Mass.: Harvard University Press.

Cuba. 1954. *Republica de Cuba. Informe general del censo de 1953.* La Habana: P. Fernandez y Cia.

Cuba. 1992. *Constitución de la República de Cuba. (Esta Constitución contiene las reformas aprobadas por la Asamblea Nacional del Poder Popular en el XI Período Ordinario de Sesiones de la III Legislatura celebrada los días 10, 11 y 12 de julio de 1992).* La Habana: Editora Política.

Cuba Commission. [1876] 1993. *The Cuba Commission Report. A Hidden History of the Chinese in Cuba.* Baltimore: Johns Hopkins University Press.

De la Sagra, Ramón. 1861. *Historia física, económico-política, intelectual y moral de la isla de Cuba.* Paris: Hachette.

Dirlik, Arif. 1996. "Chinese History and the Question of Orientalism." *History and Theory: Studies in the Philosophy of History* 35 (4): 96–118.

Dominguez, Jorge I. 1998. *Democratic Politics in Latin America and the Caribbean.* Baltimore: Johns Hopkins University Press.

El-Azm, Sadik Jallal. 1981. "Orientalism and Orientalism in Reverse." *Khamsin* 8: 5–26.

Fernández Retamar, Roberto. 1989. *Caliban and Other Essays.* Minneapolis: University of Minnesota Press.

Fong, Flora. 1997. *Nube de otoño.* La Habana: Alexis Malaguer, MA & G/Grafispaço.

Garcia, Maria Cristina. 1996. *Havana U.S.A.: Cuban Exiles and Cuban Americans in South Florida, 1959–1994.* Berkeley: University of California Press.

Guanche Perez, Jesús. 1996. *Componentes étnicos de la nacion cubana.* Coleccion La Fuente Viva. La Habana: Ediciones Union.

Grupo Promotor. 1995. *El Barrio Chino de La Habana: Proyecto integral.* La Habana: Grupo Promotor del Barrio Chino.

Grupo Promotor. 1998. *Posibilidades inversionistas en el Barrio Chino de La Habana.* La Habana: Grupo Promotor del Barrio Chino.

Jensen, Lionel M. 1997. *Manufacturing Confucianism: Chinese Traditions and Universal Civilization.* Durham: Duke University Press.

Jiménez Pastrana, Juan. 1983. *Los chinos en la historia de Cuba 1847–1930.* La Habana: Editorial de Ciencias Sociales.

Kushigian, Julia A. 1991. *Orientalism in the Hispanic Literary Tradition: In Dialogue with Borges, Paz, and Sarduy.* Albuquerque: University of New Mexico Press.

Martí, José. [1898] 1977. *Our America: Writings on Latin America and the Struggle for Cuban Independence.* Translated by Elinor Randall. New York: Monthly Review.

Ong, Aihwa. 1993. "On the Edge of Empires: Flexible Citizenship among Chinese in Diaspora." *Positions* 1 (3): 744–78.

Ong, Aihwa. 1997. "Chinese Modernities: Narratives of Nation and of Capitalism." In *Ungrounded Empires,* edited by D. Nonini and A. Ong. New York: Routledge.

Ortiz, Fernando. [1947] 1995. *Cuban Counterpoint: Tobacco and Sugar.* Durham: Duke University Press.

Ortiz, Fernando. 1975. *Historia de una pelea cubana contra los demonios.* La Habana: Editorial De Ciencias Sociales.

Peréz Sarduy, Pedro, and Jean Stubbs, eds. 1993. *AfroCuba: An Anthology of Cuban Writing on Race, Politics and Culture.* Melbourne: Ocean Press.

Prakash, Gyan. 1990. "Writing Post-Orientalist Histories of the Third World: Perspectives from Indian Historiography." *Comparative Studies in Society and History* 32 (2): 383–408.

Quesada, Gonzalo de. 1896. *Los chinos y la independencia de Cuba.* Translated by A. Castellanos. La Habana: Heraldo Cristiano.

Saco, José Antonio. 1881. *Coleccion posthuma de papeles científicos, historicos, politicos y de otros ramos sobre la isla de Cuba.* La Habana: Editorial Miguel De Villa.

Said, Edward W. 1979. *Orientalism.* New York: Vintage Books.

Said, Edward W. 1994. *Culture and Imperialism.* New York: Vintage Books.

Spivak, Gayatri C. 1996. "Subaltern Studies: Deconstructing Historiography." In *The Spivak Reader,* edited by D. Landry and G. Maclean. New York: Routledge.

Strubbe, Bill. 1995. "Start with a Dream: Rebuilding Havana's Chinese Community." World and I 10. *Washington Times,* September: 188–97.

Weber, Max. 1968. *The Religion of China: Confucianism and Taoism.* Translated by H. H. Gerth. New York: Free Press.

14

The Diasporic Mo(ve)ment

Indentureship and Indo-Caribbean Identity

SEAN LOKAISINGH-MEIGHOO

The argument of this chapter will unfold in four scenes. Each scene will lead into the next, and new concepts will be encountered within each scene. I think it necessary to follow my argument in this way if the many layers of the story I want to tell are to be appreciated. Of course, there are themes that will recur throughout, and some sort of narrative that will hold it all together. My argument is organized around the concept of what I will call the diasporic mo(ve)ment— that historical point of rupture between diaspora and home, which pins but does not fix diasporic identity in both time and space. So although this paper is about the significance of Indian indentureship in the Caribbean, there are many inter-related problems, both specific and general, ethno-historical and theoretical, that must be met along the way—the constitution of Indo-Caribbean identity, the meaning of diaspora, and even the very workings of identity.

The first act, as such, will deal with the concept of diaspora in two scenes. In starting with a discussion of diaspora as a style rather than an identity itself, I want to suggest right away that diaspora is neither an intra- nor an extra-cultural concept. That is, the concept of diaspora cannot be theorized without reference to specific cultural identities, and yet, diaspora always escapes any such reference. The meaning of diaspora does not lie either fully inside or fully outside specific cultural identities, but may only be approached through the ongoing articulation of these identities. This, then, explains the first of my chapter's excesses: in discussing Indo-Caribbean identity, we must always consider its relationship with Afro-Caribbean and other diasporic identities. And let me also spell out a corollary here, that my discussion of indentureship in this chapter offers important insights not only into Indo-Caribbean identity but into the intercultural politics of diaspora.

The second act will move on to address indentureship in particular, again in two scenes. Revisiting some of the key characters introduced in the first act, I want to further suggest that not only must any discussion of cultural identity grapple with the challenge of cultural difference, but that moreover, this challenge of cultural difference must itself grapple with its own limits. The theoretical discourse of difference has certainly proven invaluable in dislodging nationalist and fundamentalist claims based on notions of absolute identity. However, this discourse itself runs the risk of falling into an equally absolute notion of difference, an unrelenting relativism that prohibits any critical discussion of the relationships that bring together different nations, religions, and cultures. The final part of the chapter, on the comparison between indentureship and slavery within Indo-Caribbean studies, then, will attempt to confront this renewed problem of cultural identity and difference.

Yet I still have not explained the second of the excesses: my brief discussion of Indo-Caribbean religion is buried within a largely theoretical treatment of diasporic identity. But this is only apparently the case. Let us not forget, after all, that the concept of diaspora, the organizing theme of this chapter, is itself a religious one, appropriated from the Jewish tradition of textual exegesis and oral transmission. However, anyone at all acquainted with current cultural politics knows that diaspora is not "just" a religious concept anymore. But what a more critical consideration of the diaspora concept would question is that it ever was "just" a religious one, and that the religious ever has been so distinct from the secular. Rather, diaspora indicates that the religious and the secular are always already mutually implied and that the notion of religion as a discrete social practice is itself an invention of modern secularism. The implication of religion with other social practices is perhaps especially evident in the Caribbean, where issues of identity and difference along with themes of captivity and redemption seem to inform all areas of life. But let me suggest here that this relation between the religious and the secular is not at all unique to the Caribbean. What the study of Caribbean religion and culture suggests, as such, is that the object of religious studies in general must not be limited to "just" the religious, at least not in its conventional sense. And likewise, what the concept of diaspora in particular gestures toward is the importance of religious studies in the critical understanding of not only modern Caribbean but modern world culture.

DIASPORA AS STYLE

Diaspora is not the objective result of dispersal through any and all sorts of migration from an already constituted cultural center, as much as a cultural process of the articulation of both this center and its dispersal. That is, home itself is produced only through diaspora. Thus, the naturalness of diaspora as well as home must be brought into reckoning with their artificiality. This dialectical relationship between diaspora and home is radically unstable and fraught with all those tensions that so characteristically exist between those living in diaspora and those living at home. In many circumstances, communication between those in diaspora and those at home may seem to be strained beyond the possibility of mutual recognition. However, the relationship between diaspora and home must be maintained, for not only is home always present in the articulation of diaspora, but diaspora is always present in the articulation of home. As is often the case indeed, the more tenuous the bond between diaspora and home, the more tenacious is its claim. Now, this is not to say that no other sense of home may be produced besides that of the diasporic process. However, for those engaged in the formation of diasporic identities, the familiarity of home is recognized only through this cultural process.

Diasporic culture must be theoretically approached, then, as a *style* of identity formation rather than a specific cultural identity. The articulation of diasporic identities works through the popular cultural processes of recognition and repetition, substitution and subversion. The concept of style has been most carefully theorized by Dick Hebdige in *Subculture: The Meaning of Style* (1993). In analyzing the race politics and aesthetic practices of the British postwar working-class youth subcultures of reggae, rock, and punk, Hebdige offers a reading of style as "signifying practice" (117–27). Drawing from the theoretical work in semiotics of the Tel Quel group including Julia Kristeva and Roland Barthes, Hebdige argues against "the simple notion of reading as the revelation of a fixed number of concealed meanings . . . in favour of the idea of *polysemy* whereby each text is seen to generate a potentially infinite range of meanings" (117, his emphasis). The meaning of style, as such, is approached in "the *process* of meaning-construction rather than [in] the final product" (118, his emphasis). Hebdige further argues that this concept of style as signifying practice allows for a "re-think[ing] in a more subtle and complex way the relations not only between marginal and mainstream cultural formations but between the various subcultural styles themselves" (120). Thus, while Hebdige does not attend to the theoretical concept of diaspora in his study of black and white British youth subcultures, his theoretical work on style may be stretched here to accommodate the concept of diaspora.

This theorization of diaspora as style or signifying practice has some important and interrelated implications. While the concept of diaspora is highly developed in certain cultural traditions and in particular the Jewish tradition, diaspora as cultural process is not culturally specific—that is, peculiar to certain "ethnic" groups. Rather, as a set of creative practices, this style of identity formation is always receptive to collaboration and innovation, even in the process of the articulation of specific cultural identities. It is in this sense that diaspora is neither an intra- nor an extra-cultural concept, neither inside nor outside specific cultural identities, but is rather a cultural style through which specific identities are formed.

As such, diaspora cannot be said to be a new cultural form. Rather, diaspora constitutes an old and even traditional style of historically conceptualizing new and ever-changing circumstances. In some cultural contexts, including the formation of African-American, South Asian, Afro-Caribbean, and Indo-Caribbean identities, the current proliferation of cultural practices associated with the articulation of these diasporic identities is certainly a remarkably recent phenomenon. Yet even in these contexts, these practices are historically related to those much older cultural practices that articulated various versions of what may be called proto-diasporic African and Indian identities. At the same time, this current proliferation of diasporic identities is also a matter of style, for the concept of diaspora is certainly subject to trends of popularity. The widespread currency of the term itself in its varied cultural contexts indicates precisely its present fashionability in aesthetic, political, and academic practices alike.

As diaspora constitutes a particular cultural style, then, there surely exist other styles or sets of signifying practices. Popularly circulating in current cultural politics are a number of salient styles of identity formation, including those of First Nations and Latin American cultural identities, not to mention other formations in current cultural politics organized around gender and sexual, as well as national and religious, identities. Certainly, these cultural styles are not impervious to each other, and they freely infiltrate one another. Yet each of these styles as a particular set of signifying practices articulates different meanings. First Nations cultural identities are articulated through a sense of nativeness, aboriginality, or indigeneity and connection to the environment. In contrast, diasporic cultural identities are marked by a sense of exile and often alienation from the land of residence. Meanwhile, Latin American cultural identities selectively incorporate these concerns of First Nations indigeneity and diasporic alienation through the articulation of *mestizaje,* or cultural mixing. Each of these cultural styles carries certain sets of meanings as much as it works through certain sets of practices. Diaspora, as such, constitutes a particularly meaningful though currently popular style of identity formation.

THE DIASPORIC MO(VE)MENT

The theorization of diaspora as style may be extended, then, to the ontological level—that is, the level of meaning. Diasporic identities are marked by ontological significance for those who are engaged in the creative practices of their articulation. Certainly, one of the most basic though important points of Hebdige's semiotic approach to style is his insistence on the meaning of style. As he emphatically puts it, "Style in subculture is . . . pregnant with significance" (1993: 18). Similarly, the formation of diasporic identities involves the work of meaning as much as a play on meaning. Diaspora works through the subversion as well as the substantiation of identities. "Substance," therefore, is inscribed within the concept of diaspora as "style." Simply put, diaspora means something to "diasporics."

In working toward the particular meaning of diaspora, then, the work of C. L. R. James, Cornel West, and Paul Gilroy on what may be called black modernity has been most constructive for me in thinking through diaspora as ontology. For much like modernity, diaspora is based on an acute sense of *historical rupture.* And yet it is conceptually different from modernity, or at least Eurocentric modernity, in a significant way. My counter-position of diaspora and modernity as styles of identity formation in this section is primarily informed by this work on black modernity. Although of these theorists only Gilroy deals specifically with the concept of diaspora as well as that of modernity, it is important to realize that James, West, and Gilroy have all written during the period when the concept of diaspora was taken up by Caribbean, American, and British national citizens in identifying themselves culturally as diasporic Africans. While James wrote early in this period, when the concept of diaspora as adopted from Jewish tradition was just beginning to gain currency among pan-African advocates, West and Gilroy have written more recently, when the diaspora concept was being extended further by cultural communities other than the African diaspora. Of course, we are still in this historical period that is marked by the proliferation of diasporic identities.

In his appendix to the second edition of *The Black Jacobins,* "From Toussaint L'Ouverture to Fidel Castro" (1963), James inaugurates this work on black modernity in a brief though succinct argument:

> When three centuries ago the slaves came to the West Indies, they entered directly into the large-scale agriculture of the sugar plantation, which was a modern system. It further required that the slaves live together in a social relation far closer than any proletariat of the time. The cane when reaped had to be rapidly transported to what was factory production. The product was shipped abroad for sale. Even the cloth the slaves wore and the food they ate was imported. The Negroes, therefore, from the very start lived a life that was in its essence a modern life. That is their history—as far as I have been able to discover, a unique history. (392)

For James, then, modernity is constituted by the international economic system, in which the African slaves were central in terms of both production and consumption from its early beginnings. As such, James suggests that the African slaves on the Caribbean plantations, not the European capitalists or even the workers, were the first fully fledged moderns. James's theorization of modernity, then, is significantly different from and yet very relevant to my own, for I maintain that his revision of Eurocentric modernity is itself a prerogative of diasporic identity.

West also only briefly addresses black modernity in discussing his commitment to what he calls "prophetic criticism" in his preface to *Keeping Faith* (1993). West places this "prophetic vision and practice . . . at the core of [his] intellectual vocation and existential engagement" (x). Citing Du Bois's notion of double-consciousness, he posits that prophetic criticism draws from both Euro-American modernity and New World African modernity. He describes this New World African modernity as "what we get when Africans in the Americas . . . remake and recreate themselves into a distinctly *new* people" (xii–xiii, his emphasis). Recalling yet significantly revising the argument of James, West asserts, "If modernity is measured in terms of newness and novelty, innovation and improvisation—and not simply in terms of science, technology, markets, bureaucracies and nation-states—then New World African modernity is more thoroughly *modern* than any American novel, painting, dance or even skyscraper" (xiii, his emphasis). In further considering the relationship between these multiple modernities, West argues, "New World African modernity radically interrogates and creatively appropriates Euro-American modernity by examining how 'race' and 'Africa'—themselves modern European constructs—yield insights and blindnesses, springboards and roadblocks for our understanding of multivarious and multileveled modernities" (xii).

While West does not particularly address the concept of diaspora, he does deal with migration, the attendant concerns with temporality and spatiality, and the concept of home. Arguing that "[t]he fundamental theme of New World African modernity is neither integration nor separation but rather migration and emigration" (xiii), West explains that "[i]n the space-time of New World African modernity, to hope is to conceive of possible movement, to despair is to feel ossified, petrified, closed in" (xiv). He describes the search for home as historically exemplified in the Garveyite movement as the "wedding of black misery in America to transnational mobility to Africa, forging a sense of possible momentum and motion for a temporal people with few spatial options" (xiii–xiv). West's own discussion in the preface to his book is occasioned by his marriage and incorporation into a prominent Ethiopian family, raising for him "urgent issues of inheritance and rootlessness, tradition and homelessness" (x). Questioning his urge to leave America and live in Ethiopia, "the land of New World African modern fantasies of 'home'" (xv), he rhetorically asks, "Is this the urge of an émigré, an expatriate or an exile?" (x). Furthermore, embodying the dialectics of diasporic identity, West's prefatory essay is itself divided by the three headings "In Ethiopia," "In America," and lastly, "At Home."

It is Gilroy who most thoroughly deals with both black modernity and the concept of diaspora in his remarkable book *The Black Atlantic* (1993). In this work, he theorizes historical black thought on as well as current vernacular and literary cultures of modernity, also employing, like West, Du Bois's notion of double consciousness. Drawing from the work of Zygmunt Bauman, he posits the Black Atlantic diaspora as "a distinctive counterculture of modernity" (36). But Gilroy is most concerned with the relationship between modernity and diaspora in dealing with current black cultural politics. Arguing that "integral" to modernity is the "decentred and inescapably plural nature of modern subjectivity and identity" (46, 48), he further claims that postmodernity is thus "foreshadowed, or prefigured, in the lineaments of modernity itself" (42). In addressing black discourse, Gilroy critiques what he calls "Africentrism" and more specifically the sustained ideological opposition between the modern and the traditional in "Africentric" politics. He argues that the "Africentric movement appears to rely upon a linear idea of time that is enclosed at each end by the grand narrative of African advancement" in which "the duration of a black civilisation anterior to modernity is invoked" (190). Those who subscribe to Africentrism claim a "ready access to and command of tradition—sometimes ancient, always anti-modern" through which "Africa is retained as one special measure [of] authenticity" (191). Gilroy seeks to unsettle this easy acceptance of tradition as the "antithesis" (187) of modernity, "outside of the erratic flows of history" (191).

In this project, Gilroy takes up "the undertheorized idea of diaspora" (6). In doing so, he rejects the theoretical symbolization of diaspora "as the fragmentary opposite of some imputed racial essence" in "the unhappy polar opposition between a squeamish, nationalist essentialism and a sceptical, saturnalian pluralism" (95, 102). Rather, he claims that the cultural history of the Black Atlantic "explodes the dualistic structure which puts Africa, authenticity, purity, and origin in crude opposition to the Americas, hybridity, creolisation, and rootlessness" (199). Gilroy works toward an understanding of the concept of diaspora in tracing the attempts of black intellectuals to rewrite modernity:

> Du Bois, Douglass, Wright and the rest shared a sense that the modern world was fragmented along axes constituted by racial conflict and could accommodate non-synchronous, heterocultural modes of social life in close proximity. Their conceptions of modernity were periodised differently. They were founded on the catastrophic rupture of the middle passage rather than the dream of revolutionary transformation. (197)

Commenting on what may be called this diasporic revision of modernity in which James also participated, Gilroy suggests that "[t]he idea of diaspora might itself be understood as a response to these promptings—a utopian eruption of space into the linear temporal order of modern black politics which enforces the obligation that space and time must be considered relationally in their interarticulation with racialised being" (198). In his project, then, Gilroy proposes "to integrate the *spatial* focus on the diaspora idea . . . with the diaspora temporality and historicity, memory and narrativity that are the articulating principles of the black political countercultures that grew inside modernity in a distinctive relationship of antagonistic indebtedness" (191, his emphasis). His work aims to "reckon with the tension between temporalities [in black political culture] that leads intellectuals to try to press original African time into the service of their attempts to come to terms with diaspora space" (196–97). As such, Gilroy, arguing that "[d]iaspora time is not, it would seem, African [as in Africentric] time" (196), theoretically articulates and politically commits himself to "[t]he desire to bring a new historicity into black political culture" (190).

In his discussion of diaspora and modernity, Gilroy's work has most obviously stimulated my own approach to the concept of diaspora, whether or not our theoretical treatments are fully compatible. I begin with the postulation that diasporic identity is articulated through the experience of historical rupture. Yet modern identity is also based on a sense of historical rupture. Thus, diaspora and modernity are conceptually different though ambivalently related. In theorizing the relationship between the historical rupture of diaspora and that of modernity, then, the concept of history itself must be problematized through the critical consideration of *temporality* and *spatiality*.

Modern identity is based on rupture, and this historical sense of rupture is temporal. Thus, modernity is not based on the material fact of social or technological progress, but it is rather this belief in progress that characterizes modern identity. Modernity is articulated through the assertion of the newness of current times, not in any banal sense of novelty but in a profound sense of a distinct order of newness. The modern is thus cleaved from the traditional. This cleavage is marked by a specific point in time. Regardless of any disagreement over which point in time this actually was, the significant feature of modernity is that the split between the traditional and the modern is identified within a linear temporal history. The traditional in this sense as well as the modern, then, are the dialectical products of modernity. The traditional is constructed as the very nemesis of the modern, the anti-modern.

The concept of tradition, however, may be used to undermine modernity. Tradition may be revived not as the anti-modern but as an irruption into the modern through which the separation between the modern and the traditional is problematized. Tradition is commonly used in this subversive sense in diasporic politics as well as in other styles of cultural politics, such as the First Nations movement, and other forms of politics that similarly challenge modernity, such as environmentalism.

Postmodernity, then, constitutes another production of modernity. Postmodernity certainly problematizes the modern notion of progress as it signifies that modernity is not the end of history. Yet in claiming a break not only with the traditional but also with the modern itself, the postmodern is thoroughly modern precisely in that this historical break is temporalized. Thus, the logic of modernity as characterized by the linear temporality of history is not negated as much as multiplied, if not arithmetically then exponentially, in the logic of postmodernity.

Now, like modern identity, diasporic identity is based on rupture, but the concept of history and thus the meaning of historical rupture differ significantly between these identities. Whereas the concept of history in modernity is strictly temporal, history in diaspora includes the senses of both temporality and spatiality. Diaspora is thus articulated through the experience of temporal *and* spatial rupture. The traumatic significance of this rupture is condensed into a specific historical point—*the diasporic mo(ve)ment*—both a moment in time and a movement in space. This is the point that pins but does not fix, like a thumbtack on a corkboard, that perpetually unstable dialectical structure of diasporic identity. Every diasporic identity hinges upon such a mo(ve)ment. For the Jewish diaspora, the Dispersion marks this mo(ve)ment, while for the African diaspora, the Middle Passage marks it. The significance of these foundational events does not lie in their historicity as such, but is rather approached through their condensation into particular historical points, both temporal and spatial. This diasporic mo(ve)ment marks the split between diaspora and home. Now, while the concept of history in diaspora is both temporal and spatial, there is a characteristic emphasis on the latter dimension of spatiality within diasporic cultural practices.

Although the historical rupture of diaspora is thus significantly different from that of modernity, then, diasporic and modern identities are ontologically related. Certainly, the spatial dimension of diaspora is emphasized at least partly as a direct challenge to the linear temporal history of modernity. Diasporic history displaces modernist history, or rather more appropriately, diasporic history *places* modernist history. The claim to universality of modernity is challenged by diaspora in that diasporic history relativizes the linear temporal history of Eurocentric modernity. Diasporic identity introduces another history—a counter-history—into modern identity. Or rather again, as modern identity is not necessarily ontologically or chronologically prior to diasporic identity, diaspora and modernity provide counter-histories to each other.

As previously noted, West and Gilroy in comparison to James have written on diaspora during the recent period, in which diasporic identity was being claimed by various cultural communities other than the diasporic African community. The relationship between these various diasporic identities must also be critically addressed. James, in his diasporic revision of modernity, comments on the "unique history" of the "Negro" slaves (1963: 392). Similarly, West notes that prophetic criticism is "primarily based on a distinctly black tragic sense of life" (1993: x). Considering these claims of what may be interpreted as cultural specificity, then, the appropriateness of the work of James, West, and Gilroy on black modernity for my theorization of diaspora as ontology, which is not specific to the African cultural context, might well be questioned.

This issue of the relationship between diasporic communities, however, has not only recently become central to the cultural politics of diaspora. The appropriation of the very concept of diaspora from the Jewish tradition by pan-African advocates has already necessitated a primary attention to this issue. Gilroy explicitly attends to this appropriation, calling for the collaboration between black and Jewish thinkers in particular and providing an argument for "the intercultural history of the diaspora concept" (1993: 211) that effectively addresses the issue of cultural specificity. Repudiating the "pointless and utterly immoral wrangle over which communities have experienced the most ineffable forms of degradation" (212), Gilroy emphatically states:

> I want to resist the idea that the Holocaust is merely another instance of genocide. I accept arguments for its uniqueness. However, I do not want the recognition of that uniqueness to be an obstacle to better understanding of the complicity of rationality and ethnocidal terror to which this book is dedicated. This is a difficult line on which to balance but it should be possible, and enriching, to discuss these histories together. (213)

Similarly then, while the particularity of African slavery must be appreciated, this recognition must not limit the use of the black tradition in understanding the intercultural politics of diaspora. As such, the work on black modernity by James and West as well as by Gilroy constitutes a significant theoretical intervention into diasporic cultural politics in its broadest sense, not only black political discourse.

As there are indeed many diasporic identities besides African identity circulating in current cultural politics, there are certainly many diasporic histories challenging the linear temporal history of Eurocentric modernity. However, these various histories do not necessarily undermine each other, for their spatialization allows for the relative placing of all of them. Diasporic histories, as such, are *concurrent*. Furthermore, the articulation of diasporic identities challenges Eurocentric modernity precisely in its placing of modernist history as also concurrent with diasporic histories. The postmodernist break with the modern is at least partly a response to the entry of these diasporic identities into modernist political discourse. Of course, the success of postmodernism in grappling with the challenge of diaspora, as well as other such significant interventions into modernity as feminism and queer politics, is debatable.

However, this diasporic dimension of spatiality may seem to imply that these various diasporic histories are *parallel*—that is, that they never meet and are thus discrete. I argue that this is the most urgent problematic within the articulation of diaspora itself. The relative placing of diasporic histories suggests that diasporic identities coexist independently alongside of each other, each following its own linear course of historical progress. I contend that diasporic cultural identities are collaboratively produced and, refiguring the spatial imagery of diaspora, that diasporic histories are not parallel but regularly *intersect*. Even as distinct cultural identities are claimed through current articulations of diaspora, this cultural process of diasporic articulation must itself be recognized as an ontologically particular though currently popular style of identity formation.

As such, the problematic of cultural specificity may be effectively addressed through the further articulation of what may be called *critical difference in diaspora*. As the specificity of each diasporic history must be appreciated, so must the intercultural and collaborative production of diasporic identity be recognized. It is only through this interplay of "identity" and "difference" that the concept of cultural difference takes on any critical significance. For if claims of cultural specificity are regularly informed by the multiculturalist notion of absolute difference, then any politically challenging formation of diasporic identity must articulate this other sense of critical difference. Only thus may the proliferation of diasporic identities in current cultural politics be recognized not simply as an exhibitionist display of the diversity of cultures in the mosaic sense, but more saliently as a radical disruption of linear temporal historicity altogether.

INDO-CARIBBEAN IDENTITY AND THE DOUBLY DIASPORIC

One such current diasporic formation is that of Indo-Caribbean identity. The term *Indo-Caribbean* itself is rather new, its earliest appearance in print and systematic use as far as I know dating from the mid-eighties in community newspapers and books published in Toronto. Certainly, there are many "East Indians" (another loaded discursive formation of diasporic identity, of course, popularly used both within the Caribbean and throughout its diaspora) from the Caribbean who do not identify as "Indo-Caribbean." However, many such as myself have come to claim this newly formed Indo-Caribbean identity, and the term seems to be gaining popularity, particularly outside of the Caribbean in the diasporic communities of the metropolitan cities of Europe and North America.

This Indo-Caribbean identity, then, is *doubly diasporic*. For the Indo-Caribbean diaspora is founded upon two mo(ve)ments—the first marking the colonial institution of Indian indentureship in the Caribbean during the nineteenth and

early twentieth centuries, and the second the neocolonial regulation of Caribbean migration to Europe and North America after World War II until the present. In the diasporic commemoration of these historical ruptures, indentureship
and migration have become inextricably linked, the first mo(ve)ment rhetorically
figured as the crossing of *Kāla Pāni,* or the Dark Waters, upon the retrospective
occasion of the second mo(ve)ment, which as yet remains nameless and perhaps
is still unnamable. Those living in the Indo-Caribbean diaspora, then, claim the
two diasporic homes of India *and* the Caribbean. As such, those who identify as
Indo-Caribbean claim not only national citizenship in the multicultural state but
also both Indian and Caribbean cultural identities. The historical emergence of
Indo-Caribbean identity is thus intimately related to the formation of Afro-
Caribbean and South Asian diasporic identities and further informed by the encounters between these and other diasporas in the metropolitan cities of Europe
and North America.

This doubled sense of historical rupture is inscribed within the term *Indo-
Caribbean* itself, the first mo(ve)ment of indentureship recalled through the prefix *Indo-* and the second mo(ve)ment of migration through the suffix *-Caribbean.*
The recollection of India in this *Indo-* is not that of the politically independent
secular state of the same name, but rather that of the cultural space of India that
the indentured laborers left behind as home. This home of the first mo(ve)ment
in Indo-Caribbean identity, then, is significantly different than the home of the
South Asian diaspora. While the South Asian diaspora is founded upon a notion
of home that redresses the political separation between the states of India, Paki-
stan, Sri Lanka, and Bangladesh, the thoroughly diasporic notion of a culturally
integrated India still informs the articulation of Indo-Caribbean identity. What
Seecharan (1993: 34) has notably called a "Gandhian India" thrives perhaps
most strongly in the active memory of the Indian diaspora in the Caribbean.

Meanwhile, the Indo-Caribbean recollection in this *-Caribbean* is of a pan-
Caribbean cultural space. While loyalty to the state and affinity to the local remain important to many Indo-Caribbean people, as expressed in their simultaneous claiming of various national and even town or village identities, these
are qualified by this broader sense of the Caribbean. Samuel Selvon recalls the
diasporic production of pan-Caribbean identity in Britain:

> When I left Trinidad in 1950 and went to England, one of my first experiences was
> living in a hostel with people from Africa and India and all over the Caribbean. It is
> strange to think I had to cross the Atlantic and be thousands of miles away, in a
> different culture and environment, for it to come about that, for the first time in my
> life, I was living among Barbadians and Jamaicans and others from my part of the
> world. If I had remained in Trinidad I might never have had the opportunity to be
> at such close quarters to observe and try to understand the differences and preju-
> dices that exist from islander to islander. (1987: 16)

Selvon further comments that "among the immigrants abroad, when they talk of
returning home the concept has widened into the greater area rather than to any

particular island" (22). However, this articulation of pan-Caribbean identity is not unique to the Indo-Caribbean diaspora but is rather similar in other diasporic Caribbean communities. Stuart Hall likewise describes the historical emergence of Black identity during the seventies in Britain:

> Then Black erupted and people said, "Well, you're from the Caribbean, in the midst of this, identifying with what's going on, the Black population in England. You're Black." . . . People [began] to ask, "Are you from Jamaica, are you from Trinidad, are you from Barbados?" You can just see the process of divide and rule. "No. Just address me as I am. I know you can't tell the difference so just call me Black." (1991: 55)

While Hall specifically addresses the development of British black politics in this passage, his use of examples of various Caribbean national or island identities is significant in its indication of the cultural formation of a pan-Caribbean identity within Britain. As such, this diasporic home of the second mo(ve)ment in Indo-Caribbean identity is collaboratively produced by Indo-, Afro-, and other diasporic Caribbean communities.

More precisely, however, this articulation of a doubled sense of diasporic identity indicates the creative collaboration of Indo- and Afro-Caribbean communities in particular on the ontological level. For Afro-Caribbean identity is similarly founded upon two diasporic mo(ve)ments—colonial slavery, commemorated as the Middle Passage, and neocolonial migration, again nameless and unnamable. Those living in the Afro-Caribbean diaspora also claim two diasporic homes— the integrated cultural space of Africa, undivided by colonial and now postcolonial borders, and the Caribbean, in its pan-regional sense. This articulation of doubled diaspora through the formation of Indo- and Afro-Caribbean identities is distinctly different from that of other hyphenated forms of cultural identity, thus radically altering the dialectics of diaspora and home. African-American diasporic identity, for example, though as a term of identity structurally similar to the term Afro-Caribbean, is constituted through only one diasporic mo(ve)-ment, that of slavery. While the prefix *African-* recalls the historical rupture of the Middle Passage, the suffix *-American* refers not to any diasporic sense of dislocation but to national identity. Now, it is not that African Americans have not participated in any significant flow of migration since slavery. The large-scale migration of African Americans between the onsets of World War I and the Depression from the rural regions of the southern United States to the urban cities of the north is historically commemorated as the Great Migration, yet this historical episode does not discursively rupture African-American identity. It seems that American national identity is strong enough to have contained this potentially traumatic historical episode.

Both Indo- and Afro-Caribbean identities as doubly diasporic, then, further complicate the dialectics of diaspora and home on the ontological level. For these formations of cultural identity are doubly diasporic not so much in an arithmetic as in an exponential sense, or perhaps in the figurative sense through which the character of diaspora has doubled over on itself. In this stylish style of diasporic articulation, the place of home becomes even more ambiguous, its location even more slippery. Through the current international circulation of these doubly diasporic identities, what I have called an old and even traditional style of cultural identity has been radically modified, the Caribbean as a site of diaspora now transformed into a site of home, those barely traceable connections to India and Africa yet further rarefied.

INDENTURESHIP AND CRITICAL DIFFERENCE IN DIASPORA

However, this collaborative articulation of doubly diasporic Indo- and Afro-Caribbean identities certainly does not translate into any sort of cultural *equivalency* between them. Indo- and Afro-Caribbean diasporic communities enter into uneasy alliances at best when this strategy of equivalency is employed. Returning to the articulation of critical difference in diaspora, I revisit here the diasporic mo(ve)ments of indentureship and slavery, those foundational historical points through which Indo- and Afro-Caribbean cultural identities are respectively constituted. The deep ambivalence toward both diaspora and home within the formation of Indo-Caribbean identity itself is traced through a critical reading of some inaugural texts in the emerging field of Indo-Caribbean studies. This revision of Indo-Caribbean history contributes to my theoretical proposition for the articulation of critical difference in the intercultural politics of diaspora and furthermore, I suggest, may well be extended to current studies on slavery in the African diaspora and other diasporic studies.

In recently published works of Indo-Caribbean history, there is a recurrent concern with the resemblance of indentureship to slavery. While concessions are usually allowed for cultural specificity, indentureship is regularly paralleled with slavery. Thus, the Indo- and Afro-Caribbean experiences are constituted as discrete and, in a sense, replicable histories. This argument on indentureship has only recently gained acceptance within the Indo-Caribbean community, let alone the Afro-Caribbean one, yet it has quickly become a foundation in the new academic discourse of Indo-Caribbean studies. However, this parallel historical treatment of indentureship and slavery was developed well before the emergence of Indo-Caribbean studies and even before the discursive formation of Indo-Caribbean diasporic identity itself.

This line of argument on indentureship as a form of slavery was postulated and popularized by the historian Hugh Tinker in his book aptly titled *A New System of Slavery* (1974). As he states, this historical work "represents the first attempt to provide a comprehensive study of the whole process of emigration from rural India, across the seas to more than a dozen countries" (xiii), dealing with the indenture and other forms of labor recruitment of Indians in the Caribbean, Africa, and Southeast Asia. The book opens with a quote from the imperial official Lord Russell in 1840: "I should be unwilling to adopt any measure to favour the transfer of labourers from British India . . . which may lead to . . . a new system of slavery" (v). Tinker states the premise of his own work:

> The legacy of Negro slavery in the Caribbean and the Mascarenes was a new system
> of slavery, incorporating many of the repressive features of the old system, which
> induced in the Indians many of the responses of their African brothers [sic] in bond-
> age. For ninety years after emancipation, sugar planters and sugar workers . . .
> worked out the inheritance of slavery. (19)

He justifies this conclusion as well as the title of his book in describing his course
of study:

> When Lord John Russell's announcement was discovered . . . this seemed to promise
> the possibility of an arresting title: but it did not appear to represent a plain state-
> ment of the realities with which he was confronted. Only gradually did the accumu-
> lation of evidence produce the conclusion that indenture and other forms of servi-
> tude did, indeed, replicate the actual conditions of slavery. (xiv)

Tinker's work certainly constitutes a valuable historical project and is indispensable for anyone conducting research in the area of Indian labor overseas, including indentureship. Moreover, his bold argument on indentureship has been
readily adopted and widely circulated within Indo-Caribbean studies. Although
Tinker is not Indo-Caribbean himself, his book has become a fundamental
cultural text in an incipient Indo-Caribbean canon. *A New System of Slavery* is
treated as an authoritative source in Indo-Caribbean historical scholarship and
regularly featured on the book tables at community events. Indeed, much current Indo-Caribbean scholarship is informed by this argument on indentureship
as slavery, if not modeled outright upon the work of Tinker.

Brinsley Samaroo's "Two Abolitions: African Slavery and East Indian Indentureship" (1987) opens with the same quote by Lord Russell as does *A New
System of Slavery*. The stated purpose of his essay is "to add to this debate by
drawing further parallels between the systems of slavery and indentureship than
those elaborated by Professor Tinker . . . [and] further, to indicate similar moti-
vation and action among those who agitated against both systems" (25). Samaroo concludes that "[t]he movement for the abolition of indentureship bore
many resemblances to that for the abolition of slavery" and summarizes that the
historical forces "in both abolitions came together to end an era of slavery and
of a new system of slavery" (38).

Basdeo Mangru's *Indenture and Abolition* (1993), while not directly referring
to Tinker's work, resembles it in certain ways. Mangru's book also opens with a
quote, but from the Indian nationalist Gopal Krishna Gokhale in 1910, stating
of indentureship that "such a system by whatever name it may be called, must
really border on the servile" (iv). Mangru describes indentureship as "a system
the essential characteristics of which were reminiscent of slavery" (ix) and further
notes that "[t]he anti-indenture campaign in India paralleled that of the antislav-
ery movement in England" (xi). He goes on to call Indian indentured laborers in
British Guiana "semi-slaves," arguing that they, "like the slave[s], [were] regarded

merely as an instrument of production, one without any personality" (xii). He also cites Chief Justice Beaumont's statement on the entire Guianese political system as "a mercantile oligarchy founded on the foundations of slavery" (xii).

Frank Birbalsingh in his successive introductory articles to *Jahaji Bhai, Indenture and Exile,* and *Indo-Caribbean Resistance* increasingly emphasizes the parallel between indentureship and slavery, strengthening this argument from one introduction to the next. In the relatively cautious approach of his first article, he states that "[t]he first indentured immigrants occupied lodgings vacated by the former slaves, and were employed by the former slave owners. Hence the themes spawned by slavery/indenture are identical" (1988: 8). In his second article, Birbalsingh more forcefully posits a number of parallels between "the satanic device of slavery" and "the devilish stratagem of slavery's bedfellow—indenture" (1989: 9). He argues:

> For a long time, slave and indentured labour, under grossly exploitative conditions of colonial domination, bore similar dehumanizing burdens and executed the same back-breaking plantation tasks. There is much . . . to support the view that this shared colonial victimization induced common attitudes of resistance and engendered unity of political purpose in Africans and Indians. (8)

He also refers to a common "exploitation [of] those who had crossed both the 'middle passage' from Africa, and the 'kala pani' (black water) from India" (10). In his third article, Birbalsingh this time explicitly argues:

> The appalling conditions under which indentured Indian immigrants existed suggests that they were slaves in everything but name; for they lived in the very quarters vacated by the freed Africans, and performed their exact tasks. . . . Just as the brutality of slavery had provoked many slave rebellions, so did the hardships of indenture provoke resistance and retaliation. (1993: viii)

As such, the argument that indentureship parallels slavery has occupied a place of strategic importance in the articulation of Indo-Caribbean identity. Birbalsingh himself explains the complicated international political situation in which this strategy was adopted:

> [T]he better documented Afro-Caribbean suffering through slavery confer[s] a regional legitimacy that is acknowledged in the Euro-American metropolis which still controls the Third World as firmly as ever. (1988: 13)

> This condign sense of [the] historical legacy [of African slavery] . . . justifie[s] the dominance of an Afrocentric ethos in the Caribbean which, in turn, tend[s] to downplay, if not obscure the parallel Indo-Caribbean experience of indenture. (1993: xvi)

Of course, Birbalsingh is politically shrewd enough to qualify his criticism of Afrocentrism with appropriate deference to "the horror of the Atlantic slave trade, and the plight of its main victims—Afro-Americans and Afro-West Indians" and to the experience of "blacks in America and the Caribbean, who had endured the most heinous of all crimes, the trade in human beings as merchandise, across the Atlantic, for nearly four centuries" (1993: xvi).

Lastly, David Dabydeen and Samaroo in their introductory article to *Across the Dark Waters* (1996) place a heavy emphasis on the parallel between indentureship and slavery. The only subheading in this introduction is titled "A comparison with slavery," appearing rather anomalously in large, bold, and italicized print. Directly crediting Tinker, they argue that "East Indian indentureship turned out to be, as Hugh Tinker wrote, 'a new system of slavery'" (3). Dabydeen and Samaroo state that "[i]ndentureship, like slavery, furthered the creation of a new civilization in the Americas out of the blending of disparate traditions and the interaction of many peoples." Furthermore, employing a quotation by the wife of a ship captain on the preparation of indentured laborers for prospective purchasers, they simply state that "indentureship was hardly any different [from slavery]" (4).

Certainly, the project of a critical comparison between indentureship and slavery, as well as the publication of historical research on indentureship that is entailed in this project, is very valuable, and not only so as an "ethnic" concern in the academic field of Indo-Caribbean studies. However, the strategy of paralleling indentureship and slavery, *and thus Indo- and Afro-Caribbean diasporic identities,* is worth reconsidering for reasons besides the obvious legal distinctions between these labor systems and their historical variations. For this strategy affects the doubly diasporic meaning of Indo-Caribbean identity itself.

Firstly, the argument for indentureship as a form of slavery affects the meaning of Indianness, or the *Indo-* in Indo-Caribbean identity. The treatment of indentureship as slavery dismisses those choices made by Indian laborers themselves to migrate in search of employment opportunities and social mobility. The campaign of the Indian nationalists for the final abolition of indenture, achieved by 1920, and the further total prohibition of Indian labor migration, achieved in 1922, did not as such represent the interests of Indian migrant laborers. Yet in my research, only Walton Look Lai (1993: 136–37, 156, 177), however sketchily, and P. C. Emmer (1986), however problematically, challenge the assumption that indentured laborers favored the abolition of indenture. In another work theorizing the representation of Indian indentured laborers in the Caribbean, I systematically critique the politics of class, race, gender, and what I call *territoriality* in the abolition campaign of the Indian nationalists, and I further argue that Indians in the Caribbean advocated the reformation of labor migration rather than its abolition altogether.[1]

This historical reading of indentureship challenges those ideological tenets of nationalism as developed by the colonial Indian elite, which continue to inform current articulations of both Indian national identity and South Asian and Indo-Caribbean cultural identities. In thus problematizing nationalist representations of Indian culture, the diasporic commemoration of indentureship may undermine monolithic notions of Indian identity. In this sense, the *Indo-* in Indo-

Caribbean identity signifies that the Indo-Caribbean diaspora cannot be treated as a mere subcategory of the South Asian diaspora and that the meanings of Indianness are significantly different between as well as within Indo-Caribbean and South Asian identities.

Secondly, the argument for indentureship as a form of slavery also affects the meaning of Caribbeanness, or the -*Caribbean* in Indo-Caribbean identity. For this argument also relies upon the contention that Indian laborers entered the Caribbean in the same historical circumstances as did African laborers and that their responses to these circumstances of entry into the Caribbean were basically similar. This reluctance to theorize the critical differences between, let alone within, Afro-Caribbean and Indo-Caribbean diasporic experiences only marks a failure in the understanding of the relationship between Africans and Indians in the Caribbean. Indeed, writing as long ago as the publication of Tinker's work, John Gaffar La Guerre (1974) noted this failure in the Black Power movement in Trinidad, commenting that "the East Indians were asked to join with Negroes on the basis of 'blackness' and a common experience in the West Indies. Slavery and indentureship, they assumed, was enough to provide a common response to all oppression" (102). Just as indentureship and slavery do not constitute a "common experience," let me suggest similarly that indentureship and slavery are not parallel *and Indo- and Afro-Caribbean identities are not discrete*. That is, indentureship is not a replica of slavery. Rather, these diasporic histories intersect, crisscrossing and interweaving with each other in the entangled trajectories of labor migration and cultural identity.

It is not coincidental that what I have suggested is the central problematic of diaspora—the issue of cultural difference—is raised by La Guerre in his treatment of the Black Power movement and again in my own treatment of the emergence of Indo-Caribbean studies. For both of these occasions mark the historical formation of new diasporic identities, Afro- and Indo-Caribbean respectively. The argument for indentureship as a form of slavery exemplifies the problem of cultural relativization in the articulation of diasporic identities. In the diasporic spatialization of history, cultural identities are often posited as parallel, reflecting each other but never meeting. As such, the cultural politics of diaspora are often only too readily compatible with multiculturalist notions of cultural diversity, based as they are on the concept of *absolute difference*. However, the diasporic spatialization of history may be theoretically reconfigured to account for the regular intersection of cultural identities. Thus, the idea of cultural difference takes on critical significance as the current proliferation of the concept of diaspora itself becomes an important point of intersection among those engaged in this historical process. What I am arguing for, then, is the concept of *critical difference*. That is, while diaspora is a currently popular style of identity formation, a critical sense of cultural difference may yet be articulated both between and within diasporic identities. As the diasporic production of identity through the commemoration of a foundational historical mo(ve)ment is presently becoming an in-

creasingly common strategy for cultural mobilization, the success of this strategy
in resisting those newly dominant notions of multiculturalism depends upon the
negotiation of social, political, and aesthetic differences among those communities constituted through diaspora.

The theorization of this issue of critical difference in diaspora is all the more
urgent as it ultimately bears upon the historical appropriation of the concept of
diaspora itself from Jewish cultural politics. For the very use of the term *diaspora*
by Afro- and Indo-Caribbean and other diasporic communities necessitates this
articulation of critical difference. If neither the powerful concept of diaspora is
to be reserved exclusively for the Jewish community, nor various histories of
displacement and disenfranchisement are to be measured against each other or
some ahistorical ideal, then the task of theorizing the current proliferation of
diasporic identities requires not the simple collapsing of, but rather a profound
reckoning with, the politically significant differences between diasporic identities. Through this articulation of critical difference in diaspora, those absurd
competitions between diasporic communities over the claim to the most oppressive form of cultural persecution might be replaced by some mutual realization
of the political relationships between the many historical structures of dominance as well as the many historical projects of resistance.

The concept of critical difference in diaspora thus affects not only the treatment of indentureship and slavery within the academic field of Indo-Caribbean
studies, but moreover the study of Indo- and Afro-Caribbean cultures themselves in all academic fields, including religious studies. For this concept challenges conventional notions of culture altogether. Accepting the concept of diaspora as style, we have to admit that culture is not a racial or even ancestral
inheritance, but that it is continually fashioned and refashioned through the
ongoing articulation of identity. Through this particular style of identity formation, home is constructed only in a dialectical relationship with diaspora. As
such, India becomes a meaningful place for locating identity only when it has
been left behind, the very desire for the return home thus inaugurated. And the
same holds true of Africa. The notion of culture either lost or retained is thus
radically problematized by this approach to diaspora, along with the conventional assumption that Africans in the Caribbean have lost their culture while
Indians have retained theirs. Rather, both Afro- and Indo-Caribbean cultural
identities have been creatively forged through the style of diaspora.

However, we must also account for the cultural differences between Afro- and
Indo-Caribbean identities. And it is not a simple matter of time—that is, that
Africans have lost more of their culture than have Indians because they have
been in the Caribbean for a longer period. Time is not so simple, and after all,
some African cultural forms are more popular now than they ever have been
within the Caribbean. Yet certainly within the cultural field of religion, it may
well seem that Indian institutions have indeed better survived the progression of
time than have African traditions. But again, it is not so much a matter of cultural

loss or retention as the specific social conditions of slavery and indentureship through which Africans and Indians were respectively introduced into the Caribbean. The system of indenture and subsequent settlement plans for Indians in the Caribbean facilitated exchange, travel, and communication between India and the Caribbean, as was not possible under slavery or post-emancipation plans for Africans in the Caribbean. Through the periodic visitations of governmental delegations and religious missionaries from India as well as the regular travels of individuals, Indians in the Caribbean were able not to retain any primordial Indian culture as such, but rather to participate in the same international upheavals that were radically transforming Indian society itself. The Hindu traditions of Sanatan Dharma and Arya Samaj and the Muslim traditions of Sunni and Shi'a exist today among Indians in the Caribbean, then, not simply because indentured laborers arrived on the sugar plantations already belonging to one of these religious traditions. It was what may be called the invention of religion within the modern world system—the division between "orthodox" and "reform" religious systems as well as the codification of Hinduism as a religion in itself—that resulted in the development of these traditions within both India and its diaspora. The concept of critical difference thus dissolves the absolutist notion of cultural difference, according to which, on the one hand, Africans in the Caribbean take no part in tradition, while on the other, Indians take no part in the modern.

In conclusion, then, working through the theoretical possibility of critical difference in diaspora, I suggest that the better strategy for claiming Indo-Caribbean identity may be pursued through articulating the difference rather than the parallel between indentureship and slavery, and hence between Indo- and Afro-Caribbean identities. Of course, this strategy is already the more successful one, if not within Indo-Caribbean studies, then within the popular Indo-Caribbean memory. While Africans in the Caribbean generally celebrate the abolition of slavery upon emancipation, Indians have long celebrated not the abolition of indentureship but rather their *arrival* in the Caribbean. On 5 May 1938 in British Guiana, the centenary of the arrival of Indians in the colony was celebrated. The British Guiana East Indian Association had requested that the day be declared an official holiday by the government, but their attempt was unsuccessful. Nonetheless, a public ceremony, an organizational session, a number of dinners, an evening fair, a dance drama, and the opening of a library were held in celebration of the centenary (Ruhomon 1988: 248, 290–92). Similarly, on 30 May 1945 in Trinidad, the centenary of the arrival of Indians in that colony was celebrated among "[t]he greatest concourse of Indians ever to have assembled in Trinidad" (Kirpalani et al. 1995: 119). Zoning regulations were lifted, while stores in the cities and major commercial centers were closed for the day and governmental departments closed for half of the day. A procession, public ceremony, a fair, and a dance were held, with over thirty thousand people in attendance during the evening (119). Presently, the celebration of Indian Arrival Day has been regularly observed as an annual event since 1978, when the first such celebration was organized by some Indo-Trinidadians from San Juan and Curepe (Singh 1987: 4).

This commemoration of diasporic history among Indians in the Caribbean certainly contradicts the argument that indentureship and slavery are parallel, as postulated in much current Indo-Caribbean scholarship. However, this contradiction does not necessarily imply any theoretical opposition between Indo-Caribbean popular culture and academic production. Indeed, their creative interaction has characterized the historical emergence of Indo-Caribbean identity in the late eighties and through the nineties. For this contradiction exists both within the popular Indo-Caribbean memory and within the academic field of Indo-Caribbean studies. In this popular Indo-Caribbean memory, a complex type of diasporic Indian nationalism has emerged. In the international development of Indian nationalism, diasporic Indians have not simply adopted the ideology of the Indian nationalist elite. Rather, not only have diasporic Indians been instrumental in the ideological formation of nationalism within India, but furthermore Indian nationalism has been articulated in radically different ways throughout India and its diaspora. In particular, diasporic Indians have articulated a quite peculiar sort of nationalism. The territorialist insistence on compulsory residence within India has not been entrenched in the popular memory of Indians in the Caribbean—that is, to be an Indian, you do not have to live inside India. The celebration of Indian arrival in the Caribbean attests to this ambivalence toward home in the formation of diasporic identity. Now, the academic field of Indo-Caribbean studies also displays this ambivalence toward indentureship. After all, those texts by Samaroo, Mangru, Birbalsingh, and Dabydeen in which the argument for indentureship as a form of slavery has been adopted from Tinker were themselves published on the occasions of the one hundred fiftieth anniversaries of Indian arrival in Guyana (1988) and Trinidad (1995). Indeed, the diasporic theme of Indian arrival in the Caribbean permeates both Indo-Caribbean popular culture and academic production, both in diaspora and at home.

The one hundred fiftieth anniversary of the arrival of Indians in British Guiana, also marking the earliest arrival of Indians in the Caribbean colonies, was celebrated in 1988 and that of the arrival of Indians in Trinidad and Jamaica in 1995. Between these celebrations, significant changes within the Caribbean had taken place as Indians were elected heads of state in Guyana and in Trinidad and Tobago, as leaders not of "ethnic" parties but of democratic parties with leftist sympathies to varying degrees. Indian Arrival Day was officially instituted as a national annual holiday in Trinidad and Tobago, as Emancipation Day had been some years before. Thus, in both popular and official arenas of Caribbean culture, the critical difference between Indian and African diasporic identities has already in some ways been recognized. Meanwhile, in the Indo-Caribbean diaspora of Toronto and other diasporic sites, Indian Arrival Day is also celebrated annually with an increasing popularity. Perhaps Indians finally *have* arrived in the Caribbean—yet only after a second migration from the Caribbean to the metropolitan cities of Europe and North America has profoundly transformed the diasporic identity occasioned by the first migration from India to the colonies of Africa, Southeast Asia, and the Caribbean.

Note

1. See my thesis, "Dialectics of Diaspora and Home: Indentureship, Migration and Indo-Caribbean Identity" (Lokaisingh-Meighoo 1997).

Works Cited

Birbalsingh, Frank. 1988. "Introduction." In *Jahaji Bhai: An Anthology of Indo-Caribbean Literature,* ed. Frank Birbalsingh. Toronto: TSAR.

Birbalsingh, Frank. 1989. "Introduction." In *Indenture and Exile: The Indo-Caribbean Experience,* ed. Frank Birbalsingh. Toronto: TSAR.

Birbalsingh, Frank. 1993. "Introduction." In *Indo-Caribbean Resistance,* ed. Frank Birbalsingh. Toronto: TSAR.

Dabydeen, David, and Brinsley Samaroo, eds. 1996. *Across the Dark Waters: Ethnicity and Indian Identity in the Caribbean.* London: Macmillan Caribbean.

Emmer, P. C. 1986. "The Meek Hindu; the Recruitment of Indian Indentured Labourers for Service Overseas, 1870–1916." In *Colonialism and Migration: Indentured Labour before and after Slavery,* edited by P. C. Emmer. Boston: Martinus Nijhoff Publishers.

Gilroy, Paul. 1993. *The Black Atlantic: Modernity and Double Consciousness.* Cambridge, Mass.: Harvard University Press.

Hall, Stuart. 1991. "Old and New Identities, Old and New Ethnicities." In *Culture, Globalization and the World System,* edited by Anthony D. King. Binghamton: State University of New York.

Hebdige, Dick. 1993. *Subculture: The Meaning of Style.* 1979. New York: Routledge.

James, C. L. R. 1963. "Appendix: From Toussaint L'Ouverture to Fidel Castro." *The Black Jacobins: Toussaint L'Ouverture and the San Domingo Revolution.* 2nd rev. ed. New York: Vintage Books.

Kirpalani, Murli J., et al., eds. [1945] 1995. "Indian Centenary Review: One Hundred Years of Progress, Trinidad 1845–1945." Reprinted in *In Celebration of 150 Yrs. of the Indian Contribution to Trinidad and Tobago,* edited by Brinsley Samaroo et al. Port-of-Spain: Historical Publications.

La Guerre, John Gaffar. 1974. "The East Indian Middle Class Today." *Calcutta to Caroni: The East Indians of Trinidad.* Trinidad: Longman Caribbean.

Lokaisingh-Meighoo, Sean. 1997. "Dialectics of Diaspora and Home: Indentureship, Migration and Indo-Caribbean Identity." Master's thesis, York University.

Look Lai, Walton. 1993. *Indentured Labor, Caribbean Sugar: Chinese and Indian Migrants to the British West Indies, 1838–1918.* Baltimore: Johns Hopkins University Press.

Mangru, Basdeo. 1993. *Indenture and Abolition: Sacrifice and Survival on the Guyanese Sugar Plantations.* Toronto: TSAR.

Ruhomon, Peter. [1947] 1988. *Centenary History of the East Indians in British Guiana, 1838–1938.* Georgetown: 150th Anniversary Committee of the Arrival of Indians in Guyana.

Samaroo, Brinsley. 1987. "Two Abolitions: African Slavery and East Indians Indentureship."
   In *India in the Caribbean,* edited by David Dabydeen and Brinsley Samaroo. London:
   Hansib/University of Warwick, Centre for Caribbean Studies.

Seecharan, Clem. 1993. *India and the Shaping of the Indo-Guyanese Imagination 1890s–1920s.*
   Leeds: Peepal Tree.

Selvon, Samuel. [1979] 1987. "Three into One Can't Go—East Indian, Trinidadian, Westin-
   dian." In *India in the Caribbean,* edited by David Dabydeen and Brinsley Samaroo. London: Hansib/University of Warwick, Centre for Caribbean Studies.

Singh, I. J. Bahadur, ed. 1987. *Indians in the Caribbean.* New Delhi: Sterling Publishers.

Tinker, Hugh. 1974. *A New System of Slavery: The Export of Indian Labour Overseas 1830–
   1920.* New York: Oxford University Press.

West, Cornel. 1993. *Keeping Faith: Philosophy and Race in America.* New York: Routledge.

Caribbean Religions
A Supplementary Bibliography

Agorsah, E. Kofi, ed. 1994. *Maroon Heritage: Archaeological, Ethnographic and Historical Per-spectives.* Kingston, Jamaica: Canoe Press.

Allsopp, Richard, ed. 1996. *Dictionary of Caribbean English Usage.* Oxford: Oxford University Press.

Alonso, Guillermo Andreu. 1992. *Los araras en Cuba.* La Habana: Editorial de Ciencias Sociales.

Argüelles Mederos, Aníbal, and Ileana Hodge Limonta. 1991. *Los llamados cultos sincréticos y el espiritismo.* La Habana: Editorial Academia.

Aristide, Jean-Bertrand. 1990. *In the Parish of the Poor.* Translated by Amy Wilentz. Maryknoll, N.Y.: Orbis.

Aristide, Jean Bertrand. 1992. *Théologie et Politique.* Montreal: CIDIHCA.

Aristide, Jean-Bertrand. 1993. *An Autobiography.* Translated by Linda Maloney. Maryknoll, N.Y.: Orbis.

Aristide, Jean-Bertrand. 1996. *Dignity.* Translated by Carol F. Coates. Charlottesville: University Press of Virginia.

Arvigo, Rosita, and Nadine Epstein. 1994. *Sastun: My Apprenticeship with a Maya Healer.* New York: Harper Collins.

Austin, Allan D. 1997. *African Muslims in Antebellum America: Transatlantic Stories and Spiritual Troubles.* New York: Routledge.

Austin-Broos, Diane. 1997. *Jamaica Genesis: Religion and the Politics of Moral Orders.* Chicago: University of Chicago Press.

Bakan, Abigail B. 1990. *Ideology and Class Conflict in Jamaica: The Politics of Rebellion.* Montreal: McGill-Queen's University Press.

Baltar Rodriguez, José. 1997. *Los chinos de Cuba. Apuntes etnográficos.* La Habana: Fundación Fernando Ortiz.

Barnes, Sandra, ed. 1989. *African Ogun: Old World and New.* Bloomington: Indiana University Press.

Barnet, Miguel. [1981] 1998. *La fuente viva.* La Habana: Editorial Letras Cubanas.

Barrett, Leonard. 1976. *The Sun and the Drum: African Roots in Jamaican Folk Tradition.* London and Kingston, Jamaica: Heinemann and Sangster's Bookstores.

Barrett, Leonard. 1988. *The Rastafarians: Sounds of Cultural Dissonance.* Rev. ed. Boston: Beacon.

Barry, Tom, with Dylan Vernon. 1995. *Inside Belize.* Albuquerque: Resource Center Press.

Bascom, William R. 1972. *Shango in the New World.* Austin: African and Afro-American Research Institute, University of Texas.

Bastide, R. 1971. *African Civilizations in the New World.* New York: Harper and Row.

Beatty, Paul B. Jr. 1970. *A History of the Lutheran Church in Guyana.* South Pasadena, Calif.: William Carey Press.

Bébel-Gisler, Dany. 1985. *Leonora: L'histoire enfouie de la Guadeloupe.* Paris: Seghers.

Bébel-Gisler, Dany, and Laënnec Hurbon. 1975. *Cultures et pouvoir dans la Caraïbe: Langue créole, vaudou, sectes religieuses en Guadeloupe et en Haïti.* Paris: L'Harmattan.

Beckwith, Martha Warren. [1928] 1969. *Jamaica Folklore*. New York: American Folklore Society.

Beckwith, Martha Warren. [1929] 1969. *Black Roadways: A Study of Jamaican Folklife*. New York: Negro Universities Press.

Bellegarde-Smith, Patrick. 1990. *Haiti: The Breached Citadel*. Boulder, Colo.: Westview.

Benítez-Rojo, Antonio. 1992. *The Repeating Island: The Caribbean and the Postmodern Perspective*. Translated by James Maranis. Durham: Duke University Press.

Bilby, Kenneth, and Elliott Leib. 1986. "Kumina, the Howellite Church and the Emergence of Rastafarian Traditional Music in Jamaica." *Jamaica Journal* 19 (3): 22–28.

Birbalsingh, Frank, ed. 1989. *Indenture and Exile: The Indo-Caribbean Experience*. Toronto: TSAR.

Birbalsingh, Frank, ed. 1993. *Indo-Caribbean Resistance*. Toronto: TSAR.

Bisnauth, Dale. 1996. *A History of Religions in the Caribbean*. Kingston, Jamaica: Kingston Publishers, 1989. Reprint, Trenton, N.J.: Africa World Press.

Blackman, Francis (Woodie). 1988. *Methodism: Two Hundred Years in Barbados*. Bridgetown, Barbados: Methodist Church.

Bolívar, Natalia. 1990. *Los orishas en Cuba*. La Habana: Ediciones Unión.

Boucher, Philip. B. 1992. *Cannibal Encounters: Europe and the Island Caribs, 1492–1763*. Baltimore: Johns Hopkins University Press.

Bourguignon, Erika. 1973. *Religion, Altered States of Consciousness and Social Change*. Columbus: Ohio State University.

Brandon, George. 1993. *Santeria from Africa to the New World*. Bloomington: Indiana University Press.

Brathwaite, Edward. 1971. *The Development of Creole Society in Jamaica: 1770–1820*. Oxford: Oxford University Press.

Brathwaite, Edward. 1977. *Wars of Respect: Nanny and Sam Sharpe*. Kingston, Jamaica: Agency for Public Information.

Bremer, Thomas, and Ulrich Fleischmann, eds. 1993. *Alternative Cultures in the Caribbean*. Frankfurt am Main: Vervuert.

Brereton, Bridget, and Winston Dookeran, eds. 1982. *East Indians in the Caribbean: Colonialism and the Struggle for Identity*. Millwood, N.Y.: Kraus.

Bronkhurst, H. V. P. 1888. *Among the Hindus and Creoles of British Guiana*. London: Woolmeyer.

Brown, Karen McCarthy. 1991. *Mama Lola: A Vodou Priestess in Brooklyn*. Berkeley: University of California Press.

Burton, Richard. 1997. *Afro-Creole: Power, Opposition and Play in the Caribbean*. Ithaca: Cornell Univesity Press.

Cabrera, Lydia. 1958. *La sociedad secreta abakuá*. La Habana: Ediciones CR.

Cabrera, Lydia. [1954] 1993. *El monte*. La Habana: Editorial Letras Cubanas.

Campbell, Horace. 1987. *Rasta and Resistance: From Marcus Garvey to Walter Rodney*. Trenton, N.J.: Africa World Press.

Campbell, Persia. 1969. *Chinese Coolie Emigration to Countries within the British Empire*. New York: Negro University Press.

Campbell, P. F. 1982. *The Church in Seventeenth Century Barbados*. Bridgetown, Barbados: Barbados Museum and Historical Society.

Canizares, Raul. 1993. *Walking with the Night: Afro-Cuban Santeria*. Rochester: Destiny Books.

Castro, Fidel, and Frei Betto. 1987. *Fidel and Religion: Castro Talks on Revolution and Religion.* Translated by Cuban Centre for Translation. New York: Simon and Schuster.

Charles, Arthur, and Michael Dash, eds. 1999. *Libète: A Haiti Anthology.* Princeton, London, and Kingston, Jamaica: Marlus Wiener, Latin American Bureau, and Ian Randle.

Chevannes, Barry. 1994. *Rastafari: Roots and Ideology.* Syracuse: Syracuse University Press.

Chevannes, Barry, ed. 1998. *Rastafari and Other African-Caribbean Worldviews.* London: Macmillan, 1995. Reprint, New Brunswick, N.J.: Rutgers University Press.

Chuffat Latour, Antonio. 1927. *Apunte histórico de los chinos en Cuba.* La Habana: Molina y Cia.

CIPS, ed. 1998. *Panorama de la religión en Cuba.* La Habana: Editora Política.

Clarke, Colin G. 1986. *East Indians in a West Indian Town: San Fernando, Trinidad, 1930–70.* Boston: Allen and Unwin.

Clarke, Sebastian. 1980. *Jah Music: The Evolution of the Popular Jamaican Song.* London: Heinemann.

Clementi, Cecil. 1915. *The Chinese in British Guiana.* British Guiana: Argosy.

Courlander, Harold. 1960. *The Drum and the Hoe: Life and Lore of the Haitian People.* Berkeley: University of California Press.

Courlander, Harold. 1976. *A Treasury of Afro-American Folklore.* New York: Crown Publishers.

Courlander, Harold. [1939] 1979. *Haiti Singing.* New York: Cooper Square Publishers.

Courlander, Harold, and Rémy Bastien, eds. 1966. *Religion and Politics in Haiti.* Washington, D.C: Institute of Cross-Cultural Research.

Crahan, Margaret and Franklin W. Knight. 1979. *Africa and the Caribbean: The Legacies of a Link.* Baltimore: Johns Hopkins University Press.

Craton, Michael. 1982. *Testing the Chains: Resistance to Slavery in the British West Indies.* Ithaca: Cornell University Press.

Cuba Commission. [1876] 1993. *The Cuba Commission Report. A Hidden History of the Chinese in Cuba.* Baltimore: Johns Hopkins University Press.

Curtin, Philip D. 1975. *Two Jamaicas: The Role of Ideas in a Tropical Colony, 1830–1865.* New York: Harvard University Press, 1955. Reprint, New York: Atheneum.

Cuthbert, Robert W. 1986. *Ecumenism and Development: A Socio-Historical Analysis of the Caribbean Conference of Churches.* Bridgetown, Barbados: CCC.

Da Costa, Emilia Viotti. 1994. *Crowns of Glory, Tears of Blood: The Demerara Slave Rebellion of 1823.* New York: Oxford University Press.

Dabydeen, David, and Brinsley Samaroo, eds. 1987. *India in the Caribbean.* London: Hansib/University of Warwick, Centre for Caribbean Studies.

Dabydeen, David, and Brinsley Samaroo, eds. 1996. *Across the Dark Waters: Ethnicity and Indian Identity in the Caribbean.* London: Macmillan Caribbean.

Dark, P. 1973. *Bush Negro Art.* New York: Alec Tiranti.

David, Christine. 1985. *Folklore of Carriacou.* Bridgetown, Barbados: Coles Printery.

Davis, Edmund. 1977. *Roots and Blossoms.* Bridgetown, Barbados: CEDAR Press.

Davis, Kortright, ed. 1977. *Moving into Freedom.* Bridgetown, Barbados: CEDAR Press.

Davis, Kortright. 1982. *Mission for Caribbean Change: Caribbean Development as Theological Enterprise.* Frankfurt am Main: Peter Lang.

Davis, Kortright. 1983. *Cross and Crown in Barbados: Caribbean Political Religion in the Late 19thC.* Frankfurt am Main: Peter Lang.

Davis, Kortright. 1990. *Emancipation Still Comin': Explorations in Caribbean Emancipatory Theology.* Maryknoll, N.Y.: Orbis.

Davis, Kortright, and Elias Farajaje-Jones, eds. 1991. *African Creative Expressions of the Divine.* Washington, D.C.: Howard University School of Divinity.

Davis, Stephen. 1977. *Reggae Bloodlines.* New York: Anchor.

Davis, Wade. 1985. *The Serpent and the Rainbow.* New York: Simon and Schuster.

Davis, Wade. 1988. *Passage of Darkness: The Ethnobiology of the Haitian Zombie.* Chapel Hill: University of North Carolina Press.

Dayan, Joan. 1995. *Haiti, History, and the Gods.* Berkeley: University of California Press.

Dayfoot, Arthur C. 1999. *The Shaping of the West Indian Church, 1492–1962.* Mona, Jamaica, and Gainesville: Press University of the West Indies and University Press of Florida.

De la Sagra, Ramón. 1861. *Historia física, económico-política, intelectual y moral de la isla de Cuba.* Paris: Hachette.

Deive, Carlos E. 1992. *Vodu y magia.* 3rd ed. Santo Domingo: Fundación Cultural Dominicana.

Delany, Francis X. 1930. *A History of the Catholic Church in Jamaica, BWI, 1494–1929.* New York: Jesuit Mission Press.

Delince, K. 1993. *Les forces politiques en Haïti: Manuel d'histoire contemporaine.* Paris: Karthala and Pegasus Books.

Deren, Maya. 1970. *Divine Horsemen: Voodoo Gods of Haiti.* New York: Chelsea House.

Desmangles, Leslie. 1992. *The Faces of the Gods: Vodou and Roman Catholicism in Haiti.* Chapel Hill: University of North Carolina Press.

Díaz Fabelo, Teodoro. 1998. *Diccionario de la lengua Conga residual en Cuba.* Santiago de Cuba: Casa del Caribe/Universidad de Alcalá/UNESCO.

Diouf, Sylviane. 1998. *Servants of Allah: African Muslims Enslaved in the Americas.* New York: New York University Press.

Dobbin, J. D. 1986. *The Jombee Dance of Montserrat: A Study of Trance Ritual in the West Indies.* Columbus: Ohio State University Press.

Dupuy, Alex. 1997. *Haiti in the New World Order.* Boulder, Colo.: Westview Press.

Edwards, Walter, ed. 1980. *Focus on Amerindians.* Georgetown, Guyana: Amerindian Languages Project, University of Guyana.

Elder, J. D. 1988. *African Survivals in Trinidad and Tobago.* London: Karia.

Emmanuel, Isaac S., and Suzanne A. Emmanuel. 1970. *History of the Jews of the Netherlands Antillies.* Cincinnati: American Jewish Archives.

Erskine, Noel. 1981. *Decolonizing Theology: A Caribbean Perspective.* Maryknoll, N.Y.: Orbis.

Farriss, Nancy. 1984. *Maya Society under Colonial Rule: The Collective Enterprise of Survival.* Princeton: Princeton University Press.

Faulk, Nancy A., and Rita M. Gross. 1980. *Unspoken Worlds: Women's Religious Lives.* San Francisco: Harper and Row.

Fernández Martínez, Mirta, and Valentina Porras Potts. 1998. *El ashé está en Cuba.* La Habana: Editorial José Martí.

Fernández Olmos, Margarita, et al., ed. 1997. *Sacred Possessions: Vodou, Santería, Obeah, and the Caribbean.* New Brunswick, N.J.: Rutgers University Press.

Fernández Robaina, Tomás. 1990. *El negro en Cuba (1902–1958).* La Habana: Editorial de Ciencias Sociales.

Fernández Robaina, Tomás. 1997. *Hablen paleros y santeros.* La Habana: Editorial de Ciencias Sociales.

Fewkes, Jesse Walter. [1907] 1970. *The Aborigines of Porto Rico and Neighboring Islands*. New York: Johnson Reprint Corporation.

Foster, Byron. 1994. *Heart Drum: Spirit Possession in the Garifuna Communities of Belize*. 2nd rev. ed. Belize: Cubola Productions.

Fraginals, Moreno. 1991. *El ingenio*. La Habana: Editorial de Ciencias Sociales.

Fried, Morton H. 1956. "Some Observations on the Chinese in British Guiana." *Social and Economic Studies* 5 (1): 54–73.

Galembo, Phyllis. 1998. *Vodou: Visions and Voices of Haiti*. Berkeley: Ten Speed Press.

Garvey, Marcus. 1986. *Philosophy and Opinions of Marcus Garvey*. Edited by Amy Jacques-Garvey. 2 vols. New York: Atheneum.

Gates, Brian, ed. 1980. *Afro-Caribbean Religions*. London: Ward Lock Educational.

Genovese, Eugene. 1979. *From Rebellion to Revolution: Afro-American Slave Revolts in the Making of the Modern World*. Baton Rouge: Louisiana State University Press.

Gibbs De Peza, Hazel Ann. 1999. *My Faith: Spiritual Baptist Christian*. Saint Augustine, Trinidad: School of Education, University of the West Indies.

Gilroy, Paul. 1993. *The Black Atlantic: Modernity and Double Consciousness*. Cambridge, Mass.: Harvard University Press.

Glazier, Stephen D. 1980. *Perspectives on Pentecostalism: Case Studies from the Caribbean and Latin America*. Washington, D.C.: University Press of America.

Glazier, Stephen D. 1983. *Marchin' the Pilgrims Home: Leadership and Decision-Making in an Afro-Caribbean Faith*. Westport, Conn.: Greenwood Press.

Gmelch, George, and Sharon Bohn. 1997. *The Parish behind God's Back: The Changing Culture of Rural Barbados*. Ann Arbor: University of Michigan Press.

Goldson, Terence O. B. 1997. *Warmed Hearts: Stories of Early Methodism and Its Heroes and Heroines in Jamaica*. London: Avon Books.

Gonzalez, Nancie. 1988. *Sojourners of the Caribbean: Ethnogenesis and Ethnohistory of the Garifuna*. Urbana: University of Illinois Press.

González-Wippler, Migene. 1982. *The Santeria Experience*. Englewoods Cliff, N.J.: Prentice Hall.

González-Wippler, Migene. 1989. *Santeria: The Religion*. New York: Harmony.

Goodridge, Sehon. 1981. *Facing the Challenge of Emancipation: A Study of the Ministry of William Hart Coleridge*. Bridgetown, Barbados: CEDAR Press.

Gordon, Shirley G. 1996. *God Almighty Make Me Free: Christianity in Pre-Emancipation Jamaica*. Bloomington: Indiana University Press.

Gordon, Shirley G. 1998. *Our Cause for His Glory: Christianisation and Emancipation in Jamaica*. Kingston, Jamaica: Press University of the West Indies.

Greene, Ann. 1993. *The Catholic Church in Haiti: Political and Social Change*. Ann Arbor: Michigan State University Press.

Gregory, Howard, ed. 1995. *Caribbean Theology: Preparing for Challenges Ahead*. Mona, Jamaica: Canoe Press.

Gullick, C. J. M. R. 1985. *Myths of a Minority: The Changing Traditions of the Vincentian Caribs*. Assen, Netherlands: Van Gorcum.

Gutiérrez, Carlos María. 1972. *The Dominican Republic: Rebellion and Repression*. New York: Monthly Review.

Hamid, Idris. 1971. *In Search of New Perspectives*. Bridgetown, Barbados: Caribbean Ecumenical Consultation for Development.

Hamid, Idris. 1980. *A History of the Presbyterian Church in Trinidad, 1898–1968*. San Fernando, Trinidad: St. Andrew's Theological College.

Hamid, Idris, ed. 1973. *Troubling of the Waters*. San Fernando, Trinidad: Rahaman Printery.

Hamid, Idris, ed. 1977. *Out of the Depths*. San Fernando, Trinidad: St. Andrew's Theological College.

Handler, Jerome S., and Frederick W. Lange. 1978. *Plantation Slavery in Barbados: An Archeological and Historical Investigation*. Cambridge, Mass.: Harvard University Press.

Harricharan, John T. 1981. *The Catholic Church in Trinidad: 1498–1852*. Vol. 1. Port of Spain: Inprint Caribbean.

Helg, Aline. 1995. *Our Rightful Share: The Afro-Cuban Struggle for Equality, 1886–1912*. Chapel Hill: University of North Carolina Press.

Henderson, John S. 1981. *The World of the Ancient Maya*. Ithaca: Cornell University Press.

Henry, Frances. 1983. "Religion and Ideology in Trinidad: The Resurgence of the Shango Religion." *Caribbean Quarterly* 29 (3–4): 63–69.

Henry, Frances, ed. 1976. *Ethnicity in the Americas*. The Hague: Mouton Publishing.

Herskovits, Melville J. [1937] 1971. *Life in a Haitian Valley*. New York: Anchor-Doubleday.

Herskovits, Melville J., and F. S Herskovits. 1934. *Rebel Destiny: Among the Bush Negroes of British Guiana*. New York: McGraw-Hill.

Herskovits, Melville J., and F. S Herskovits. 1936. *Suriname Folklore*. New York: Columbia University Press.

Herskovits, Melville J., and F. S Herskovits. 1947. *Trinidad Village*. New York: Knopf.

Heumann, Gad. 1994. *The Killing Time: The Morant Bay Rebellion in Jamaica*. London: Macmillan Caribbean.

Hill, Robert. 1983. "Leonard P. Howell and Millenarian Vision in Early Rastafari." *Jamaica Journal* 16 (1): 24–39.

Hoffman, Léon-François. 1989. *Haïti: Couleurs, croyances, créole*. Montreal: CIDIHCA.

Holzberg, Carol S. 1987. *Minorities and Power in a Black Society: The Jewish Community of Jamaica*. Lanham, Md.: North-South Publishing Co.

Honychurch, Lennox. 1995. *The Dominica Story: A History of the Island*. London: Macmillan.

Horowitz, Michael M. 1963. "The Worship of South Indian Deities in Martinique." *Ethnology* 2 (3): 339–46.

Horowitz, Michael M., ed. 1971. *Peoples and Cultures of the Caribbean*. New York: Natural History Press.

Horowitz, Michael M., and Morton Klass. 1961. "The Martiniquan East Indian Cult of Maldevidan." *Social and Economic Studies* 10 (1): 93–100.

Houk, James T. 1995. *Spirits, Blood and Drums: The Orisha Religion in Trinidad*. Philadelphia: Temple University Press.

Houtart, F., and A. Rémy. 1997. *Les référents culturels à Port-au-Prince: Étude des mentalités face aux réalités économiques, sociales et politiques*. Port-au-Prince: Centre de recherche et de formation économique et sociale pour le développement (CRESFED).

Hulme, Peter, and Neil Whitehead, eds. 1992. *Wild Majesty: Encounters with Caribs from Columbus to the Present Day: An Anthology*. Oxford: Oxford University Press.

Hurbon, Laënnec. 1972. *Dieu dans le Vaudou Haïtien*. Paris: Payot.

Hurbon, Laënnec. 1980. "Le double fonctionnement des sectes aux Antilles: le cas de Mahikari en Guadeloupe." *Archives de Sciences Sociales des Religions* 25 (50–1): 59–75.

Hurbon, Laënnec. 1987. *Comprendre Haïti: Essai sur l'état, la nation, la culture*. Paris and Port-au-Prince, Haiti: Karthala and Deschamps.

Hurbon, Laënnec. 1989. "Enjeu politique de la crise actuelle de l'Église." *Chemins critiques* 1 (1): 11–22.

Hurbon, Laënnec. 1994. "Nationalisme et démocratie en Haïti." *Chemins critiques* 3 (1–2): 7–30.

Hurbon, Laënnec. 1995. "Haïti et la politique du St.-Siège." In *Tous les chemins ne mènent plus à Rome,* edited by R. Luneau and P. Michel. Paris: Albin Michel.

Hurbon, Laënnec. 1997. "Rôle et statut du religieux dans les luttes haïtiennes de sortie de la dictature." In *Religion et démocratie,* edited by P. Michel. Paris: Albin Michel, 210–37.

Hurbon, Laënnec. 1998. "Gnadenlose Liebe zum Volk. Irrwege der Demokratie." *DU, die Zeitschrift der Kultur* 2 (Feb.): 68–72.

Hurbon, Laënnec, ed. 1989. *Le phénomène religieux dans la Caraïbe.* Montreal: Éditions du CIDIHCA.

Hurbon, Laënnec, ed. 1996. *Les transitions démocratiques.* Paris: Syros.

Hurston, Zora Neale. [1938] 1990. *Tell My Horse: Voodoo and Life in Haiti and Jamaica.* New York: Harper and Row.

Jacobs, C. M. 1996. *Joy Comes in the Morning: Elton George Griffith and the Shouter Baptists.* Port of Spain: Caribbean Historical Society.

Jahn, Janheinz. 1961. *Muntu: An Outline of the New-African Culture.* Translated by Marjorie Grene. New York: Grove Press.

James, C. L. R. 1989. *The Black Jacobins: Toussaint L'Ouverture and the San Domingo Revolution.* 2nd rev. ed. New York: Vintage-Random House.

James, Joel, José Millet, and Alexis Alarcón. 1998. *El Vodú en Cuba.* 2nd ed. Santiago de Cuba: Editorial Oriente.

Jan Voorhoeven, J., and Ursy M. Lichtveld, eds. 1975. *Creole Drum: An Anthology of Creole Literature in Surinam.* Translated by Vernie A. February. New Haven: Yale University Press.

Jones, Grant. 1989. *Maya Resistance to Spanish Rule: Time and History on a Colonial Frontier.* Albuquerque: University of New Mexico Press.

Karner, Frances P. 1969. *The Sephardics of Curacao.* Assen, Netherlands: Van Gorcum.

Kerns, V. 1983. *Women and the Ancestors: Black Carib Kinships and Ritual.* Urbana: University of Illinois Press.

Khan, K. Rahamat. 1978. *Reflections on the Caribbean: Toward Liberation and Mission.* Ducansville, Penn.: Capitol Press.

Kilson, M. L., and R. I. Rotberg, eds. 1976. *The African Diaspora: Interpretive Essays.* Cambridge, Mass.: Harvard University Press.

Kirk, John. 1989. *Between God and the Party: Religion and Politics in Revolutionary Cuba.* Tampa: University of South Florida Press.

Klass, Morton. [1959] 1988. *Cultural Persistence in a Trinidad East Indian Community.* Ann Arbor, Mich.: University Microfilms International.

Klass, Morton. 1996. *Singing with Sai Baba: The Politics of Revitalization in Trinidad.* Boulder, Colo.: Westview Press, 1991. Reprint, Prospect Heights, Ill.: Waveland Press.

Knight, Franklin. 1990. *The Caribbean: The Genesis of a Fragmented Nationalism.* New York: Oxford University Press.

Korom, Frank J., and Peter J. Chelkowski. 1994. "Community Process and the Performance of Muharram Observances in Trinidad." *Drama Review* 38 (2): 150–75.

Kremser, Manfred, ed. 1996. *African-Caribbean Religions.* 3 vols. Wien: WUV-Universitätsverlag.

Lachatañeré, Rómulo. 1992. *El sistema religioso de los afrocubanos.* La Habana: Editorial de Ciencias Sociales.

La Guerre, John G., ed. [1974] 1985. *Calcutta to Caroni: The East Indians of Trinidad.* 2nd ed. St. Augustine, Trinidad: University of the West Indies Extramural Studies Unit.

Laguerre, Michel S. 1980. *Voodoo Heritage.* Beverly Hills: Sage Publications.

Laguerre, Michel S. 1989. *Voodoo and Politics in Haiti.* London and New York: MacMillan and St. Martins.

Lampe, Amando. 1997. *Breve historia del cristianismo en el Caribe.* San Jose, Costa Rica: CEHILA: Universidad de Quintana Roo.

Las Casas, Bartolomé de. 1992. *A Short Account of the Destruction of the Indies.* Translated by Nigel Griffin. London: Penguin.

Lawson, Winston Arthur. 1996. *Religion and Race: African and European Roots in Conflict— A Jamaican Testament.* New York: Peter Lang.

L'Étang, Gerry. 1994. "Présences de l'Inde dans le monde." Paris: L'Harmattan/GÉREC/ PUC.

Levine, Robert M. 1993. *Tropical Diaspora: The Jewish Experience in Cuba.* Gainesville: University Press of Florida.

Lewis, Gordon K. 1979. *Gather with the Saints at the River: The Jonestown Holocaust.* Río Piedras, Puerto Rico: Institute of Caribbean Studies.

Lewis, Gordon K. 1983. *Main Currents in Caribbean Thought: The Historical Evolution of Caribbean Society in Its Ideological Aspects, 1492–1900.* Kingston, Jamaica: Heinemann.

Littlewood, Roland. 1993. *Pathology and Identity: The Work of Mother Earth in Trinidad.* Cambridge: Cambridge University Press.

Look Lai, Walton. 1993. *Indentured Labor, Caribbean Sugar: Chinese and Indian Migrants to the British West Indies, 1838–1918.* Baltimore: Johns Hopkins University Press.

López Springfield, Consuelo, ed. 1997. *Daughters of Caliban: Caribbean Women in the Twentieth Century.* Bloomington and London: Indiana University Press and Latin American Bureau.

López Valdés, Rafael L. 1985. *Componentes africanos en el etnos cubano.* La Habana: Editorial de Ciencias Sociales.

Lowenthal, David. 1972. *West Indian Societies.* London: Oxford University Press.

Luneau R., and P. Michel, eds. 1995. *Tous les chemins ne mènent plus à Rome.* Paris: Albin Michel.

Mahabir, Noor Kumar. 1985. *The Still Cry: Personal Accounts of East Indians in Trinidad and Tobago during Identureship (1845–1917).* Tacarigua, Trinidad: Calaloux Publications.

Malik, Yogendra K. 1971. *East Indians in Trinidad: A Study in Minority Politics.* Toronto: Oxford University Press.

Mangru, Basdeo. 1993. *Indenture and Abolition: Sacrifice and Survival on the Guyanese Sugar Plantations.* Toronto: TSAR.

Martinez-Fernandez, Luis. 1995. "The Sword and the Crucifix: Church State Relations and Nationality in the Nineteenth-Century Dominican Republic." *Latin American Research Review* 30 (1): 69–93.

Mattibag, Eugenio. 1996. *Afro-Cuban Religious Experience: Cultural Reflections in Narrative.* Gainesville: University Press of Florida.

Mbiti, John. 1970. *African Religions and Philosophy.* London: Heinemann.

McDaniel, Lorna. 1998. *The Big Drum Ritual of Carriacou: Praisesongs in Rememory of Flight.* Gainesville: University Press of Florida.

Menéndez, Lázara. 1990. *Estudios afro-cubanos.* Vol. 2. La Habana: Facultad de Arte y Letras, Universidad de La Habana.

Métraux, Alfred. [1959] 1972. *Voodoo in Haiti*. Translated by Hugo Charteris. New York: Schocken.

Midy, F. 1989. "Haïti; La religion sur les chemins de la démocratie; L'affaire Aristide en perspective; Histoire de la formation et du rejet d'une vocation prophétique." *Chemins critiques* 1 (1): 23–44.

Mitchell, David I., ed. 1973. *With Eyes Wide Open*. Bridgetown, Barbados: CADEC.

Montilus, Guérin. 1989. *Dompin: The Spirituality of African Peoples*. Nashville: Winston Derek Publishers.

Moore, Brian L. 1987. *Race, Power and Social Segmentation in Colonial Society: Guyana after Slavery, 1838–1891*. New York: Gordon and Breach Science Publishers.

Moore, Brian L. 1995. *Cultural Power, Resistance and Pluralism: Colonial Guyana, 1838–1900*. Montreal and Kingston, Jamaica: McGill-Queen's University Press and Press University of the West Indies.

Morrish, Ivor. 1982. *Obeah, Christ and Rastaman: Jamaica and its Religion*. Cambridge: James Clarke.

Moutoussamy, Ernest. 1987. *La Guadeloupe et son Indianité*. Paris: Éditions Caribéennes.

Mulrain, George M. 1984. *Theology in Folk Culture: The Theological Significance of Haitian Folk Religion*. New York: Peter Lang.

Murphy, Joseph. 1988. *Santería: an African Religion in America*. Boston: Beacon Press.

Murphy, Joseph. 1994. *Working the Spirit: Ceremonies of the African Diaspora*. Boston: Beacon Press.

NACLA, ed. 1995. *Haiti: Dangerous Crossroads*. Boston: South End Press.

Nérestant, M. 1994. *Religions et politiques en Haïti*. Paris: Karthala.

Nettleford, Rex. 1970. *Mirror, Mirror: Identity, Race and Protest in Jamaica*. London and Kingston, Jamaica: Collins and Sangster's.

Nicholls, David. 1979. *From Dessalines to Duvalier: Race, Colour and National Independence in Haiti*. Cambridge: Cambridge University Press.

Niehoff, Arthur, and Juanita Niehoff. 1960. *East Indians in the West Indies*. Milwaukee, Wisc.: Milwaukee Public Museum.

Nunley, John W., and Judith Bettleheim, eds. 1988. *Caribbean Festival Arts*. Seattle: University of Washington Press.

Obenga, Théophile. 1985. *Les Bantu: Langues-peuples-civilisations*. Paris: Présence Africaine.

Olwig, Karen. 1985. *Cultural Adaptation and Resistance on St. John: Three Centuries of Afro-Caribbean Life*. Gainesville: University Press of Florida.

Olwig, Karen. 1993. *Global Culture, Island Identity: Continuity and Change in the Afro-Caribbean Community of Nevis*. Chur, Switzerland: Harwood Academic Publishers.

Ortiz, Fernando. 1951. *Los bailes y el teatro de los negros en el folklore de Cuba*. La Habana: Ediciones Cardenas.

Ortiz, Fernando. [1924] 1990. *Glosario de afronegrismos*. La Habana: Editorial de Ciencias Sociales.

Ortiz, Fernando. 1991. *Estudios etnosociológicos*. La Habana: Editorial de Ciencias Sociales.

Ortiz, Fernando. [1947] 1995. *Cuban Counterpoint: Tobacco and Sugar*. Translated by Harriet de Onís. Durham: Duke University Press.

Osborne, Francis J. 1988. *History of the Catholic Church in Jamaica*. Chicago: Loyola University Press.

Ouensanga, Christian. 1983. *Plantes médicinales et remèdes créoles*. 2 vols. Paris: Désormeaux.

Owens, Joseph. 1979. *Dread: The Rastafarians of Jamaica.* Kingston, Jamaica: Sangster's Book Stores, 1976. Reprint, London: Heinemann.

Paquette, Robert, and Stanley Engerman, eds. 1996. *The Lesser Antilles in the Age of European Expansion.* Gainesville: University Press of Florida.

Patterson, Orlando. 1973. *The Sociology of Slavery: An Analysis of the Origins, Development and Structure of Negro Slave Society in Jamaica.* London: MacGibbon and Kee, 1967. Reprint, Kingston, Jamaica: Sangster's Bookstores.

Paul, Emmanuel C. 1978. *Panorama du folklore haïtien: présence africaine en Haïti.* Port-au-Prince: Fardin.

Perez Sarduy, Pedro, and Jean Stubbs, eds. 1993. *Afro-Cuba: An Anthology of Cuban Writing on Race, Politics and Culture.* Melbourne: Ocean Press.

Petitjean Roget, Henri. 1994. "Éléments pour une étude comparée des mythologies Taïnos et Caraïbes insulaires (Kalinas) des Antilles." *Espace Caraïbe* (2): 91–107.

Pezeron, Simone Maguy. 1993. *The Carib Indians of Dominica Island in the West Indies.* New York: Vantage.

Phillippo, James M. 1843. *Jamaica: Its Past and Present.* London.

Plaskon, Judith, and Carol P. Christ, eds. 1989. *Weaving the Visions: New Patterns in Feminist Spirituality.* San Francisco: Harper and Row.

Pollard, Velma. 1994. *Dread Talk: The Language of Rastafari.* Kingston, Jamaica: Canoe Press.

Portuondo Zúñiga, Olga. 1995. *La virgen de la caridad del cobre: símbolo de cubanía.* Santiago de Cuba: Editorial Oriente.

Post, Ken. 1970. "The Bible as Ideology: Ethiopianism in Jamaica, 1930–1938." In *African Perspectives,* edited by C. Allen and R. W. Johnson. Cambridge: Cambridge University Press.

Poupeye, Veerle. 1998. *Caribbean Art.* New York: Thames and Hudson.

Price, Richard, ed. 1973. *Maroon Societies: Rebel Slave Communities in the Americas.* New York: Anchor-Doubleday.

Price, Richard, ed. 1990. *Alabi's World.* Baltimore: Johns Hopkins University Press.

Price-Mars, Jean. [1928] 1983. *So Spoke the Uncle.* Translated by Magdaline Shannon. Washington, D.C: Three Continents Press.

Quesada, Gonzalo de. 1896. *Los chinos y la independencia de Cuba.* Translated by A. Castellanos. La Habana: Heraldo Cristiano.

Ramesar, Marianne Soares. 1994. *Survivors of Another Crossing: A History of East Indians in Trinidad, 1880–1946.* St. Augustine, Trinidad: University of the West Indies.

Ramsay, James. 1784. *An Essay on the Treatment and Conversion of African Slaves in the British Sugar Colonies.* London: James Phillips.

Rauf, Mohammad A. 1974. *Indian Village in Guyana: A Study of Cultural Change and Ethnic Identity.* Leiden, Netherlands: E. J. Brill.

Rodney, Walter. 1983. *The Groundings with My Brothers.* London: Bogle L'Ouverture Publications.

Rotberg, Robert I., ed. 1997. *Haiti Renewed: Political and Economic Prospects.* Washington, D.C., and Cambridge, Mass.: Brookings Institution Press and World Peace Foundation.

Rouse, Irving. 1992. *The Tainos: Rise and Decline of the People Who Greeted Columbus.* New Haven: Yale University Press.

Rowe, Maureen. 1980. "The Women in Rastafari." *Caribbean Quarterly* 26 (4): 13–21.

Ruhomon, Peter. [1947] 1988. *Centenary History of the East Indians in British Guiana, 1838–1938.* Georgetown: 150th Anniversary Committee of the Arrival of Indians in Guyana.

Russell, Horace O. 1993. *Foundations and Anticipations: The Jamaica Baptist Story, 1783–1892.* Columbus, Ga.: Brentwood Christian Press.

Ryan, Selwyn. 1991. *The Muslimeen Grab for Power: Race, Religion and Revolution in Trinidad and Tobago.* Port of Spain, Trinidad: Inprint.

Ryan, Selwyn, ed. 1991. *Social and Occupational Stratification in Contemporary Trinidad and Tobago.* St. Augustine, Trinidad: Institute of Social and Economic Research, University of the West Indies.

Saco, José Antonio. 1881. *Coleccion posthuma de papeles cientificos, historicos, politicos y de otros ramos sobre la isla de Cuba.* La Habana: Editorial Miguel De Villa.

Samaroo, Brinsley, ed. 1996. *Pioneer Presbyterians: Origins of Presbyterian Work in Trinidad.* St. Augustine, Trinidad: Institute of Caribbean Studies, University of the West Indies.

Samaroo, Brinsley, et al., eds. 1995. *In Celebration of 150 Years of the Indian Contribution to Trinidad and Tobago.* Port of Spain, Trinidad: Historical Publications.

Sankeralli, Burton, ed. 1995. *At the Crossroads: African Caribbean Religion and Christianity.* Port of Spain: CCC.

Schwartz, Barton M., ed. 1967. *Caste in Overseas Indian Communities.* San Francisco: Chandler Publishing.

Scott, Jamie, ed. 1996. *"And the Birds Began to Sing": Religion and Literature in Post-Colonial Cultures.* Amsterdam: Rodopi.

Seaga, Edward. 1969. "Revival Cults: Notes towards a Sociology of Religion." *Jamaica Journal* 3 (2): 3–13.

Seecharan, Clem. 1993. *India and the Shaping of the Indo-Guyanese Imagination 1890s–1920.* Leeds: Peepal Tree.

Seecharan, Clem. 1997. *"Tiger in the Stars": The Anatomy of Indian Achievement in British Guiana 1919–29.* London: Macmillan.

Semaj, Leahcim Tufani. 1980. "Rastafari: From Religion to Social Theory." *Caribbean Quarterly* 26 (4): 22–31.

Shepherd, Verene. 1993. *Transients to Settlers: The Experience of Indians in Jamaica 1845–1950.* Leeds, England: Peepal Tree.

Siddhantalankar, Satyavrata. 1969. *Heritage of Vedic Culture. A Pragmatic Presentation.* Bombay: D. B. Taraporevala.

Simpson, George Eaton. 1978. *Black Religions in the New World.* New York: Columbia University Press.

Simpson, George Eaton. 1980. *Religious Cults of the Caribbean: Trinidad, Jamaica and Haiti.* 3rd ed. Río Piedras, Puerto Rico: Institute of Caribbean Studies.

Singaravélou. 1975. *Les Indiens de la Guadeloupe: Études de geographie humaine.* Bordeaux: CNRS.

Singaravélou. 1987. *Les Indiens de la Caraïbe.* 3 vols. Paris: L'Harmattan.

Singh, I. J. Bahadur, ed. 1987. *Indians in the Caribbean.* New Delhi: Sterling Publishers.

Singh, Kelvin. 1988. *Bloodstained Tombs: The Muharram Massacre 1884.* London: Macmillan Caribbean.

Smith, Ashley. 1984. *Real Roots and Potted Plants: Reflections on the Caribbean Church.* Williamsfield, Jamaica: Mandeville Publishers.

Smith, M. G, Roy Augier, and R. Nettleford. [1960] 1978. *The Rastafari Movement in Kingston, Jamaica.* Mona, Jamaica: Extra-Mural Studies, University of the West Indies.

Sosa Rodríguez, Enrique. 1982. *Los ñáñigos.* La Habana: Casa de las Américas.

Speckmann, J. D. 1965. *Marriage and Kinship among the Indians in Surinam.* Assen, Netherlands: Van Gorcum.

Stephen, H. 1986. *De Macht van de Fodoe-Winti.* Amsterdam: Karnak.

Stephen, H. 1992. *Lexicon van de Winti-Kultuur.* Amsterdam: Stephen.

Stephen, H. 1996. *Geneeskruiden van Suriname.* Amsterdam: Drihoek Uitgeverij.

Stewart, Robert. 1992. *Religion and Society in Post-Emancipation Jamaica.* Knoxville: University of Tennessee Press.

Taylor, Douglas. 1951. *The Black Caribs of British Honduras.* New York: Viking Fund Publications in Anthropology.

Taylor, Patrick. 1989. *The Narrative of Liberation: Perspectives on Afro-Caribbean Literature, Popular Culture and Politics.* Ithaca: Cornell University Press.

Taylor, Patrick. 1990. "Perspectives on History in Rastafari Thought." *Studies in Religion* 19 (2): 191–205.

Taylor, Patrick. 1992. "Anthropology and Theology in Pursuit of Justice." *Callaloo* 15 (3): 811–23.

Thomas, Eudora. 1987. *A History of the Shouter Baptists in Trinidad and Tobago.* Ithaca, N.Y., and Tacarigua, Trinidad: Calaloux Publications.

Thompson, J. Eric. 1970. *Maya History and Religion.* Norman: University of Oklahoma Press.

Thompson, Robert F. 1983. *Flash of the Spirit: African and Afro-American Art and Philosophy.* New York: Vintage-Random House.

Titus, Noel. 1998. *Conflicts and Contradictions: The Introduction of Christianity to the Sixteenth Century Caribbean.* London: Minerva.

Toussaint, H. 1992. "Église catholique et démocratie en Haïti." *Problèmes d'Amérique latine* 4 (Jan.–Mar.): 43–60.

Trouillot, Michel. 1990. *Haiti, State against Nation: The Origins and Legacy of Duvalierism.* New York: Montlhy Review Press.

Turner, Mary. 1982. *Slaves and Missionaries: The Disintegration of Jamaican Slave Society, 1787–1834.* Urbana: University of Illinois Press.

Turner, Terisa E. 1994. *Arise Ye Mighty People! Gender, Class and Race in Popular Struggles.* Trenton, N.J.: Africa World Press.

Van der Burg, Cors, and Peter van der Veer. 1986. "Pandits, Power and Profit: Religious Organization and the Construction of Identity among Surinamese Hindus." *Ethnic and Racial Studies* 9 (4): 514–28.

Vertovec, Steven. 1992. *Hindu Trinidad: Religion, Ethnicity and Socio-Economic Change.* London: Macmillan Caribbean.

Waddall, H. M. [1863] 1970. *Twenty-Nine Years in the West Indies and Central Africa: A Review of Missionary Work and Adventure, 1829–1858.* London: Frank Cass.

Warner-Lewis, Maureen. 1991. *Guinea's Other Sons: The African Dynamic in Trinidad Culture.* Dover, Mass.: Majority Press.

Warner-Lewis, Maureen. 1995. *Trinidad Yoruba: From Mother Tongue to Memory.* Tuscaloosa: Alabama University Press.

Waters, Anita M. 1985. *Race, Class, and Political Symbols: Rastafari and Reggae in Jamaican Politics.* New Brunswick, N.J.: Transaction Books.

Watty, William. 1981. *From Shore to Shore.* Kingston, Jamaica: CEDAR Press.

Wedenoja, W. 1989. "Mothering and the Practice of 'Balm' in Jamaica." In *Women as Healers: Cross Cultural Perspectives,* edited by C. S. McClain. New Brunswick: Rutgers University Press.

Wilentz, Amy. 1989. *The Rainy Season: Haiti since Duvalier.* New York: Simon and Schuster.

Williams, Brackette F. 1991. *Stains on My Name, War in My Veins: Guyana and the Politics of Cultural Struggle*. Durham: Duke University Press.

Williams, Eric. [1944] 1964. *Capitalism and Slavery*. London: Andre Deutsch.

Williams, J. J. [1934] 1979. *Psychic Phenomena of Jamaica*. Westport, Conn.: Greenwood.

Williams, K. M. 1981. *The Rastafarians*. London: Ward Lock Educational.

Williams, Lewin. 1994. *Caribbean Theology*. New York: Peter Lang.

Wilson, Samuel, ed. 1997. *The Indigenous Peoples of the Caribbean*. Gainesville: University Press of Florida.

Wood, Donald. 1968. *Trinidad in Transition: The Years after Slavery*. New York: Oxford University Press.

Wooding, Charles J. 1979. "Traditional Healing and Medicine in Winti: A Sociological Interpretation." *ISSUE* 9 (3): 35–40.

Wooding, Charles J. 1981. *Evolving Culture: A Cross-Cultural Study of Suriname, West Africa, and the Caribbean*. Washington, D.C.: University Press of America.

Wooding, Charles J. 1988. *Winti, een afroamerikaanse Godsdienst in Suriname: Een cultureel-historische analyse van de cosmologie en het ethnomedische systeem van de Para*. Rijswijk, Netherlands: C. J. Wooding.

Yawney, Carole. 1982. "To Grow a Daughter: Cultural Liberation and the Dynamics of Oppression in Jamaica." In *Feminism in Canada: From Pressure to Politics*, edited by A. Miles and G. Finn. Montreal: Black Rose Books.

Contributors

Petronella Breinburg is Head of the Caribbean Centre, Goldsmiths College, University of London. She has written articles on Dutch Caribbean culture and has authored collections of Surinamese folktales and fiction writing, including *De Winst van het Lakoe spel, Legends of Suriname,* and *Stories from the Caribbean.*

Frederick Ivor Case teaches Caribbean Studies and French at New College, University of Toronto. He is the author of *The Crisis of Identity: Studies in the Martinican and Guadeloupean Novel* and has published numerous articles on Francophone-Caribbean and African literature, religion, and culture.

María Margarita Castro Flores, a researcher with the Centro de Estudios Sobre América in Havana, is pursuing postgraduate studies at El Colegio de Mexico. She is co-author of *Movimientos comunitarios en Cuba: Un análisis comparativo* and has published articles in the areas of religion, gender, and ethnicity.

Barry Chevannes is Dean of Social Science at the University of the West Indies, Mona, Jamaica. He is the author of *Rastafari: Roots and Ideology* and the editor of *Rastafari and Other African-Caribbean Worldviews.*

Arthur C. Dayfoot, former principal of St. Andrews Theological College in Trinidad, is a retired minister of the United Church of Canada. He is the author of *The Shaping of the West Indian Church: 1492–1962.*

Juanita De Barros teaches at York University in Toronto. She completed a doctorate in History on "public space" in colonial Guyana.

Yvonne B. Drakes is founder and Queen Mother Bishop of the Trinity Divine Spiritual Baptist Church in Toronto. She is a founding member of the Spiritual Baptist Faith of Canada.

Eva Fernandez Bravo was a leading *espiritista* (spiritualist) in Santiago de Cuba until she passed away in 1997.

Laënnec Hurbon is *directeur de recherche* with the Centre National de la Recherche (CNRS), Paris. He has published numerous books and edited works on Haitian religion, culture, and politics, including *Voodoo: Search for Spirit, Dieu dans le vaudou haïtien, Comprendre Haïti: Essai sur l'état, la nation, la culture,* and *Les Transitions démocratiques.* He is editor of the journal *Chemins Critiques.*

Abrahim H. Khan is a fellow of Trinity College, University of Toronto, where he teaches the philosophy of religion and comparative religion. He is the author of *"Salighed" as Happiness? Kierkegaard on the Concept Salighed* and has published many articles on Christianity, Islam, and Hinduism.

Sean Lokaisingh-Meighoo is a doctoral candidate in the Graduate Programme in Social and Political Thought at York University in Toronto. He completed a master's thesis on Indo-Caribbean identity and is currently engaged in research in the area of postcolonial theory.

Althea Prince completed a doctorate in Sociology, focusing on the work of C. L. R. James. An essayist, short story writer, and novelist, she is the author of *Being Black, Ladies of the Night and Other Stories, How the East Pond Got Its Flowers,* and *How the Starfish Got to the Sea.*

Deloris Seiveright is Archbishop Doctor Mother Superior of the Shouters National Evangelical Spiritual Baptist Faith in Toronto and Hamilton.

Frank F. Scherer is a doctoral candidate in the Graduate Programme in Social and Political Thought at York University in Toronto. He completed a master's thesis in Anthropology on the Chinese in Cuba and is currently engaged in research on Cuban culture and ideology.

Judith Soares is academic coordinator of the Women and Development Unit of the University of the West Indies in Barbados. She completed a doctorate in Political Science on religious fundamentalism and politics in Jamaica and has published articles on related topics.

Patrick Taylor teaches Caribbean Studies and Religious Studies in the Division of Humanties at York University in Toronto. He is the author of *The Narrative of Liberation: Perspectives on Afro-Caribbean Literature, Popular Culture and Politics* and the co-editor of *Forging Identities and Patterns of Development in Latin America and the Caribbean.*

Index